Further prais

"Rachel Moran takes us where no hell of being prostituted, into what happens after the door closes and you're alone with a john, into the experience itself—and into survival and escape. Anyone who believes 'sex work' is chosen or a job like any other should read *Paid For* for its exposure of misinformation and myths alone. But the book is more: Moran writes so well that her story will scorch your heart, even as you realize this is a first: hers is a voice that has never been heard before."

—Robin Morgan

"Through her profoundly personal account, Rachel Moran unmasks the extreme violence of the commercial sex trade. Her solution—penalizing the demand for commercial sex by holding pimps, brothel-keepers, and buyers accountable for the harm they cause—comes from both her first-hand experience and a deep analysis of the realities of prostitution. I salute Rachel for her courage, candor, and commitment in writing this game-changing book."

—Yasmeen Hassan,
global executive director, Equality Now

"From one survivor to another, *Paid For* got to the heart of what sex-trafficked and prostituted women face on a daily basis. Rachel, you spoke for those survivors who can't speak for themselves, and for those who have been lost to the life."

—Vednita Carter, founder and
executive director, Breaking Free

"*Paid For* is a political weapon of such force and magnitude you almost feel you need a permit to carry it around!"

—Taina Bien-Aimé, executive director,
Coalition Against Trafficking in Women

"Rachel Moran demolishes the 'Pretty Woman' myth with the stark reality of the lived experience of her young years in prostitution. This memoir makes a strong case for the Nordic model law that criminalizes the buyers whose money drives the trade that treats women as objects for sale."

—Terry O'Neill, president, National Organization for Women

"*Paid For* is a deeply moving personal story combined with a brilliant analysis of the forces that drive the commercial sex industry—a 'must-read' for all."

—Jessica Neuwirth, founder,
Equality Now and Donor Direct Action

"With rare courage and candor, Rachel Moran strips away the many falsehoods and fictions that disguise sexual slavery as 'sex work' and shows it for what it really is—human exploitation and degradation. The power of Moran's narrative is that it is at once deeply personal and smartly political, as she reclaims her life and self-worth by owning her own story and demands realistic public policy solutions to save others from the complacency and complicity that have made sex-trafficking possible and even acceptable. In the great tradition of antislavery literature, from Frederick Douglass and Harriet Jacobs to today, Moran confronts us with truths that we dare not ignore and with guides on organizing that we all can, and must, support. She wants us to become abolitionists. After reading *Paid For*, we will know why we should."

—Randall Miller and Stacey Robertson,
co-directors, Historians Against Slavery

PAID FOR

My Journey Through Prostitution

RACHEL MORAN ∾

W. W. Norton & Company
New York • *London*

Copyright © 2013 by Rachel Moran
First American Edition 2015

For information about permission to reproduce selections from this book,
write to Permissions, W. W. Norton & Company, Inc.,
500 Fifth Avenue, New York, NY 10110

For information about special discounts for bulk purchases, please contact
W. W. Norton Special Sales at specialsales@wwnorton.com or 800-233-4830

Manufacturing by RR Donnelley Westford
Production manager: Louise Mattarelliano

Library of Congress Cataloging-in-Publication Data

Moran, Rachel.
Paid for : my journey through prostitution / Rachel Moran. — First
American edition.
    pages cm
ISBN 978-0-393-35197-2 (pbk.)
1. Moran, Rachel. 2. Prostitutes—Ireland—Dublin—Biography.
3. Prostitution—Ireland. I. Title.
HQ188.A5M67 2015
306.74082—dc23

                         2015009736

W. W. Norton & Company, Inc.
500 Fifth Avenue, New York, N.Y. 10110
www.wwnorton.com

W. W. Norton & Company Ltd.
Castle House, 75/76 Wells Street, London W1T 3QT

1 2 3 4 5 6 7 8 9 0

This book is dedicated to my parents, who did the best they could, and to my aunt Margaret, without whom I simply would not have the life I have today.

Sewers are necessary to guarantee the wholesomeness of palaces, according to the fathers of the Church. And it has often been remarked that the necessity exists of sacrificing one part of the female sex in order to save the other and prevent worse troubles . . . a caste of 'shameless women' allows the 'honest woman' to be treated with the most chivalrous respect. The prostitute is a scapegoat; man vents his turpitude upon her, and he rejects her. Whether she is put legally under police supervision or works illegally in secret, she is in any case treated as a pariah.

SIMONE DE BEAUVOIR, *THE SECOND SEX*

CONTENTS

ACKNOWLEDGEMENTS   xi

PART ONE

1.   The First Question   1

2.   Childhood Social Exclusion   12

3.   My Mother's Illness   18

4.   A Web of Dysfunction   24

5.   Homelessness   36

6.   The First Day   47

PART TWO

7.   Submerging in Prostitution   57

8.   Layers of Negativity   64

9.   The Interplay of Depravity   75

10.   The Myth of the High-Class Hooker   90

11.   Prostitution's Shame, Violation and Abuse   101

12.   The Violence Inherent to Prostitution   120

13.   Survival Strategies   129

14.   Dissociation and the Separation of Self   138

15. The Myth of the Happy Hooker   151

16. The Myth of Prostitutes' Sexual Pleasure   162

17. The Myth of Prostitutes' Control   169

18. The Losses of Prostitution   180

19. Misconceptions About Prostitution   192

20. Legalisation and Decriminalisation   205

21. The Normalisation of Prostitution   222

PART THREE

22. Integrating Myself into Society   237

23. Depression and Suicide   249

24. The Damage to Relationships and Sexuality   254

25. Aftershocks   266

26. The Last Question   282

EPILOGUE   290

AFTERWORD   296

SPACE   297

ACKNOWLEDGEMENTS

Foremost, I need to thank my son who, in telling me to write this book in my own name, showed himself to be more of a man than many who are decades older than him. I'd also like to thank my friends, who know who they are, and Fergal Tobin and all at my Irish publishers Gill and MacMillan, for believing in this book from the outset. I'd like to thank Amy Cherry and all at Norton for embracing this book and for being a joy to work with, and Catharine MacKinnon for recommending it to Norton in the first place, and for her long-standing and impassioned stance against the cruelty and inhumanity of the sex trade.

I would like to record my gratitude for the work of the women who've come before me, from Josephine Butler to Andrea Dworkin, and the many women, like Kathleen Barry, who've made hugely significant contributions along the way.

I want to thank all the sex-trade survivors, feminist activists and allies I have come to know, both in Ireland and abroad, who are far too numerous to mention but whose courage and conviction continually bolsters my own. In particular I would like to thank the women who work with me in SPACE International (Survivors of Prostitution-Abuse Calling for Enlightenment) and the activists who sit with me on our Board: Vednita Carter, Julie Bindel, Norma Ramos and Agnete Stroem.

Finally, I would like to acknowledge the men who speak out against the sex trade, in particular Former President Jimmy Carter. The sex trade damages all of humanity, and we need men to fight against it alongside us, for their sakes and our own.

| PART ONE

Chapter 1 ～

| THE FIRST QUESTION

What makes the simple act of shaming or blaming people complicated is the knowledge that they each had a specific history, and the more we know about it, the easier it becomes to understand why they did what they did.

RICHARD HOLLOWAY, *GODLESS MORALITY*

This book will not read in the style of a traditional memoir; it is not intended to. I have not written about prostitution with the sole focus on my own experience, because this issue is bigger than I am, and it is bigger than my place within it. My seven years in prostitution have brought me to the conviction that prostitution is also a collective, not a purely individual, experience. Therefore, I am writing this book in a manner that alternates between the personal and the universal. We women shared much more than our clients and our secrets. We shared an experience, the threads of which were so common that I have come to realise they form a pattern that makes up the basic shape of the prostitution experience. It presents a horribly ugly image.

I pay no respect or accommodation to the glamorising or sensationalising of prostitution. These are not true depictions of prostitution. They are not even caricatures; they couldn't be, because caricatures are nothing more than amplified truths, and glamour bears no resemblance to the truth here. My assessment of prostitution and my opinions of it I take from the years I spent enduring it and everything I ever saw, heard, felt, witnessed or otherwise experienced at that time. There was no glamour there. Not even the flicker of it. Not for any of us.

There is always a first question asked of the prostituted or formerly prostituted woman. It is always the same one. People want to know: 'How did you get into it?' I believe it is the first question because humans are

creatures in need of the comfort of a linear trajectory, and it is difficult to
answer because human lives are just not lived along those lines. Another
problem with that question is that it can never be fully answered in the
space of one conversation, and certainly not in the space of one sentence, as it is asked. It is just too complex to condense without losing
something vital of the answer. The truth is, there is no one reason, there
is a web of reason, and each part of it, each glimmering thread, is equally
important to the overall balance of *how* you got into prostitution.

The purpose of this book is to take something bad and try to alche-
mise it into something good. The 'something good' here is in the sharing
of this understanding for the benefit of those who want an awareness
of it, but who have never and will never experience it for themselves.
There is something good in that; I can sense it. There is something good
in exposing prostitution for what it really is. It is the illumination that
comes from shining a light in dark places. It is the essential honesty in
showing the outlines as they truly are.

Men who use prostitutes superimpose upon prostitution an image of
it which to them is satisfactory, agreeable and pleasing. This image will
vary from man to man. The only things which remain consistent are
the fantasy element involved and the reality that shifting male perceptions do nothing to alter the experience of prostitution for the women
involved. Their realities remain, concrete and immovable. It is my intention, with this book, to lay those realities before the reader.

I do not expect any of this to be easy, because there is another reason why the answering of the 'first question' is particularly difficult: it is
because it involves an unavoidable reaching into the self, a painful emotional excavation. The honest answering requires a feat of penetrative
inward searching in areas you don't want to dig, precisely because you
know what you will find. But as the most precious artefacts are those
which must be hollowed from the ground, the most valuable words are
often those which must be laboriously quarried from the self. So I am
going to have to be very thorough. I am going to have to dig.

To go back to the start, to begin to answer that first question: my home
life as a child was textbook dysfunctional. My parents were both patients

of the local psychiatric hospital, St Brendan's. It is situated within walking distance of where we lived, in a council housing estate on the north side of Dublin city.

HSE records show that my mother was 'thought to be schizophrenic' and that she was an out-patient of the hospital. My father was sometimes an out-patient, sometimes an in-patient, depending on how his manic depression was affecting him at any given time.

They were also both in the grip of active addiction; my mother to prescription drugs, my father to the lure of compulsive gambling. I don't blame my parents and I know they weren't bad people, they were sick people. These facts are simply facts and I harbour no desire to play them for tears. I record them here only because they are central to an understanding of how I became involved in a harmful, depressing, destructive lifestyle that would have been scarcely imaginable to me the day before I first embarked upon it.

I am writing this work as a person who is still in a stage of transition, working towards being secure with my place in society. It is a difficult journey, because it is not as if I am going back anywhere; I am journeying towards somewhere I never was to begin with: our lives as children set us utterly apart from mainstream society and we were raised both painfully aware of it and numbly accepting of it. We understood it. It was our position in the world. My life as a child primed me for prostitution in that it primed me to continue to live outside the sphere of what was normal. It also primed me for any other socially unacceptable or unusual pastime or pursuit; it just happened that several factors of timing and circumstance fell perfectly in place so that prostitution presented itself both as a solitary option and a viable one.

I grew up feeling as though I was separated from the world and all its inhabitants as if by something absolutely solid, but which I could not see, smell, or touch. By the time I was a young teenager in prostitution, this sense of disconnectedness from the world operated so strongly that I could go into a hairdresser to have my hair cut, but I couldn't possibly imagine being the woman holding the scissors. I could go into a bar and order a drink, but I could never imagine standing behind the bar serving it. There was a sense of adequacy, of normalcy, of decency inherent to those socially acceptable positions, and I suppose the sad thing is that, deep down, I felt I had no adequacy, I had no normalcy, and I was not decent.

There was a strangely familiar rhythm, in one particular way, in working as a prostitute: I was not reaching outside of my own belief system. I was not challenging the negative self-image I had been raised with and had carried with me all my life. Of course it caused me much suffering in the longer term, but at that time, in a sense, it was easier to accept that it would not be possible for me to assimilate into society than to set about the very frightening task of accepting my own potential. For me, that didn't even feel like an option, because I hadn't the slightest clue how that could possibly be done or even what the first step towards achieving it might be. Life is, or ought to be, a participatory experience, but it is possible for a person to be so damaged by early lifetime exclusion as to believe their only role in life is that of an observer.

By the time prostitution took its place on the stage of my life, on one of the deepest levels, the likelihood of our co-existence had already been cemented. The journey towards prostitution was complex but its advent in my life was simple. I very quickly learned how to share the stage with it. It was as if we'd rehearsed together before we'd ever met.

'Lifestyle' really is a more appropriate term as compared to 'profession' in relation to prostitution. When we think of the term 'lifestyle', certain imagery is called to mind. We might think of cocktails, coffee and croissants. Or we might think of yachts and harbours; the relaxed and stimulating holidays of the well-to-do. We might think of childcare and mortgages and the daily commute. That is not the imagery I want to call to mind here. When it comes to lifestyle, most of us, even prostitutes, don't think of women down on their knees in backstreets and hotels. This doesn't fit the view of lifestyle in the public consciousness. But it should, because 'lifestyle' simply means 'the way in which one lives,' and this is not an occupation that can be left outside your front door. A worker in another industry can come home and take off the 'teacher's cap' as it were, but complex tapestries of factors mean a prostitute can't do the same thing.

Firstly, it is not possible to discuss what you do openly, so you are bound by a secrecy which has the very distinct effect of distancing you from members of 'normal' society. The company of other prostitutes is the only company in which you can be honest, discuss the sort of day you've had, your plans for next week, the awful experience you had the night before, etc. It is the only company in which you will certainly not be ridiculed for what you do. It is the only company in which you will be met with total understanding as to how you got there, why you stay there, and why you might never get to leave.

You are pushed into the company of one group of people, and, simultaneously, out of the company of others. There is no one reason for this; there are many. As a prostitute, you're generally a night worker; you sleep well into the day, when 'normal' members of the public usually go about their work. When they are returning home and winding down for the day, you are not always long up and are often only gearing up for your 'day'. This is a simple practicality that separates you from society, and is in no way the most pervasive.

Drug and alcohol abuse are endemic. We are all used to the stereotype of the heroin addict who enters street prostitution to feed her habit. This happens in prostitution, I've seen it; but what I've seen far more regularly is women developing addictions in prostitution that they never had in the first place, usually to alcohol, valium and other prescription sedatives, and to cocaine. These substances are used to numb the simple awfulness of having sexual intercourse with reams of sexually repulsive strangers, all of whom are abusive on some level, whether they know it or not, and many of whom are deliberately so. These substances offer an effective release and escape. The level of drug and alcohol abuse in prostitution is not at all surprising to me; in fact, given the circumstances, I would expect it. This chemical escapism is encouraged strongly, although often unwittingly, by the women themselves. As in any walk of life, people influence each other and where there is present in the same community of people both the need for escapism and the constant example of it, the writing really is on the wall.

Becoming drug or alcohol dependent further separates the working prostitute from 'average' society on an emotional and psychological level and, in a lot of cases, the substance dependence accelerates the degree of time a woman must give of herself to prostitution as the addiction increases in intensity and presents a hunger that only money can feed. The effect is obvious: prostitution has caused a practical barrier in the form of an addiction, which has the cumulative effect of forcing her further into prostitution and further away from mainstream society.

The sense of 'otherness' for the woman ensnared in this lifestyle is so strong that she begins to regard herself as so utterly different from other members of society that it does not feel possible or feasible on any level to partake in that society. By that I mean it does not feel possible to get a regular job, to undertake education, or sometimes even to form relationships with people outside her sphere of reality. It is not possible, while earning an illegal living, to honestly obtain a mortgage or business loan, etc., further removing her from the remit of what it is to be considered a 'normal' functioning member of the public.

I believe this is especially true in the case of someone such as myself, whose first regular income was from prostitution and therefore had experienced no other occupational reality.

It was, I can attest, something I considered totally unimaginable, that I could ever be any kind of functioning part of the society I saw around me every day, and that was something that both caused and channelled a great deal of resentment on my part. If, while walking down to the red-light zone in the early evening, I saw a group of young women walking together in the uniform of one of the local banks (as often happened around the Baggot Street area) I would be struck by a great wave of jealousy and resentment that tore through me in a way I could scarcely justify or describe. I know today, at a distance of years and after a great deal of examining my own feelings, that I felt very keenly that they were accepted members of a world I had been excluded from, and I absolutely hated them for it.

I can testify that this sort of resentment further excludes the prostitute, because not only is she not part of society, but she also regards herself at odds with it. Society, in turn, confirms the hostilities. Attitudes and opinions directed towards prostitutes are almost never positive. A prostitute is only accepted within the sphere of prostitution, so, paradoxically, she begins to feel safe in the place in which it is least safe to be.

The years go by; her friendships with other women of her trade have become longer, therefore more solidified, and there is often no positive aspect to the companionship of other people that makes itself apparent to her. Personally I had a wider remit than that, and I am glad of it, but that sense of being closed off to those outside of prostitution did exist in me to some large degree and I witnessed its existence to a near total degree in others.

After some years have passed, it suddenly occurs to you that you cannot explain those years in any sort of official capacity. For example, if a working prostitute attempts to compile a cv, she'll quickly find herself staring at blank pages that are impossible to fill. She realises she has taken a road from which it is impossible to return. Somewhere along the path, when she wasn't even looking, a gate snapped shut behind her. It seems that now there is no way back. Besides being a criminal in the eyes of the law, she now finds that she cannot explain herself on any level to officialdom, so she is further removed from society and this has the effect of affirming and compounding what she has always felt; she is further separated and alone and apart, she is further depressed, she is further removed from the general public and the downward spiral continues, on and on and on.

So really, because all these facets combine to create a sub-culture which she is now thoroughly a part of, because she now exists in the 'world' of prostitution, 'lifestyle' is an entirely more appropriate term than 'trade', and certainly more so than 'profession'.

Luckily for me, my sense of personal identity must have been stronger than my sense of identification with the underbelly of society, even at the worst of times, either later, when I was an 'escort' and cocaine addict, or in my early teens on the streets and seeing a disgusting number of 'clients' per week.

Although I could not imagine being a part of the society around me, I had a very clear sense of who I was as an individual, and that was very fortunate for me because losing the sense of yourself, of who you actually *are*, is the easiest thing in the world for a prostitute. Apart from existing in a world that would have been previously unimaginable to you and the separation from your sense of self that inevitably comes with that, the battle is from without, as well as within, in that society conspires to convince you of your new status as an unworthy piece of shit.

Slut, tramp, brazzer, whore . . . these terms apply to you now in the most authentic sense of their meanings and it is easy to become separated from who you are, to forget who you were; and of course you can trace the trajectory of the transition, but you can never take back the person you were before that evil evolution took place.

The sad thing is the social stain that is left upon you, but the important thing is to remember that it really only exists in the perceptions of people; and so if you can manage to read the perceptions of others as of little value to you, and you can undertake the more difficult task of nullifying negative perceptions of your own, then it is possible to come out the other side of prostitution and at least make some decent effort at taking back what is left of who you were. Those remnants, unfortunately, can be hard to find, and more difficult still to identify upon recovering.

I spent seven years in prostitution and I've been fourteen years out of it now, but though I'm out of it twice as long as I was in it, it is still, unavoidably, one of the clearest, most formative experiences of my life. It shapes and forms you in particular ways. This is a hard thing to acknowledge for someone who doesn't wish to be defined by that experience, but if somebody who has been through this has any wish to be honest about its consequences, an acceptance of that fact is paramount.

It was a university of sorts. I learned a lot, probably more than I'm aware of. I honed abilities that I was previously unaware even existed, and which I still use, often semi-consciously, to this day. The knack of getting a man off as quickly as possible (though hardly a skill), was one of the first things you learned, for the simple fact that time was money and the quicker a man climaxed, the quicker you could move on the next man and the next man's money. This is an awareness you would acquire with regular clients, whose sexual penchants you were used to. I have no need to do that today. The act of sex with somebody you love and the act of sex within the punter/prostitute dynamic are about as different as it is possible to imagine. In fact, I doubt it would be imaginable for someone who hadn't experienced the depth of that distinction. I know I couldn't have dreamt it, before I had experienced it for myself.

Another of the things I acquired through prostitution was a much-heightened sense of people's intentions. That has served me well, both in and out of prostitution. It has also changed me, and served as a reminder of how I am changed.

This was not a benign alteration, and the road to that change was a long one. It began not with the first time I performed sex for money, but with the dysfunction of my family. The next steps on that road were educational disadvantage and adolescent homelessness. It is a familiar story in prostitution. It is the most common one I have ever known. I will detail my experience of it now, and you can believe that the stories of innumerable others are echoed within it.

I wavered between writing this book anonymously and in my own name for a long time. I considered the issue of anonymity and I wondered: if secrecy and shame are the threads woven together to make up the fabric of this garment, and secrecy dissipates upon disclosure, does the garment itself disintegrate? Will revealing my identity possibly, in any way, free me of shame? Would that it might, but shame exposed is not shame dispersed. In my darker moments I think identifying myself will only change the texture of this garment and have it emerge in a new incarnation, a single-threaded fabric, consisting simply of shame which has been laid bare. Which is true? Maybe both are, and it is a pointless wondering.

I could never get comfortable with the idea of writing this book anonymously though. I felt that to write it publicly was simply to share the shame between myself and my son and the rest of our family, yet I could find no peace in anonymity, so, for a long time, I was troubled. I just wanted to tell the truth, but how could I consider my account truthful if it were stamped on the cover page with a name that was not my own? Would I not have been guilty of presenting its readers with a dishonesty before they'd even opened to the first page?

Publishing this account under a pseudonym felt to me for a long time as though I had accepted the challenge of telling the truth and failed at the first hurdle. I resented it. I resented it dreadfully. Over and over I paired my first name together with a multitude of surnames in an effort to find a pseudonym. I did this because I thought if I kept my first name, I wouldn't feel so badly about not being able to publish it under my full name. It didn't work, and on reflection, why should it? My first name paired with any other is still not my name. I felt there was no arguing with the necessity of a pseudonym, and yet there was no end to that nagging conviction that to have my account published under any other name would be to not bear witness fully, to not own my account fully. I could find no peace in being represented by any of these names. What to do about that?

Eventually an answer came. I would use my partner's surname. The moment he suggested it, I knew it was the only name in the world I would not resent on the cover of this book. So there it was, and that was fine, except he and I broke up during the writing of the book and I was back to square one, wondering what to call myself.

I decided to end the mental struggle and to choose a name that expressed qualities I liked. Queen Maeve was an Irish warrior queen, and I know that the truths I'm presenting here will fly in the face of a lot of the nonsense that's circulated about prostitution, so I felt I could do with a bit of her energy. Also, folklore has it that Queen Maeve once demanded an interlude during battle because she got her period. She was not prepared, even by nature itself, to be put at an unfair disadvantage to the men. I liked her style. I've always thought the surname Conway had a certain melodic ring to it and felt it sat nicely with Maeve. I found, when looking up the meaning of 'Conway', that it had two possible meanings, one being 'fearsome warrior', so the names seemed to fit well together.

Yet, even though I'd settled on a pseudonym, that did not quell certain fears of mine about making these truths public. If examining the truth about prostitution has been one type of pain, laying these truths before the public is another. This former type of pain has accompanied me constantly through every line I've written and it will only leave after I've typed the last full stop. Thinking about actually publishing the book, laying these truths before the public, is a different kind of pain and it is made up of different components; there is a constant low-level negative feeling, the fears and paranoia of being exposed. There is a sense of defensiveness, the expectation of being judged. There is, of course, shame. Today that feels as if it is abating, but not all days are like this one, and shame, I have come to find, is more stubborn than grief. Shame does not ebb away slowly over time; it sometimes hides its face for a while, seeming to slink out of sight, only to stride purposefully back out of the shadows and onto the centre-stage of your life, as real and alive as it was the first day you saw it. Grief can and does pull this nasty little stunt too, but it has not the persistence or longevity of shame.

I imagine shame to wear a mask, like something you'd see at Hallowe'en. Its image is always ugly. I cannot see it very clearly today, but I know that does not mean it has gone away. I have decided not to wear a mask here, not even one I like in some ways, because to take my mask off is my way of confronting shame and daring it to do the same thing. That is why I've decided to tell the world my name is Rachel Moran.

Chapter 2 ⌒

CHILDHOOD SOCIAL EXCLUSION

We know the world only through our relationship to it.
DR M SCOTT PECK, *THE ROAD LESS TRAVELLED*

There were significant world events that occurred during a time when I would have been old enough to comprehend and remember them, but I never did, because of my separation from society, both practical and literal. Two good examples would be the fall of the Berlin Wall and the end of apartheid in South Africa. Even now, after all these years, I find myself making excuses. Why do I not remember the fall of the Berlin Wall? Do I not remember it was all over the television and it was all anybody could talk about? How come I don't remember the end of apartheid? Don't I remember how we Irish played our part in applying international pressure against it? Don't I remember the anti-apartheid workers' strike at Dunnes Stores? Those are the kind of questions a person in my position dreads, because the truthful answers are banging around in our heads, much louder than the lies we use to conceal them.

Here are those truths: I do not remember the end of apartheid because in 1993 I was busy working as a prostitute and developing a drug problem. I was living a lifestyle wholly outside of communal norms and felt neither welcome nor inclined to participate in society on almost any level. Foreign politics was a long long way from the conversations we prostitutes would have among us and buying newspapers and watching the news was something that simply wouldn't have occurred to me, or to most of us, in those times. Is it any wonder? Why would anyone wish to engage with a world that collectively shunned them?

I do not remember the fall of the Berlin Wall because, though we had a working television in the house at that time, on 9 November 1989, when the Wall came down, my father had been dead less than a week and my mother's schizophrenia was on a startling upswing. My father had committed suicide by throwing himself from the fourth floor of a block of flats and my mother had reacted in a manner that was creepy and horrifying: she was pleased about it. I was too disturbed and stunned to have any time for what might be happening elsewhere in the world. I could only just keep my wits about me enough to concentrate on what was going on inside our own front door. My mother had taken to dancing, literally dancing, in a crazed untrained tap-step all about the house, singing and laughing about the wonderful new freedom afforded by her recent widowhood. Please forgive the tone of bitterness, I do not know how to erase it, but that is the 'liberation' I remember from the week that saw the collapse of the Berlin Wall.

What I've been talking about here is familial dysfunction and the way in which it can separate you from the world, and can lead to social exclusion. It is such a short leap from one to the other that it is easy to confuse the two. In fact, there is no leaping involved; they literally blend into each other as they overlap. Familial dysfunction breeds social exclusion in the most thorough and painstakingly meticulous manner I can imagine, because it takes each child born into that household and schools them all the moments of their life to understand and accept that they and the world they occupy are wholly separate and apart.

I have heard a lot of nonsense spoken about how children 'don't know any better'. Children *do* know better, and they know better in a hundred ways and for a thousand reasons. You actually come to your first consciousness, as a toddler in a dysfunctional home, with the sense that this home is different from others. In my family's case, we encountered practical examples of our own poverty every day and we knew from the earliest age that it set us apart from those around us. Also, occasionally the world outside our community would intrude upon our lives to confirm the fact. For example, that happened every year in the form of the budget. My mother would be interested in two things: would there be a rise in the cost of tobacco? And would there be a rise in the rate of social welfare? She was not interested in petrol prices because she couldn't dream of owning a car, even if she could drive, which she couldn't. She was not interested in anything to do with interest rates or mortgages, because she couldn't conceive of owning her own home. She was not interested in the tax rates that affected those in employment because her husband was almost always out of work and since she'd had her children she'd never had a job; nor was she interested in policies that affected trade, commerce or the business world because she was an uneducated housewife from the disadvantaged classes and inhabited an entirely different sphere of reality. Most of what was discussed was not relevant to us and never had been. The budget was just another way of officialdom reminding us that we were different.

So our status in society was very clear to us, even as very young children. Our situation as the offspring in a family with mentally ill people at the helm was equally clear. Mental illness on the scale that afflicted my parents would be impossible not to be aware of, even at the youngest age, and most especially in the case of my mother.

My father's manic depression meant that he would often, for extended periods, sink into a very morose state where he'd simply sit and stare at nothing for long stretches of time and I knew that this was not normal. I'd never seen any adult, besides my mother, do that. Otherwise, her illness was altogether different and I was acutely aware of the differences in their behaviour. Her illness would actually be impossible not to detect, even for the youngest of young children, because it involved such fantastical breaks from reality. Her delusions would involve supposed occurrences that couldn't possibly have happened, things that broke the laws of nature; gravity, for example. It was very clear to me that she was someone who saw things that didn't happen. What was also very clear was that other adults did not discuss these things, so obviously they were people who did not experience things unless they *had* happened. The disparity between the behaviour of my mother and that of the teachers at school (who really were the only other consistent example of adulthood we had during our childhoods) was so cavernously wide as to be indisputable evidence that there was something wrong with her; but I had known even before I'd had the example of other adults that there was something wrong with our mother.

Her descent into illness escalated very rapidly in my early years and I clearly remember asking her one day when she was going to get better. She looked at me in a manner that was wide-eyed and innocent and slightly perplexed, as if she wondered where I might have gotten such an idea. She told me that she was not sick. That was the day I realised my mother was sick but was unaware of it. I don't know for certain how old I was that day, but we had that conversation in the sitting room in my grandfather's city-centre flat and we moved out of there when I was four years old. My mother's twelve-year addiction to the prescription tranquiliser Mogadon, in tandem with her untreated schizophrenia, produced symptoms and behaviours that would have been impossible to mistake for anything other than a severe form of sickness. I knew it was not normal for her to lie in bed until 6 p.m. each and every evening of her life. This she put down to insomnia; in fact, it was just one of the many symptoms of mental illness combined with addiction.

There are a million little ways to feel socially excluded as a child. Here are some of my memories of that: never having a pencil in school, always having to borrow one, or if I did have one, it being about an inch-and-a-half long, chewed to bits and the subject of mockery and derision; rarely having a book; always having to share someone else's or 'look in' as the teacher would say, and battling feelings of humiliation and the conviction that I was intruding and regarded as a nuisance; never having any knickers to wear and hoping, especially in the school yard, that nobody had any cause to find out; never having any socks; wearing my father's, which would be doubled over to compensate for their size and withering with shame in PE when I had to take my shoes off. Having to answer the teacher when she asked me in front of the whole class why I wasn't wearing my school jumper in the middle of January, when the truth was I hadn't got one; and, if I was late and knew all eyes would be on me, counting backwards from ten outside the classroom door because it helped to steel myself against the shame of being stared at. All of these things caused me to understand that I was separate and apart from my classmates.

Of course I couldn't apply the correct terms to what was happening to me then. All I knew was that I was regarded as different in my neighbourhood and different in my school, for obviously justifiable reasons. I saw that the situation was wrong, and I was right in thinking that it was; but my mistake was in believing I was part of that wrongness.

There would come a time in my adult life when I'd study criminology and sociology, but I had lived these things long before I'd ever read about them. Later, studying those subjects in an environment that was so detached and divorced from them, was a strange and surreal experience.

I know that my own journey into prostitution was strongly encouraged by economic deprivation and social disadvantage. These lacks generally affect males and females slightly differently. While they will strongly encourage both genders into a life of criminality, the exact type of crime will often differ along gender lines. Men, in my experience, are more likely to become drug dealers, women drug couriers. Where theft is concerned males are more likely to become armed robbers, whereas the majority of shoplifters I've known have been female. As gender differences relate to prostitution, men are far more likely to be found attempting to control and profit from it by taking on the role of pimps than they are likely to sell their own bodies.

I have witnessed in others levels of destitution and economic lack that could, in my opinion, justify criminality having been breathed into them, and I have seen this many times in my lifetime. To give one example, I will have to move forward in time: a few years after I got out of prostitution and about a year or so after I'd returned to education, I was walking down Parnell Street when a homeless man approached me. He was filthy, dressed in rags and had a long dirty matted beard. He looked at least forty years old, possibly forty-five. He spoke to me and the words that came of his mouth hit me with the shock of a slap. He said, 'Rachel, do you not remember me? It's me, John!' He said all this with a huge delighted smile on his face. He was so happy to see me. Past the beard and the dirt and the roughened skin I saw his eyes, the same piercing blue, the same liveliness behind them, sparks of the same merry and mischievous light. It was indeed John.

John and I had been in a psychiatric assessment centre for adolescents during the summer of 1990. We'd both been fourteen at the time. I'd been placed there because I'd been suspended from a hostel, thrown out of a foster home and expelled from school all in the space of a few weeks. There were a dozen or so other kids in the centre but John and I had a great connection. We were always laughing. There was a little one-roomed school on the grounds and there came a point where I had to force myself not to look at John in class any more because any time we made eye contact the pair of us would end up laughing and getting into trouble with the teacher. In the end I got sick of being psychiatrically assessed and walked out of there. I hadn't seen John since then and ten years had passed between that day and the day I met him on Parnell Street. Ten years, and he had aged thirty. He told me that he'd been homeless since he'd turned eighteen. When a boy in care turned eighteen, he was expected to be able to take care of himself. He could either sink or swim. Many sank, as John did.

We talked for a good few minutes and then he held his arms out for a hug. I hugged him, and was nauseated by the smell of him, and the guilt hit right after the smell. I cried as I walked away.

I'm sure the day I walked away from John he went right back to whatever he'd been doing; and I'm sure he stole and scammed his way through life any way he could, just as I had done when I'd been similarly desperate.

I have heard it said that economic deprivation and social exclusion have nothing whatever to do with the existence of criminality and that the latter can be explained simply by the presence of evil. I met many young people like John in the early 1990s. I *was* a young person like John in the early 1990s. I know what happened to bring us to where we were and I know evil had nothing to do with it.

Chapter 3 ~

|MY MOTHER'S ILLNESS

She had secluded herself from a thousand natural and
healing influences; that, her mind, brooding and solitary,
had grown diseased, as all minds do and must and will
that reverse the appointed order of their maker . . .
CHARLES DICKENS, *GREAT EXPECTATIONS*

The symptom of my mother's illness that was most obvious and most overt was a terrible fear of the world, and she was afraid both for herself and for her children. It was this fear that caused her to confine us to our home, so that the five of us were only allowed to go to school and to the local shops, very rarely anywhere else. We were not allowed to play with or interact with any of our neighbours' children. A 'hello' to any of our neighbours would have been taken as a sign of disrespect to our mother—by her, of course—so we were raised knowing to keep silent on our way in or out of the estate where we lived in north Dublin inner city. This was noted by the locals, along with our filthy ragged clothes, and naturally we were marked out as different. We were treated as such by the neighbours' children and (though I doubt they truly understood what they were doing) the cruelty of their daily taunts seriously compounded our sense of isolation. This in turn fuelled our mother's tendency to keep us isolated. But this was just one manifestation of an illness that became more marked as it displayed itself in increasingly disturbing ways.

When I remember back over my childhood I see that it was like a living yardstick; an eerily accurate mode of measurement by which to gauge the progression of an unquiet mind. For example, I developed a fairly severe stutter in a short space of time as a child of about eight or nine. It didn't last long. That was a matter of luck I'd imagine, as my mother's technique of language correction was to hit me in the face with such force each time I stuttered that I would see blinding flashes of light like great bursts of electric lightning which, together with the pain, would leave me trembling in shock and fear. I have to give it to her though; it was effective. She literally frightened the stutter out of me, and I've never had a recurrence of it since.

One of my most brutal memories of childhood is of opening our kitchen door and finding my mother lying unconscious in a monstrously huge puddle of her own blood. I was about nine at the time. I remember, even though I wasn't a very small child, that the blood seemed like a small lake, extending three or four feet out from her body in all directions. I don't remember what happened after that, but I do remember her arriving home several days later in the same coat she'd been wearing, now covered in maroon-coloured dried blood and her muttering some nonsense about having had to receive a four-pint blood transfusion due to her chronic anaemia. There was no reference made by either of us to the truth, which was that she had tried to kill herself and had very nearly managed it.

Where does the fragmentation of a dysfunctional family begin? I believe it begins before the family does. I believe the wounds are already there, waiting to be cut into existence by the meeting of two unsuitable people and the birth of the children they go on to create with a love that is potent in its powers of destruction. What happened was that my parents both reached out for the comfort of love, as all humans do, and that unfortunately they just happened to reach for it within each other. Of course I regard myself fortunate that flawed and fractured love existed, otherwise I would not be here to record the outcome. As strenuous as life has sometimes been, and as emotionally arduous as it was in the beginning, it is my life and I have always loved it. There were times when I loved it more in the having than in the living; still, it's been a rare day I considered letting it go.

Some of the terms that are used around family dysfunction would not be accurate in reference to my family. Terms like disintegration, degeneration, deterioration seem to refer to the destruction of something that was at one time healthy or whole. My family did not break down: my family was born broken.

My father had his first nervous breakdown at eighteen, some fourteen years before he met my mother. My mother had begun acting strangely some time during her teens, the best part of ten years before she met my father. These two people, both afflicted by serious mental illness, met and paired together as adults, my mother being twenty-four, my father thirty-two at the time.

My father's first breakdown had landed him in St Brendan's psychiatric hospital and his manic depression was diagnosed there and then. His family were keenly aware that any woman he settled with would have to be a stabilising influence in his life, and my poor mother, with her untreated schizophrenia, was probably the one woman in all of Dublin who least fit the bill. But they did meet, they did marry, and the manifestations of my mother's illness continued unabated and roared through her marriage and the childhoods of her children like the ocean in all of our ears.

Another expression of her sickness would have been the evening, a day or two after our father's suicide, when she sent me and my older brother to our father's bed-sit to collect whatever was useful of his belongings. We were thirteen and fourteen at the time. It was in Rathmines, on the south side of the city. The main street was dominated by the neon lights of the Swan shopping centre. I had never seen them before that, and every time I've seen them since they've brought me back to the darkness of that November night. It was only about eight o'clock, but the sky was black and those lights shone bright against it so as to bring to mind the video games and pinball machines you'd see in an arcade.

When we got to the bed-sit it was just that, another one-roomed hovel with a paltry attempt at a kitchenette in one corner and a single bed in the other. We'd seen many of these over the years, a new one each time my parents split up, which was often. That was just the last time our family was physically fractured, and as for the regular dissolution of our family; I remember the cruelty of it, the way it was accepted without question that whenever the family broke down, my father was always the disposable member. I have always carried with me, heavily, like a weight, a deep compassion for separated fathers. It is easy to see why.

So we stood there in his bed-sit, looking around. We'd never been in this one before. It was particularly small and of course, being the last place he would ever occupy leant it a distinctive sort of melancholy; a feeling of pitiful sadness with the shameful smell of poverty and degradation all bound up with that awful sense of finality that only death brings. There was, besides the elements that made it unique to the death of my father, a heavy sombre atmosphere, a sort of sensory aroma of fatality I'd never experienced before.

We'd been instructed to take anything that was of any use or value. There wasn't much. We hardly spoke while we were there and when we did it was very quietly, as though we knew what we were doing would have offended our father, and no doubt it would have, though I can see now, through my adult eyes, that he'd have been much more offended for our sakes than his own. But there was shame then, at that time, and I wonder could my mother, in her sickness, possibly have known I'd feel like a vulture picking over my own father's bones?

We scrunched closed packets of cornflakes and sugar and took them home to our mother, who inspected her meagre inheritance with glazed, emotionless eyes. Though I could see no ordinary mourning in them, I could see something very deep in her eyes that told me she held the whole universe behind them, and all the grief that was in it.

There are too many painful memories, and I will not recount them all, because they are not all necessary. I will only recount what is necessary to show the reader how and why things came to be as they were, and I don't believe the excavation of every old bone is required in order to do that. But this image, this is important: two children walking back to a bus stop on a winter's night carrying light bags, each gram of which weighed as shameful. This is important to an understanding of how and why it could not have been hoped we'd grow up without encountering great adversity in our lives.

Sometimes, when I am feeling very embittered, I feel assaulted by the assertions of others that my mother will 'always be my mother'. I regard them as the pious ramblings of people who haven't got a clue what it feels like to be raised by a paranoid schizophrenic. I contend then that you can sweeten stale cream till it's edible, but no amount of sugar stops it being sour cream. I resent them, I do; these people who maintain that my mother will always be my mother.

I once worked with a woman who had two grown daughters, young women in their twenties. She spoke about them daily: what they'd been up to, what they'd gone through, what was going on in their lives. She recounted their experiences and the advice she'd administered to steer them through work problems and social problems and their heartbreak with men. Regardless of what trials they were going through, I couldn't help but think how lucky they were, those heartbroken daughters.

I have often wondered what a normal mother/daughter bond is, but because circumstances have placed me so removed from that concept, I do not wonder this with any overt sense of sadness; just simple curiosity, tinged with an abstract sort of regret. I wonder what that is like, and when I see grown women having a laugh or a hug or a conversation with their mothers, I find myself looking with concentration at what they are doing. I watch their facial expressions and make an effort to decode their body language. There is inquisitiveness there, paired with a sense of puzzlement. I am trying to understand what it is they are experiencing. I am trying to decipher dynamics I know nothing about. It interests me, but it leads to melancholy feelings.

As far as fully rounded emotional maturity is concerned, in many ways my mother was a young girl while I was, and I've no doubt she still is to this day. We don't see anything of each other any more and, sad as it is, that is what works best for me right now and no doubt for her too. For my part, to a very great degree, I have moved away from my feelings of blame-filled bitterness. It's been widely commented that there comes a time when a person stops thinking of their parents as parents and starts viewing them as people, and I believe it's when that happens that the inclination towards pity shifts from you to them. When I think about my parents now, the overwhelming feeling I have for them is sorrow: just that; sorrow and compassion. I was surprised by the force of the compassion for my mother when it did hit. I almost hadn't been expecting it. I had always known some part of me felt sorry for her but I didn't look too deeply into that, the same way when you break a bone you make it your business not to flex the limb.

|A WEB OF DYSFUNCTION

*It is hard for children to withhold assent from their
mother—to stand far enough apart to judge that what
she is doing is not part of nature.*
              NUALA O'FAOLAIN, *ARE YOU SOMEBODY?*

My parents were not to blame for my becoming involved in
prostitution. As I have said, they were sick people, not bad
people. It is the background of dysfunction that acts as a
gateway to that lifestyle and while sometimes such an environment can
be attributed to the moral failings of parents, I truly believe that was
not so in my case. Yes, they made choices that negatively influenced the
direction of my life, but they didn't act alone. They were directed themselves by very powerful influences quite beyond their control. Mental
illness, addiction and poverty existed as the trio of primary roots in our
experience of dysfunction, and those were not threads of experience
with which my parents or any parents would wish to be familiar, much
less intentionally desire or invite.

Whatever my parents got wrong, they must have gotten something
right, because they reared five intelligent children who went on, after
some adversity, to form decent and relatively emotionally healthy lives.

I used to think I knew what it was to come from as horrible a background as it was possible to know. I found out very quickly upon leaving
home that I had no such knowledge. I met young teenage girls during
my own early teens who had been horribly abused, physically and sexually, and bore obvious physical and emotional scars to prove it. I came
to discover that sexual molestation was commonplace among the girls I

met and existed in a lot of cases as the primary reason they had fled their homes.

I had, thankfully, no such experience; my father was a decent man. So if I hold a mirror up and look at where I've been and contrast and compare childhoods by that barometer, I have very little to gripe about. Still, though, conditions of consistent dysfunction act as a catalyst for future problems and if there is one thing I resent my mother for it is that she raised us in such a way as to be totally unskilled in dealing with the world, before turning us out, as fledgling humans, straight into the thick of it.

These resentful feelings are there because I am only human and I can hardly be expected to be happy about it, but they are partnered with the knowledge that my mother did the best she could. And I wonder, if I were raising five children while struggling with an untreated mental illness along with a decade-long addiction to prescription drugs, and all this in the midst of extreme poverty, would *I* have done a better job? Could I even have found the strength to do an equal job? Somewhere inside myself, I doubt it.

Looking at the three root causes of our family's experience of dysfunction, now, when enough years have gone by to still my resentment to a degree that some level of contemplative analysis is possible, I can see how they worked together in a supportive triangular formation; and I can see how that formation nurtured itself and each of its separate components.

Mental illness, addiction and poverty: active addiction is the surest route to extreme poverty and its function can only be accelerated when the people in its grip are poor to begin with. Mental illness, of course, reduces the capacity for rational thinking, which lessens the likelihood of those suffering from it engaging in any sort of successful struggle against either it or the grip of addiction.

Poverty itself is an aggravating factor in mental illness, and it was especially so in the 1970s and 80s, when the only in-patient treatment available was substandard and wholly inadequate. Also, in a household with five young children, poverty creates the perfect breeding ground for depression, a central element of mental illness, which the depressive addict will then attempt to alleviate with their substance of choice, the use of which will further aggravate their mental condition. Poverty provokes a desire for escapism, which encourages addiction; and mental illness incapacitates, making employment less likely, therefore copper-fastening poverty.

Really, I could go round in loops all day, uncovering further and deeper reasons how and why those three elements nurtured each other, but there is no need: my parent's problems were clearly relentless; besides, it is an upsetting thing to examine the impossible maze that ensnared those two people who loved me. 'What hope had they got?' The question is a cry that is angry and impassioned, but the answer comes back low-spoken in a tone that is factual and cold: 'They had none.'

I know that I was mentally and emotionally abused on a daily basis until I was fourteen years old. That abuse came about not by way of deliberate intent on the part of my parents, but rather as a consequence of the conditions their illnesses conspired to create. That truth, unfortunately, wasn't enough to alleviate the damage the abuse was responsible for, and why should it have been?

If somebody has spent their first fourteen years of life in a state of almost constant tension, physically and mentally stiff, as if continually braced against some oncoming storm, how much smaller is the leap into a situation which will place them in circumstances to which they will respond and react as they have always done? In this way and for this reason, prostitution was much more feasible for me than for the child of a non-dysfunctional home.

For all the tensions and stressors of my childhood, I do not claim, among the children my parents reared, to have drawn the short straw; not by a long way. For a large portion of my childhood, almost as much as she needed to have somebody on whom to vent her frustrations, my mother was in need of somebody to hold in high regard. That position was mine for a long time and retaining my 'post' involved the execution of particular types of patience and cunning merged together to form an unsavoury skill. Dealing with a mentally ill woman in such a way as to benefit yourself and your position within a dysfunctional household is a skill indeed and every day for me presented both the necessity and the opportunity to practise it.

The negative side of my mother's nature, her all-consuming animosity, was in many respects something akin to a flame. It had to consume; it couldn't survive otherwise, and just like fire, you could blow it away and it would live elsewhere, as long as it had somewhere else to go and something else to feed upon.

I could see what aggravated her, she made that very clear, and I deduced that the best way to play the game was not only to behave so as to deflect negative attention from myself, but also to actively direct her aggression onto the other children so as to make doubly sure that I would remain unscathed. I deflected attention from flaws she might perceive in me by way of regular selfless acts, such as cleaning the house from top to bottom while she was in bed asleep, and also by exploiting through encouragement seeds of derision that existed in her mind, directed at my brothers and sisters. All of this had to be executed in a very subtle manner because schizophrenics are hyper-perceptive and if she had ever discovered the ruse that would have spelled disaster for me; so I had to learn to gently encourage these ideas that my siblings were bad, misbehaved and unruly.

Because she had made a confidant of me, and treated me as an adult and an equal, it was often only a matter of responding agreeably to her never-ending diatribe about my siblings' characters and behaviours. These perceived flaws existed only in her imagination, but whenever she would express them, I would deliberately encourage them. It was a constant exercise in manipulation on my part, and by dint of simple practice, I eventually became very good at it. It was, in essence, a struggle for a position of relative ease within the household. There were so many stressors in our lives at that time, from within and without, that a position of some favour with our mother was very enviable and I was prepared to resort to ruthlessness in order to attain it. It was a survival tool that I honed as a child in response to an appalling daily reality; but still, to this day, I am deeply ashamed of it.

One example of an outside stressor was the fact that we were known by the other children in the estate simply as 'The Knackers'. They'd dubbed us with that title in response to our permanently dirty hair and tattered clothes, which were passed from one child to the next, regardless of what sort of state they were in.

They called us this to our faces on a daily basis for the ten years I lived in that house. A couple of days after my youngest brother was born in June 1989, I went to the local shop to buy a packet of nappies for him. My older brother had had his first ride home in a police car that day. He'd been caught shoplifting in the local supermarket and my mother was at her wits' end about what the neighbours would say. I personally couldn't understand why she'd give a damn about the neighbours or what they'd have to say; it wasn't as if we could number any friends among them.

So anyway, I walked into the shop; I was thirteen at the time. There were three or four of the neighbours' children, all around my age, standing huddled together in a group in the middle of the shop floor and I heard the boy with his back to me say, very distinctly: 'You know the young fella out of the knackers' house? He just got brought home in a police car.' At that moment, one of the children he was speaking to spotted me and elbowed him in the ribs. They all glanced at me quickly, looked away, and fell silent. I passed them without a word or a look and made my way to the counter.

It was a shock of revelation; a very undesirable kind. I paid for the nappies in a sort of daze and walked out of the shop and all the way home still reeling from the realisation that they hadn't only called us 'Knackers' to our faces with the intent to insult; it was also simply a term of reference, a means of identification. 'Knackers' was what we actually *were* to them. It is not a term I could ever use in reference to the Travelling people.

Years later, in prostitution, on hearing prostitutes casually referred to as 'whores', I was imbued again with the understanding that an insult cuts much deeper when it is not intended to insult, when it is presented as a simple term of reference with no intention to affront. The prostitute knows that she lives in a society which, however saturated with sexual imagery, is still steeped in the veneration of virginity, and has the wit to know that since she is placed on the opposite end of that spectrum she will not find herself venerated any time soon. When someone castigates women like me for their histories, I just think quietly to myself: you could have been me, I could have been you, and isn't the whole world made up of junkies who just never got strung out?

But anyway, this is an example of the sort of banishment and shunning we lived with as children; this was an enormous part of our daily reality, this experience of being ostracised by our neighbours' children on the one hand and being refused permission to mix with them on the other. In this way, we really only had one reality to which we could identify and belong, and that was within the home. Inevitably we would develop all the psychological problems that living in such an environment entails, constant and ensnared witnesses as we were to the sickness that raged within its walls.

Of course, sheer poverty set us further apart and compounded our sense of otherness in ways that operated beyond the physical realities and practicalities of economic lack. I remember Brother Luke's of Bow Street well. Our mother used to send us down there when we were children to ask for food and to explain that our family couldn't afford any. As young as we were, we understood the nature of begging. It humiliated us, yes, but we were inured to it so that what might have been a sharp sting to other children was just a dull thud in us.

I remember so well that old medieval-looking street off Smithfield. The brother there (I'm not sure if he was Brother Luke himself) would move around the kitchen swathed in his huge brown cassock that skimmed the floor as he wrapped meat and packed tins and cut great lumps of butter from an enormous block. I used to wonder what all that food was for; he never kept anything in small amounts. Years later I found out it was a food centre for the homeless.

I can't remember him ever saying a word. He may have taken an oath of silence, I don't know, but I always got the impression that the sight of us depressed him, and probably it did, but it more likely just saddened him. His silence frightened me then, but I can see now that he was a very kind man.

I remember one Christmas week he gave me and my sister so much food we could scarcely carry it and had to keep stopping for rest breaks all the way home. The load we carried made a forty-minute journey out of a ten-minute walk. It was so much the more awkward because he'd given me an enormous cake and I had to carry it so that it wouldn't get mashed in the box while managing half a dozen bags strung along either arm. There was no top on the cake box and I remember the neighbours' children gawking at us as we walked in and the keen sense of prestige involved in being seen carrying an enormous cake, coupled with the relief that they didn't know where it came from.

I'd often be sent around to the St Vincent de Paul who would hold a clinic in a building adjoining our local church one day a week; I think it was a Friday. There was a dim waiting room with a scruffy terracotta-tiled floor and I remember clearly the humiliation of sitting alongside the other people on the benches that lined the walls. I was not humiliated, for the most part, because of waiting there for charity, as we were all waiting for the same reason; but the sting was in being the only child in that room, because I could decode from the adults' sidelong glances that my unaccompanied presence there spoke volumes about what was going on at home.

My mother's propensity to treat me as though I were ten years my senior began at a very early age and I'm sure it had a great deal to do with my feeling older than I was all throughout my childhood and adolescence. From the age of about eight, she would send me alone to visit my father during his stays in the psychiatric hospital. That was always a dismal experience, as he would be medicated and was always deeply depressed, often to the point of immobility. I also had negative associations with St Brendan's on account of earlier memories I had of my mother sitting crying on the white benches of its grounds. One particular day though, it went well beyond the depressing.

My father was usually located in the day wards, which was the term for the downstairs dormitories that housed patients who had signed themselves in for treatment. I wasn't aware of the existence of any other wards at that time.

When I approached the desk that day and asked to see my father there was a delay I hadn't experienced before. Normally, on giving his name, I would be directed to his bed. The nurse behind the desk went off and came back with a man who was tall, dressed in white, and of a heavy build, with a big belly that protruded far over his belt. A male nurse, though I hadn't any idea who or what he was, ignorant as I was that there was any such thing at the time.

He guided me towards a lift I'd never been in and through what seemed to me then to be huge steel doors. The lift seemed extraordinarily large and was sheeted with steel and standing inside its metal walls as the lift moved slowly upwards, I just knew that something was wrong.

The lift doors opened and the man walked me out into a hallway. The walls were cream and a dead-looking green. Straight away there was the sense that this was a place so different from downstairs it was scarcely imaginable that anyone could make the transition simply by way of a lift.

Just as the nurse was about to walk towards my father's bed, which I couldn't see as it was behind a cubicle wall, the most intimidating person I had ever seen lumbered by. He was enormous in stature, seemed about six-and-a-half feet tall, with huge arms and shoulders. But it was his walk, not his stature, which exuded a sense of menace. He put one foot in front of the other in the manner of zombies walking in the movies and his eyes just stared straight ahead; he seemed to have neither time nor trouble for looking in any other direction.

He opened his mouth and emitted a sort of deep guttural moaning sound that resonated more horribly than anything I'd ever heard as it bounced back off the walls, and the last I remember of him was looking as the back of his head as he moved onwards up the hall and I started to walk again, beside the nurse who'd temporarily stopped to clear his path. That in itself had struck fear into me; that the nurse, whom I'd regarded as an authority figure just seconds before, had deferred power to this man.

We walked on and I saw that bodies lay in beds all around the ward, or sat up in bed, just staring with a spaced-out resignation that rendered them little more than statues that somehow managed to breathe, and a great air of misery and utter hopelessness permeated the air and made it heavy, so that I felt physically pressed against by it.

When we got to my father's bed the nurse walked away and left me there. Everywhere I looked I saw dead colours; shadows of grey, dirty shades of cream, and that horrible decomposing green. I remember thinking how unwell my father looked while he made the gargantuan effort of lifting his head off the pillow. I kept saying, 'Dad, Dad', and pulling at his shoulder, and eventually he slowly raised his head and looked at me. I saw that he was heavily medicated. His eyes were glassy and unfocused and as he recognised me I thought I saw them cloud with shame. He managed the briefest of conversations before he sank back beneath the fog. I cannot remember what was said, but I know that if I could, recounting it would not take up more than a couple of lines. I'm sure he must have asked after my mother, because that was always his first question when he hadn't seen her in a while.

I didn't know what to do. I sat on the edge of the bed in the end and stared at the cubicle wall till enough time had passed that seemed reasonable for a visit. I stood up and said goodbye to him and then I went looking for the nurse.

When I got home I told my mother about the man who'd frightened me in the hospital and she said to me: 'Your father is afraid of that man because he beats him.' That was a typical example of her thoughtless wounding tongue, and all I could think about after that was my father being beaten by that man, and thinking about it, for a long time, I couldn't stop wishing I had hugged my sleeping father.

Memories of childhood are connected to us by a secret door, which we rarely consider. We travel back to those places, summoned, whether or not we are desirous of making the journey. The key to this portal morphs and changes from moment to moment. To that time, for me, the key might be that particular shade of loathsome green in a public toilet; tomorrow it might be a pretty white-painted bench in a public park. But whatever is responsible for bringing me back there in my mind serves the same purpose, to forcibly cause me again to experience that sense of stepping out of a lift and into a nightmare. I have never liked lifts, but I've never shared that common fear of a sense of forced enclosure. I would imagine that fear engulfs the moment the doors begin to close. I feel the stab of anxiety at the opposite moment, when the doors begin to open.

To this day I don't understand why I was allowed, alone, at that age, into the secure ward of a mental hospital. But then Ireland was a different place in the mid-1980s, and I'd imagine people scarcely knew what to do when confronted with a young child presenting herself at a mental institution, obviously deeply assured that she had every business to be there. Had they not allowed me in, I'd just have a different dismal memory; I'd be remembering the day I wasn't allowed in to visit my father. I'd be remembering wanting to go in and comfort him and not being allowed to do that; and that is the thing about severe family dysfunction: when the problems come from within, there is almost nothing that can be done to make things better from without. That is not to say that kind-natured strangers did not sometimes try: they did, and the memory of their actions stays with me to this day.

I remember when my youngest sister spent several weeks in Cherry Orchard hospital in 1985. She was suffering from some sort of virus and was five at the time. I made the two-legged journey there to visit her alone, as my mother never had any time for that sort of thing and my parents were separated at the time. When the day came for me to collect her and bring her home, I found, to my horror, at the bus stop on Westmoreland Street, that I had lost the pound note my mother had given me for our bus fare. It was about seven or eight o'clock in the evening but it was wintertime and already very dark. There was no turning back and I got the bus to Cherry Orchard and decided to worry about how to get us both home when I got there. (I cannot remember if I had change enough to get that bus or if I had to make my case to the bus driver. I'd say it was probably the latter, because I do remember talking to him, which wouldn't have been necessary otherwise.)

I got off the bus and walked up the long dark road lined with poplar trees that seemed, against the night sky, to be menacingly tall and resolved that there was nothing for it but to appeal to someone's sense of charity. I made my way into the hospital and when my sister and I were getting ready to leave, I explained to the nurse that I had lost our bus fare, told her how far we had to go, and asked if she'd be able to give me the money for the bus home. The look on her face was one I'd seen on many faces and it was something that made me deeply uncomfortable, that I had that effect on people; that my presence so often worked the features of strangers into that same sense of affronted appal. They were little stabs, those expressions. She called a taxi for us and paid the driver in advance. I remember on the taxi ride home feeling warm, grateful and ashamed.

Of course there were good times: I remember (and strangely this memory induces the greatest sadness of all) my mother sitting on my father's knee as they kissed and cuddled and hugged to the tune of Kris Kristofferson's 'Loving her was Easier (Than Anything I'll Ever do Again)', which played loudly on the old vinyl record player. I saw this scene more than once and I came to identify that song very clearly as an expression of their love. To this day I cannot listen to it without battling a tidal wave of emotion, the origins of which I'm certain, but the transition of a happy thought into tears confuses me still.

I did love Christmas-time as a child, poverty or not. I adored the smell of the pine trees. I still do. When we lived in the city centre my mother would take me into O'Connell Street and Henry Street shopping and I would be mesmerised at the sight of all the lights.

I remember one Christmas, after we'd moved out of town, my father bringing home a tree so tall he had to practically saw it in half in order to make it fit into the kitchen, which was like walking into a forest by the time he'd completed the operation. I felt as if I was in Narnia and I know that my enduring insistence on buying a huge genuine tree every December has its origins in that day.

Sometimes my father would play silly games with us where he'd fashion a ridiculous looking hat out of some old cloth and style himself as a wizard and he'd stand there asking us questions. If we guessed the right answer we'd win a chocolate bar out of a bag he'd be holding.

If ever, in the morning time, there'd be hot porridge or gas in the heater, you could be sure my father was responsible for it. He'd line us up on the wooden benches and place the heater opposite us so we could warm our legs. If there was any jam in the house, he'd put a dollop of it in the porridge, which my mother derided as a common low-class habit he'd picked up back in the days when he'd been running around Cabra

West with the arse hanging out of his trousers. This view of his upbring-
ing was, like so many other things, a fiction of her mind.

Sometimes I used to sit on the stairs outside the sitting room listening to my father playing guitar. I have never heard anyone play like that.
My father was a great jazz guitarist and had been a member of several
Irish showbands, including the Dublin City Showband. If, during my
parent's frequent fights, my father couldn't afford to move out, he would
retreat to the sitting room and live there, like it was his own little flat. It
was filled with his records, guitars, amps and other musical equipment.
He had everything you could need in there for a little self-contained flat,
including the sofa he slept on. He even bought his own kettle, and I used
to sit outside listening to him play. He never found out about that.

On and off for a couple of years my mother was in the habit of allowing me to stay up a bit later than the other children. Sometimes we'd pot
plants together. I felt very close to her during those times and regardless of the absence of a mother-daughter bond, I did, and do, love my
mother.

It is difficult, both in the practical and the emotional sense, searching
for the good times among the memories of a dysfunctional childhood.
It is rather akin to hunting for pretty pebbles among the mass of shingle
and shale of an enormously large beach. When you find them, they are
lovely and precious because they're rare; but their very rarity reminds
you how much crap surrounded them and kept them hidden. Their
purity though, is so much the more beautiful for the contrast with all
that surrounds them. And just now it hits me; maybe in this last line I
have solved the riddle of those Kris Kristofferson tears.

Chapter 5 ∾

| HOMELESSNESS

We humans are so constituted that we need a sense of our own social significance. Nothing can give us more pleasure than the sense that we are wanted and useful. Conversely, nothing is more productive of despair than a sense that we are useless and unwanted.

DR M SCOTT PECK, *PEOPLE OF THE LIE*

I think people usually use the term 'homelessness' without ever really being able to understand what that means. I think they do so because homelessness, like prostitution, is not a place in life that is possible for someone to fully comprehend unless they've been there. A caring person will be moved by compassion to sympathise with the homeless, but unless they've been homeless themselves, they cannot truly empathise in the sense that they feel another's suffering. Not to be flippant, homelessness actually means sofalessness, chairlessness, table-lessness, TV-lessness, fridgelessness, cookerlessness, showerlessness (a dreadful condition) and, worst of all, bedlessness.

The word 'homeless' seems to present the condition as a single lack, but homelessness is actually many individual deficiencies combined. The worst of them are emotional; but to mention the physical challenges first: the single worst bodily aspect of homelessness is exhaustion. It is caused by several different factors including sleep-deprivation, hunger, and a constant need to remain on the move.

I had left my family home a couple of months after my father's suicide. Within weeks of my father's death, my mother's paranoia and propensity for scapegoating had reached fever pitch and were wholly concentrated on me. She assailed me verbally each and every day. In our constant rows she regularly spat out the suggestion that I should contact a social worker and find myself a hostel. The more I thought about her suggestion, the more it made sense to me. I was very scared about walking out into the world and striking out on my own, but my home life was simply intolerable and I knew I could not stay, so I did exactly as she suggested. I went down to the local health centre and asked to see a social worker. I felt very determined, as though I was finally taking control of my own life, but I crumpled into a mess of tears when I began explaining to the social worker why I was there. I kept repeating, 'I have to get out of there; I just have to get out of there'. She had me out of there within a week, and so began the dizzying experience of living in State care.

My first placement was in a Salvation Army-run hostel in the city centre called Lefroy House. I was homeless sporadically over the span of the following eighteen months, between the ages of fourteen and fifteen-and-a-half. Whenever my stay in a hostel or B&B would come to an end, I would usually find myself homeless again. Near the beginning of my stints of utter destitution I lived a very solitary existence, not mixing with anybody, not approaching anybody, not asking for help, and, consequently, not receiving it.

Sometimes I walked out of hostels, other times I was thrown out. I was never violent, but I was absolutely immovable when there were rules I didn't want to cooperate with; I was a very determined girl, and I had a mouth on me. Nonetheless, I cannot condone some of the reasons that were put forward for telling me to leave, like walking in with one shoe on because I'd just received a beating, or being found to have been hoarding tablets in a jar in my room in case I ever wanted to commit suicide.

Suicide did cross my mind in childhood. The most obvious display of that was the time I had swallowed my mother's sleeping tablets. I was eleven at the time. It was 1987 and one of my abiding memories of the month I spent recovering in Temple Street children's hospital was Whitney Houston's 'I Wanna Dance with Somebody' playing on the TV in the ward. I loved the energy and the positivity of that song; it lifted my spirits to listen to it while watching Whitney bouncing around singing.

It wasn't as if I could forget who I was in the hospital though; I'd often be reminded by different things. One night, during the early hours, I woke up after having wet the bed and had to get up and tell the nurse. It was embarrassing and I was glad all the other children were asleep, but while the nurse was changing the sheets the girl in the bed beside me woke up and asked what was going on. I felt very humiliated because this girl was a few years younger than me and none of the other children ever wet the bed.

I'd always be reminded I was a different sort of child at visiting hours. I received two or three visits in the space of the month, from my father, and he brought one of my sisters with him on one occasion. I never saw, nor expected to see, my mother.

The other children's families were present every visiting hour and when they'd go, they'd leave behind big bottles of minerals and sweets and fruit and there'd often be cards and balloons. After a week or two one of the nurses realised that my locker was always bare and after that, I had a jug of diluted orange that she'd keep topping up from the kitchen.

The difference between the other children's plastic bottles and my glass jug was certainly not lost on me. Nor was the difference between my hospital-issue nightclothes and the other children's pyjamas from home. I was very conscious of how different I looked and how different my bed looked compared to the other children's. I perceived my glass jug as a symbol of the charity I was used to from the St Vincent de Paul and elsewhere and unless I was very thirsty, I would nearly have preferred it to be empty. The nurse who put it there was a kind person though. I remember her well. She more or less took me under her wing and would bring me around with her while she was doing her work. I remember one day slapping her belly and laughing after she'd told me in a dismal tone that she'd reached ten stone and wasn't happy about it. I thought she looked lovely and was worrying about nothing. She'd give me sweets sometimes. I distinctly remember her handing me a packet of Cadbury Eclairs one day when she took me out for a walk in the grounds; Cadbury Eclairs reminded me of her for a long time after that.

I actually really enjoyed my time in the hospital and only got upset when it was time to go home. To this day, unlike most people, I find great comfort and reassurance in the smell of hospital disinfectant.

When the day came for my father to bring me home, I'll never forget the shock I got on seeing my mother. She had always dyed her hair black but she'd nearly always have a thick strip of whitish grey at its roots. She was sitting at the kitchen table looking as if she'd aged twenty years in the four weeks I'd been gone. She was very heavily sedated on sleeping tablets and had cut all the black out of her hair. She raised her head slowly to look at me and when her stoned eyes focused on mine she slurred: 'Look at what you've done to me'. The feeling that followed that would be difficult to describe, but was in no way uncommon. It was a deep, deep disturbance in the pit of my soul. Fear mixed with the deepest sort of concern. I was scared of her and for her at the same time.

I suppose, in a sense, my mother is still frightening me today. It frightens me that I share one aspect of her mental illness: a propensity towards deep and abiding depression.

When I became homeless, the first shock to me was the constant ceaseless need to remain in transit, and finding somewhere to simply *be* was a far bigger problem than I could have previously imagined. Nowhere you go are you left alone. Nowhere can you expect that luxury, because of course, all the private places of the world are closed to you and all the public places offer no privacy. Many of them do not even grant you admittance.

As to the problems of finding somewhere to sleep: there is just literally nowhere that covers the needs even the tiniest and shabbiest of bed-sits would provide. There is nowhere that offers dryness, safety, cleanliness, warmth and comfort. A park bench may be dry, if it is not raining, and it may be clean, if you are lucky, but it is not safe, warm, or comfortable. The underside of a bush may be dry, again, if the weather is with you, but it is not safe, clean, warm, or comfortable.

I slept in many different such locations, each as pathetic as the last. I once fell asleep on a bus that had been parked at a depot with the doors open and awoke to find myself driving through the then-green fields of west Dublin in the early hours of the morning. I hadn't a clue where I was and it was a rude awakening all right, but I reckoned it was worth it; it was the most comfortable night I'd spent in some time.

I once spent a half hour or so in a fitful sleep on the cold tiled floor of a toilet cubicle in McDonald's on O'Connell Street. I hadn't been able to find anywhere to sleep the night before and was utterly exhausted so I went in there as soon as they'd opened their doors to sell Egg McMuffins for breakfast. I reckoned that at least in the toilet I'd be bolted in and safe. I was woken up and thrown out by a member of staff who'd come in to clean the toilets, and that brings me to the real and deepest damage of homelessness: the loneliness. It is the experience of being utterly unwanted, of your very presence being an undesirable commodity in all places and situations. Wherever you are, as a homeless person, you are unwelcome. When a person is homeless, their sense of social significance is reduced to zero. It doesn't exist. Their sense of themselves is of being worthless and unwanted; a social pariah, an exile, an outsider whose very body is an unwanted intrusion they must carry with them wherever they go. They are unwanted in the most literal sense of the term. They are redundancy embodied. I felt all these feelings in homelessness. All homeless people do. It is unavoidable.

When I eventually ended up meeting another homeless girl, a couple of years older than I was, it was quite by accident. She was a friend of another girl I'd been in a hostel with, and I'd been introduced to her briefly six months or a year before. Recognising each other and finding ourselves in the same predicament, it made sense to stay together for safety and companionship, though the truth of the matter was neither of us particularly liked the other from the start and by the time we parted ways neither of us could stand the sight of each other.

We quickly teamed up in the shoplifting we'd already been at individually in order to sustain ourselves. We'd steal food, which of course we'd eat, but together we progressed to converting into cash stolen clothes, perfumes and inexpensive jewellery, which we'd rob from the major department stores in town. As a shoplifter, I was highly prolific but totally without skill. I actually once found myself in Store Street garda station twice in the same day. The only deception I was gifted at was coming up with an increasingly fantastical array of bogus names and addresses. I could think up anything on the spot and make it sound credible and in fact, if I had been able to apply the same skill to shoplifting, I probably never would have been caught in the first place. There was memory involved also; I always had to remember the face of the arresting garda and match the name I'd given to the face I'd given it to. I suppose the guards didn't pay much attention to us kids, having as they did much more serious matters to attend to, which would explain why this kind of messing was possible.

I had presented myself as Lisa Simpson on the day the ruse was finally blown, which happened when my brother was escorted in the door as I was getting ready to walk out of it. We roared laughing and greeted each other by the front desk with high enthusiasm, not having seen each other in a year or so by that time. Of course, a garda asked who we were to each other and when my brother announced that we were brother and sister, they realised the disparity in the surnames and that someone was clearly lying. I was promptly marched back to the cells, the joy of the reunion significantly soured.

I knew I'd never get away with lying in Store Street after that, so I began stealing on the south side of town, where if I was caught (which I'd come to accept as an occupational hazard) I'd be brought to the garda station in Pearse Street. Although my behaviour was deliberately designed to exasperate, there was no malicious intent on my part. I had a generally good-natured attitude towards the police and knew that I was the guilty party and presented a pain in the arse they had to deal with.

At that point, when I was regularly stealing, life was in some ways a good deal better than it had been during the previous year. The physical lacks of my life were abating to some extent, but the emotional ones tormented as ever and it wasn't long before I discovered the synthetic solace of drink. Before long, as soon as we'd sold the last of our shoplifted wares around the flats complexes and housing estates, it would be time to go to the pub and get drunk. I was a tall and well-developed girl, and the laws were laxer then, and I never had any trouble getting served. In fact, I'd often get served until the early hours of the morning when I'd be steaming drunk.

My friend and I began staying with people she knew in a rented flat in the city centre. I would never be anything approaching happy there. It was somewhere to sleep, and some of the people were nice enough, but I was starting to dislike her more and more and some of the people she'd introduced me to left a lot to be desired. We had been staying there for weeks and I'd been feeling it was time to move on since the first night we arrived. Eventually I did, after I discovered she'd been robbing me.

When I write about the days of my youth I can feel it coming back to me; or parts of it, and rarely the good parts. I can feel myself slowing down, reverting back to that awkward, shy and utterly under-confident young person, desperate for escape and for relief, and I can feel my writing change as a result.

When I dwell on my place in those times I make a transition to the person I once was and never want to be again, and I actually feel myself stripped of the strides I've since made, because this recounting is not possible without reliving, and this reliving involves the mental stripping away of all the days between those days and this one.

When I theorise on the routes into and out of those experiences, I am the me of today and I feel the indifference of distance; when I recount specific incidences I am the me of yesterday, and I feel again that awful sense of becoming numb and nullified. To write this book is to take a journey into somewhere I don't want to go, but must. I have to visit this place one last time before I'll earn my own blessing never to have to come here again.

Homelessness: my memories of it echo a time utterly imbued with the absence of prospects and vibrate with the opus of loss. It is joylessness, and for many, hopelessness also. I remember it still, usually at night, when I am lying between the white cotton sheets of my warm and comfortable bed. I think of all the people out there wandering around cold and shaking, hungry and thirsty, lonely, tired and broken in spirit, and I shudder in my warm bed and say a quick prayer for them; and the last thing I feel before sleep is guilt, because the last thing I do is try to rid my mind of their image.

That prostitution is a documented consequence of homelessness is not at all surprising to me, since all of the teenaged girls I knew (including myself) had come to it from a place of homelessness and destitution; but it might be newsworthy to some people, so I will include some documentary evidence of that here. This particular quote is quite chilling to me, as it could have been written to describe my situation exactly:

> 'Homelessness is a recognised entry route into prostitution, which, in the case of young people and children, is often a result of running away (Home Office, 2004a). Running away can be an attempt to make a positive move, a means of breaking away from an intolerable home life in order to make a fresh start. It can also be seen as an attempt to exercise control over the situation. However, while a young woman may be making an attempt to be assertive, she would simultaneously be increasing her vulnerability to manipulation.' (Cusick et al, 2003)

The above findings were published in a British Home Office report and reproduced in the 2005 Ruhama[1] research report, 'The Next Step Initiative'. The link between teenage homelessness and prostitution is so abundantly clear that even if I had never worked as a prostitute I would still understand the existence of it, because homelessness is so thoroughly and relentlessly traumatic a person will take any route, however dangerous or disgusting, to escape it.

The desperation of homelessness is so pronounced that those afflicted by it are sometimes willing to risk death for the release of escaping it for a single night. I know this is true because one evening a friend took a deliberate overdose in front of me to secure herself a hospital bed for the night. The plan was that she would be kept in the hospital and I would be allowed to wait for her overnight in the waiting room. I told her she was mad but she was determined to go through with it so I told her I'd make sure she was okay. She took an entire box of Feminax (female pain-relief medication) that she'd stolen from a chemist. There was a moment of hilarity in it, morbid and all as the situation was, because she'd taken the overdose on the south side of the quays and she wanted to be taken to the Mater hospital on the

---

1   Ruhama is the only group that provides frontline services to prostituted women in Ireland and has been working with them for over twenty years.

north side, so to avoid being taken to St James's hospital, I had to half-carry her over the Ha'penny Bridge.

We didn't expect that she'd be kept in more than one night. We just thought she'd have her stomach pumped and that would be the end of it. The plan worked out all right for her and her health was not affected, thankfully, but she was kept in the hospital for several days and after the first night I was told to leave the waiting room, so I was right back where I started, except now I was alone again.

In homelessness, you are not invisible to people, but rather not worth looking at. Most people regard you in this way; most, but not all. I will never forget the day another teenager gave me a fiver while I was trying to sleep on the steps of Best's in O'Connell Street. There is a short period of respite between about six and half-seven in the morning in summertime during which it is relatively safe to sleep in public if you are in the centre of town. This is because it is not dark, the shops have not opened yet so it's not too busy to prevent you sleeping, but also there are enough people around so that you're unlikely to be molested in your sleep. It was about seven o'clock in the morning the day that girl approached me and I had been walking around all night and was utterly exhausted, but couldn't sleep properly on the cold stone steps. I had been trying to sleep in a sitting position with my arms folded on my knees and my head in them when she shook me gently by the shoulder. I looked up at her. She smiled a soft sort of smile and handed me something. I put my hand out only out of reflex. I'd never begged while I was homeless and I had no idea she was handing me money until it was in my palm and she'd turned to walk away. She was only about eighteen or nineteen and seemed to be at the tail-end of a wild night out. I remember distinctly thinking how she was only a girl, a few years older than I was. I remember the stab of receiving compassion, somehow different from the days of my childhood, not as acute. Probably because it was so unexpected; the first thing I had experienced on having been roused from sleep, or probably because it had been given without my having to ask for it. I remember watching her shiny chestnut hair as she walked down O'Connell Street, and I remember feeling a peculiar blend of shock and love. I waited till McDonald's was open and bought myself some breakfast. That was over twenty years ago. The woman that girl became has most likely forgotten me. I have never forgotten her.

It probably sounds like a funny thing to be considering as a lack when faced with so many more pressing ones, but when I was homeless I really missed reading. Because I am someone who loves books and reading it was something that I really missed. You might think you can read anywhere, but when you're homeless without a penny to your name you can't buy a book to begin with; the odd bit of money you come across you'll immediately convert into food. I used to look longingly into bookstore windows and really wish I could go in and read a book, but I would not do that for fear of a staff member coming along and reminding me I was not in a library and the shame I knew would result from that. I knew I couldn't join a library either because you cannot do anything in this world without an address.

People who've never been homeless would not relate to this and some of them might think me mad, but these days I have a home and once in a while I reach out and spread my hand flat on its walls and reflect to myself that I can touch it, I can actually *feel* it, the thing I wanted so badly back then.

One of the strangest things about my experience of homelessness, and probably one of those most worth recording, is the feelings I remember of my very first time on the street. There was the feeling of an irresistible and seductive pleasure to destitution in disguise, but it was a fragile creature and it perished like a little bird in the depths of an unendurable winter. I had morphed destitution into freedom in my own mind, but the ruse didn't last long.

There was cold, I remember that, and the suddenly awful changeability of the Irish weather; how rain and sleet would assail you by turns and then the sudden appearance of the sun would warm the wet off your clothes, only for the iron grey clouds to roll again over the wide-open roof of everything.

If my autonomy itself was vulnerable, I myself was more so, and I felt it then, as freedom morphed into destitution; I felt it in the bones of me, though I could not have articulated it to anyone and wouldn't have anyway, for shame.

Chapter 6 ~

| THE FIRST DAY

I wonder if I've been changed in the night? Let me think.
Was I the same when I got up this morning? I almost
think I can remember feeling a little different. But if I'm
not the same, the next question is, "Who in the world
am I?" Ah, that's the great puzzle!
LEWIS CARROLL, *ALICE'S ADVENTURES IN WONDERLAND*

I first began working as a prostitute on a warm sunny afternoon in mid-August 1991. That afternoon changed unutterably every day of the subsequent seven years and, after that, will influence all the days, however few or many they may happen to be, so it's hardly surprising that it is burned on my brain. My 21-year-old lover's suggestion, which I had been mentally struggling with for hours, suddenly seemed viable, practicable, and even attractive in some of its components.

'I could be that woman,' I thought. 'I could be strong enough to do that. It would put an end to this wandering, this never knowing where I am to sleep, whether it'll be this sofa or that bench. It would put an end to the constant pining for some fucking food or a cigarette and to the shoplifting I've never been any good at. It could all be over if I am just strong enough to do this.' In that way, I morphed it into a matter of courage, and I didn't have a chance after that.

My boyfriend was as homeless as I was, and we were sleeping in the home of a friend of his, off the Infirmary Road, just minutes' walk from Benburb Street, then a well-known spot for prostitutes to work. I'd been with him less than a week.

'But I wouldn't know where to go,' I said.

'I do,' he replied. 'Come on, I'll show you.'

I followed him. And so the 'decision' was made, and within an hour I was standing on Benburb Street, back after my first job, and now, officially, a whore.

The first job, of course, is one you'll never forget. I don't remember much about the second, and nothing of the third, but this is the loss of a new virginity of sorts, and, as they say, you never forget your first.

He was about mid-forties, probably a bit older, and he had a balding head and wore spectacles. He pulled in in a white car and my boyfriend told him through the open window on the driver's side: 'Take it easy, it's her first time.'

I remember cringing at those words as the car pulled away; the hypocrisy of the pretence at caring, after where he had just taken me.

I consider myself very fortunate to have met that particular man as my first client, as he taught me a lesson I never forgot in all the years it remained relevant. The going rate, according to my lover's enquiries from one of the other girls, was ten pounds for a hand-job, fifteen for a blow-job and twenty for full sex. That man paid me thirty pounds to pull his prick with one hand, while leathering the arse off him with a thin flexible branch he'd stripped from a nearby tree as we stood concealed in woodland at the edge of the Phoenix Park. And so, from the very first job, I deduced that the perverts were where the money was. I was right.

I decided after that first job that I couldn't do full sex. I could still smell his prick on my hand and the experience itself had been as disgusting as to be scarcely bearable. Imagining those fuckers moving around inside me was just far too much; the thought of it made me feel physically ill. So I spent the first day doing hand-relief alone and 'graduated' to blow-jobs within the next couple of days.

I don't know what's happening on the streets now, but in 1991, almost all the girls used condoms for fellatio. The reality was that selling oral sex was a disgusting practice, condoms or not, but I continued to do both on a near-daily basis. That situation continued for two years: it was that long before I had sexual intercourse for money.

My memories of that first day are splintered and broken. I know I did about six or seven jobs. I remember at one point getting out of one car and into another before I had time to alert my boyfriend that I was back from the last job. This happened because a car stopped right beside me just as I'd gotten out of the last one and he was standing at the far end of the street. I decided that it'd be all right and went ahead and got in the car. When I got back, he was angry and panicked that something had happened to me. In my naïveté I interpreted this as caring, rather than the fear for his own skin he was more likely feeling.

That night, when I lay down beside him to go to sleep, tears came from some indefinable place inside me. I'd have had trouble even naming it, the thing that was hurting me. I felt as though I'd woken up as one person that morning and was going to sleep as another; and in many ways, that was exactly what had happened.

These words are coming much more slowly now. At this moment I am experiencing what must be the literary version of stuttering. I will write a line and stare at it for ten minutes. A decent-sized paragraph is an arduous feat. I am sure a psychiatrist, if I had one, would be interested to dissect the material that must be wrung out, but I don't need a psychiatric dissection of the subject matter; I know why this is hard for me: Entering prostitution is to slip from one world to another and to remember the transition is to mourn again the loss of something pure, something good.

I remember one other thing that really bears recording. It reminds me of the very odd feelings I had, so ill-matched to the situation, when walking out into my very first day of homelessness. Strangely, and conversely, in the moment I allowed myself to be coerced onto my first red-light street, I felt a surge of powerful decisive direction. I felt, for the first time since I had walked out of my mother's house, as though I were taking control. How stupid I felt when, in some later year while casting a contemplative look over the past, I realised that that feeling had been in response to giving my control away.

Prostitution is widely recognised among those who have conducted research into it as a sphere of life often entered into by young teenaged girls who have left home much younger than is usual or recommendable. I know this now. I didn't know it when I most needed to.

The major problem as I see it now was that the place I had come from made any extremity a perceived possibility. I was so ignorant of the nature of the world that to have gone on to be wildly successful in some respectable fashion seemed to have been every bit as likely as to have stepped, as I did, from the footpath straight into the gutter. I was so innocent I suppose, I just didn't realise how close I was to the edge.

I understood, to a much minimised degree, the way the world worked. I knew while I was living in hostels that I was on the lower rungs of the social ladder; homes for the teenagers of dysfunctional backgrounds are clearly not distinguished places to be. I knew that at that time, I was living a lifestyle I didn't want as opposed to one that I did, but the handicap on my part was one of perception: I simply didn't comprehend the link between the conduct of today and the consequences of tomorrow.

As I see it now, I was balanced on the outermost edge of society and the likelihood was always that I would encounter much adversity. I wildly underestimated the struggle ahead and the dedication and clarity of mind it would take to avoid such a probability; and that really was where the matter of misjudgement came strongest into play: I did not regard a future of disadvantage and destitution as a probability, but rather a possibility, as likely as any other outcome. In fact, it was more than a probability, much more. At fifteen, I had a well-developed body and a pretty face: the twin worst curses God could put on a homeless young girl. The likelihood always was that men would seize the opportunity to exploit me sexually, but when I first became homeless, I was patently unaware of that. I see prostitution now as an enemy that was able to sneak up on me because I hadn't the wit to expect it.

A term which is commonly used by the proponents of prostitution is 'consenting adults'. It's a term that needs to be examined closely; firstly because it is not possible to consent to a lifestyle you don't comprehend. It is only possible to consent to a lifestyle as you imagine it to be, and it is not possible to grasp an accurate comprehension of prostitution until you are already immersed in it. Secondly, many of the prostituted are not adults, and so are in no position to 'consent' to any form of sex with an adult. Also, a huge proportion of adult prostitutes were, like me, not adults when they first 'consented' to it.

The problem with recording an account like this is that it involves so many memories resurfacing. For the time being I'm just going to have to learn to deal with them. I tell myself that if I could live with the reality of these things as they were happening I'm sure I can find a way to deal with the memory of them. The difference is I do not wear that same armour any more. I am not telling myself the lies that are necessary for a prostitute to protect herself with, so in actual fact the memories are sometimes more painful than the events as I am no longer shielded from the fullness and exactness of their nature.

You understand the nature of your surroundings as a prostitute, but you make great efforts not to dwell on it. While recording your history in prostitution, you must necessarily dwell on it, and that is the difference. In this way, the sense of reliving is somehow deeper on a psychological level than the original experience itself. Not to say that it is more damaging, but that it requires a person to reach more deeply into themselves, to examine their feelings thoroughly and to reach a deeper understanding of the damaging elements of the original experience.

It is well-documented that humans have the capacity to psychologically numb themselves in circumstances which they find threatening or traumatic. As Dr M Scott Peck wrote (in his fascinating study of human evil, *People of the Lie*): 'In a situation in which our emotional feelings are overwhelmingly painful or unpleasant, we have the capacity to anesthetise ourselves'.

Before even that first day was out, I was already actively engaged in the process of shutting out the reality of what I was experiencing. Beyond that, I now perceive that before I had even arrived on Benburb Street, I was already engaged in the process of shutting out the reality of what I was about to do. I put a different shape on it, a different face on it; a face which was acceptable to me.

The true face was very different. On Benburb Street, because the rates were so low and because I did not do full sex, I would often have to have my body used by up to ten men before I would make even a hundred pounds. For this reason working on Benburb Street was a particularly gruelling, dreary and miserable experience, especially as the winter months came in. It is difficult to describe how hollow a woman feels after she has been used sexually by ten different men. Of course the experience rarely stopped at the agreed-upon hand-relief or oral sex. Even when a man has accepted that he will not be putting his penis in you, he often has no compunction about shoving his fingers or other objects in you, and mauling you and biting you and trying to shove his tongue down your throat and everywhere else. I knew by the rabid dog-like behaviour of one particular client that he'd have liked nothing better than if he'd bit and sucked my nipples till they'd gushed blood. Years later I opened a newspaper and read that he'd been charged for trying to rip a prostitute's nipples off with his teeth. They made me sick, these supposedly 'ordinary'² clients. This was the case from the first day I stepped out onto the street. There was nothing ordinary about them as far as I was concerned and if I'd never thought there was any body of men out there who'd make me long to meet perverts, the supposedly 'ordinary' clients of prostitution taught me different.

Men with unusual sexual proclivities were less common on the streets, but I hadn't forgotten them and I always took the opportunity to make a regular client out of a man like this. They exhibited significantly less disrespect for women and simply made life easier. Although not all women will accommodate them, the benefits of seeing men with unusual requests is well known in prostitution circles. Since I had become aware of this, I began dressing in a manner that was designed to attract them. I wore a lot of leather and miniskirts with studded hipster belts, red lipstick and stiletto heels or thigh-high boots. I knew I looked like the quintessential whore, but I told myself I couldn't have cared less about that and anyway, I saw no sense in dressing demurely while I was standing on a red-light street in broad daylight selling my body for money. Who would I have been fooling? I reasoned that if I wanted to attract men with extreme tastes, I had to dress the part, and I was right. For this reason men who wanted to be

---

2   The term 'ordinary' here refers to men who pay for sexual acts that would not be considered sexually perverse, i.e. intercourse, fellatio etc., as opposed to men who pay for sexual acts that would be considered outside the norm, like bondage, sadomasochism, etc.

dominated gravitated towards me. Strange as it may sound, I counted myself lucky.

I remember the first girl I ever met on Benburb Street. She was the woman my partner had asked about the rates I could expect to charge. She was twenty-seven, slim and attractive, well dressed with longish fawn-brown hair tied up carefully and stylishly and her make-up was always perfectly applied. I remember her for several reasons. Firstly, because she was the first prostitute I ever met. Secondly, because she stood out on the street as a woman who took great care of her appearance, which was unusual there; and thirdly because she was uncommonly kind to me, always asking how I was and if everything was all right. She was the only woman I had met there at that point who, beyond showing me no animosity, actually offered me kindness. Finally, I remember her because she was raped and beaten by a man who picked her up on Benburb Street within weeks of my having arrived there. It was a particularly horrible attack. He raped her repeatedly and beat her to within an inch of her life. I remember the older women talking about it and about how she should have gone to the guards. They seemed to understand though, why she never did, which was something that was beyond my comprehension at that point.

She started abusing heroin directly after that. The transformation was immediate and shocking. The weight fell off her. She'd been a slim girl to begin with but now she was a walking skeleton. Her hair became greasy and lank and she never tied it up any more. Her skin was deathly pale and without a trace of make-up. Her clothes were no longer clean or pressed and she stood on the street smoking cigarettes one after the other with an empty vacant stare in her eyes and she had no kind words for me any more, or for anyone.

In my childish mind, I read so much into the fact that she never tied her hair up. I remember looking at it hanging around her shoulders and feeling that this was a concrete symbol that she was not the same woman, that there'd been some awful and irreversible alteration in her. I remember while looking at her feeling the thrill of an unnameable fear. The change in her was so complete, I felt as if her spirit had gone to some dark place there was no coming back from, but I wanted her to come back because I liked her and she was the only bit of comfort I had on that street. Sometimes she'd give me a watery smile when I stood near her and offered her a cigarette, but it was brief, gone almost before it arrived and never followed by conversation. Her addiction accelerated at an astonishing rate and worsened until she was barely recognisable as the same person and eventually I came to understand that there was no reason she should be, because she wasn't.

I know today the fear I felt when I looked at her was the amplification of my already-present sense of the hugely destructive nature of what I was involved in. She was my first real example of that devastation and the living embodiment of something I was coming to understand I ought to be *very* afraid of. Above all, I thought that it was so sad, such a pity; such a waste of life. I don't know what ever became of her, but I would be surprised if she were not dead now.

| PART TWO

Chapter 7 ～

SUBMERGING IN PROSTITUTION

Almost anything is easier to get into than to get out of.
AGNES ALLEN

However much you try to adapt to your new life (or new 'skin' as it feels to you), some incident will occur to shock you into realising how very much things have changed. I was standing on Benburb Street just weeks after I'd started working as a prostitute when a group of about five or six girls walked by wearing the green uniform of my old secondary school. It was the same school I had attended before having been expelled nearly a year before and is situated less than ten minutes' walk from Benburb Street.

It was September and the new school term had just begun; so I hadn't seen that sight before, at least not from this vantage point. I stared at them walking by, with a sense of wonderment mixed with a melancholy that had no power of expression I am aware of in the English language, and I felt like those months had been aeons and those girls like ghosts I was seeing from another time.

Was it me that had changed? Or had the whole world changed around me? At fifteen, I felt like it had. Of course today I know that it was I who had changed and because of that my perceptions had altered also.

A year later I would stand on a corner of Waterloo Road, which was heavily lined with trees, and be reminded of the North Circular Road, which was densely tree lined also and which I had walked twice a day on my way to and from primary school. I would kick those leaves and wonder why they didn't make the same sound as the ones I had kicked on my way to school. And why, when it had been raining, they didn't smell the same, and though of course they did, there was something altered in the essence of that smell: it had lost its innocence.

The truth is the leaves on the ground of a prostitute's patch are not the same as the leaves on the path she walked to school because she perceives them differently, and there is a very acute sense of their being altered. They don't look the same. They don't smell the same. They don't sound the same when you step on them.

For me, their magic was gone and they were just musky-smelling leaves, sodden and rotting on the ground. I often felt like everything around me had altered but in small flashes of lucidity I would realise that the world was still the same, it was just me who was different; contaminated. I realised then that the leaves weren't beautiful any more because I was looking at them through different eyes.

When those moments of clarity came I would feel that all of nature and literature and everything I had loved before I'd become a prostitute was still there and still the same, but not open to me any more because I was different now, and those thoughts were even more hurtful, even more devastating than the notion that all about me was changed and gone. These feelings were omnipresent, but they operated like a tide, sometimes forcefully roaring and sometimes receding to the point where they were but a gentle whispering reminder that something was wrong.

I would walk home from the red-light district along the canal-side in the early hours of the morning and the water was like black ink shot through with little flashes of light. The street lamps were not harsh; they burned a soft, warm amber, and the trees that lined the canal were silhouetted against deep-navy night skies. I wanted to love that walk, and some part of me did, but it was in a very sad way, because the scene emitted a peace that I was excluded from. I felt estranged, lost . . . utterly forgotten.

Some days I still sought refuge in the literature I loved and in long walks in parkland and then something would change with a soundless click and I would be cut off again from any sense of belonging to the world. In my earlier years in prostitution, I could connect best to who I was and what I enjoyed when I was alone.

I did rail against the oppressive nature of prostitution; I think we all did to some degree. You'd carry your secret around with you, day in, day out, when in 'respectable' society and you would try to integrate yourself into it just for the day, or perhaps the afternoon. But though nobody else would know about it you always would. Sometimes the veneer would crack. This would happen, for instance, when you came eye to eye with another prostitute in public. If you didn't know her personally and she was in company, you would just look away, an unwritten but much understood rule of etiquette among prostituted women. If she was alone and you didn't know her personally, you would recognise one another with nods that would be barely discernible to an observer and continue on your way. If you did know her and you both got on well, the likeliest outcome would be a day spent laughing and drinking away yesterday's earnings.

The thing that filled me with such panic, whenever I allowed myself to think about it, was that I could see no way out. I could see no end to this, but equally, I knew there'd have to either be an end to it or an end to me, because I could not live this way forever. I had begun smoking cannabis at fourteen in my first hostel and I used that and other substances to hide from the reality I could find no way to escape from; and so I numbed myself, as I submerged in prostitution.

I say 'submerged' in prostitution because you are wholly immersed in it to the point where you feel that it is the only avenue of life open to you. I know in my heart, though I haven't experienced them all, that this is true of all obviously illicit ways of earning a living. How likely is it that the bank-robber will wake up one morning and suddenly decide to strive for a life of social normalcy? And how alien a concept would this surely feel to him? The society he would be attempting to integrate himself into does, after all, include banks! Illicit ways of making money will always set those involved in opposition to both acceptable society and those who inhabit it. There are two different and distinct spheres of life in this world; they are the socially acceptable and the socially unacceptable, and you need to have occupied the latter before you can fully appreciate the depth of the distinction between the two. They are so vastly far apart, these two different worlds that occupy the same space.

Another of the features of submerging in prostitution is to experience a lack of self-worth, because of your position in the world. None of us are built or equipped to feel cheerful whilst we accept banishment and shunning from the rest of society.

The standards of life which we all desire, that of being happy, fulfilled and content, begin to slip away from the woman in prostitution because she does not experience these for herself or see them evidenced in the lives of the women around her. When something is less attainable it is less often reached for. I got to the point early on in prostitution where I saw being happy as simply unrealistic, and I was right. I didn't know any women who were happy in prostitution and I didn't meet any in later years either. There are no 'happy hookers' in my experience.

Submerging in prostitution, for me, involved having my life narrowed down so that everything came back to prostitution, which was by then the central point. It seemed to invade and pervade everything. It dictated my sleeping habits, the clothes I bought, the conversations I had, the things I did *not* do as much as the things I did.

I measured out time not in hours or minutes of the day, but counting down the hours until work: five hours until work, four hours, three—and I would feel the same sickening shudder, intensifying the closer it got to the time to sell myself. When I was on Waterloo Road, the time I'd go down to the street would depend on the time of year, because the punters came out as soon as it got dark. That meant that in summer I could still be working at four o'clock in the morning and I would have my body used by between around six and twelve men. Sometimes I thought, 'What if this is all there is, forever?' When that thought surfaced my heart hammered against my ribs. It felt like a bird against the walls of a room it's flown into by mistake; demented in equal measure by the fear of what enclosed it and the desperation to escape.

I first heard the term 'child prostitute' long after I had begun working as one myself, and it is not a way that would ever have occurred to me to describe myself in my early teens. I had no problem identifying with the 'prostitute' part of the term; I knew what I was doing and what it made me, but I never felt like a child at that time. I had always felt older than my years and by the time I was fifteen, I was a young woman in my own mind. It is only now, as the mother of a child older than I was then, that I can see how young I really was.

I told all of the men I met my age at that time. I did this for a reason: because it had the almost universal effect of causing them to become very aroused and to climax easily, which was good news for me because it meant that the experience was over with quickly. There was one man though, who didn't take the bait. Paradoxically, he drove a large white van; the vehicle recognised amongst street prostitutes as the transport of choice of violent perverts. Nonetheless, when I told him I was fifteen, he turned his van around pronto and brought me back where he'd found me, arguing all the way that he didn't want to leave me there, I should be at home or in school, and was there nowhere else he could drop me? Thousands of men's faces have merged into a featureless nothingness, but I have never forgotten his.

I wonder could he ever know what it meant, what it cost, when he picked me up the following year.

I had wanted to be all the things a young teenage girl wants to be. I wanted to be a model and an actress. I'd told the staff about my aspirations in the first hostel I lived in, Lefroy House. They'd photographed me and taken me to a model agency near Baggot Street Bridge. I was fourteen at the time and only 5 feet 6 inches tall. I was told to come back at sixteen when I might have grown the two inches necessary to reach the required industry minimum height. I didn't go back at sixteen. By that time I was working as a prostitute just minutes' walk from Baggot Street Bridge and the life of somebody respected, even admired, was a reality that I couldn't apply to myself in my own mind. It was the opposite of how I felt about who I was. In any case, I hadn't grown the required two inches. I was 5 feet 7 inches at that time, as I had learned from having been measured in the Bridewell garda station the previous year, the first time I'd been arrested for soliciting.

Is it possible to call a fifteen-year-old a 'child'? I suppose there would be people who believe that a pair of developing breasts and a clitoris which is beginning to function make up the most significant components of a woman. I am not of that school of thought, and I've always regarded with suspicion anyone who goes out of their way to make a distinction between a sexual interest in pre-pubescent children and young teenagers.

As far as breasts and genitalia are concerned, though I had well-developed breasts at fifteen and I presume my clitoris was capable of orgasm, I didn't even know that what was behind that fold of skin was my clitoris and as far as masturbation was concerned, I literally wouldn't have known where to start. But more than that, I wasn't capable of making adult choices and decisions. The really important signifiers of adulthood are not breasts and genitals, as anyone who has reached adulthood should know.

Of course now, all these years later, as a mother, I can see that a person of fifteen is a child, end of story—but I still struggle with the image of myself as a child then. It may be that it is too painful to comprehend fully, but since my own child turned the same age, that image has become much harder to turn my face away from. The mind inevitably makes comparisons. I think about how young my son was at fifteen, how illequipped to deal with the world. I think how much growing he had left to do, and how fragile his sense of self was, however well that might have been hidden behind teenage bluster and bravado. Every now and again, since he turned fifteen, I look at him and think of what I was doing at his age, and what was done to me. I think of the repulsive way it felt in my body, how it hurt in my heart and how it warped my mind; and I've come to find that it is not possible to consider how much of my young life was contaminated without acknowledging how young I was at that time.

So I find myself forced to confront that, but as stark a reality as that is, there is actually something here that's deeper, more troubling for me, because there was a certain upshot to my having been inducted into this lifestyle, a certain influence that it had: it caused me to believe that this was the only way for me—that I was *fit* for nothing else.

You get submerged in prostitution on all levels, including the things it teaches you about yourself. I see now that to have believed those things was to have been submerged in a lie.

|LAYERS OF NEGATIVITY

*All of the women spoke of attempting to keep themselves
separate from the act and identity of prostitution.*
'THE NEXT STEP INITIATIVE', RUHAMA RESEARCH
REPORT ON BARRIERS AFFECTING WOMEN IN
PROSTITUTION, IRELAND, 2005

I was photographed pornographically. That is a difficult thing for me
to write. I have thought about that, about how it would feel for me
to look at those pictures now. It would hurt me to see them and
to know that others would see them. I know that. But it would also be
educational and worthwhile, because I am quite sure I could contort my
own face to resemble the dummy image of female sexuality required of
me as I shifted from one pose to the next, all the while steeling my mind
against an almost tangibly present sense of degradation. I think it might
be enlightening for people to see that that face can be matched to these
words.

About six months after I'd first started working the northside red-light
district of Benburb Street, I met a girl there who worked both sides of the
city. We hit it off, became friends, then flat-mates, and she introduced
me to the city's southside streets.

Marginally more money could be charged per job, but it certainly
did add up over the night. They were also far busier streets in terms of
the volume of punters, presumably because men were more comfortable
doing what they did in the dark, and also because the southside district
was more widely known and did not carry the same stigma of Benburb

Street. There wasn't the same degree of unfortunates, junkies, alcoholics and such, patrolling the area for business.

My new friend had been working on Burlington Road for a couple of years by then, but bringing me there caused a lot of trouble for her. I hadn't long turned sixteen, quickly became very much in demand, and in the matter of a few weeks we had to consider the threat that our faces would be slashed to such a degree as to render us incapable of generating any business at all. We braved it out for a few more weeks, but with no desire to be maimed for life we eventually agreed between ourselves to take our enterprising spirits over to the next street, which ran parallel to the side of the Burlington Hotel—Waterloo Road.

Waterloo Road was empty of prostitutes, though it had at one time been a red-light street. It was an upmarket Dublin-4 residential road and we knew that we would have an uphill struggle there. Business would be sure to slow almost to a stop. Few men went to Waterloo Road looking for prostitutes, but we reasoned that it was in such close proximity that some of them would have to be driving up and down it on their way to and from Burlington Road, the Pepper Canister, Fitzwilliam Square and the canal area; so what we hoped to do was to turn it into part of the red-light zone again and carve out a niche for ourselves there, where, following the prostitutes' law of proximity, the other women could not reasonably object to us working there as we were not infringing upon anybody's specified space.

We knew that we would be making next to nothing until such a time as the punters cottoned-on to the fact that this area was again open for business and we had no idea how long or how short a time that might be. We also knew that we would encounter much hostility and objection from the residents of that street, who would surely not be pleased to see their pleasant residential road being infected with lowlifes such as ourselves, whom they no doubt felt were too close for comfort already.

We chose the natural place to stand, the corner of a footpath at the entrance to a long laneway. This would be convenient for doing business with what are known as 'walkers'; men who walk rather than drive to their destination and intend to do business in the open air. It was also the natural place to choose as we had more than one route to use in order to extract ourselves from the situation if needs be, and I suppose that is indicative of the mentality of the prostitute; you're always comforted to have an escape route should things go wrong, which suggests, of course, that you always anticipate that they may.

Business did pick up there and it didn't take nearly as long as we'd imagined. Perhaps the women hadn't been gone from there as long as we'd thought. We had been right in assuming that Waterloo Road was a well-traversed route for the punters and it didn't take them long at all to adjust to the restored nature of the street; just the matter of a week or two. For the residents however, it took far longer.

Now, at this point in my life, I can understand the situation from the residents' perspective. As the mother of a teenager, I would be deeply unhappy if a number of prostitutes decided to stake their new patch yards from my front door. I don't want the danger and the negativity of prostitution enveloping my home like that. I don't want to live with the fear that one of the men seeking out these women might happen to be a dangerous pervert who also entertains a penchant for children. I don't want to have to worry about the hygiene aspect or the pure revulsion factor of people throwing used condoms on the footpath outside my front door, as some prostitutes and clients unfortunately do. Personally I never did that, and nor did the girl I worked with. We always put them down the shore. It was the best compromise for the sake of the neighbours that I could come up with, as carrying them on my person all night and disposing of them in my bin at home was not something I was prepared to do. So yes, I can understand why some of the residents so vigorously objected to our presence there: I just wonder if it ever occurred to them that some part of us vigorously objected to our presence there more than they ever could.

We'd only been standing on Waterloo Road a couple of days and, I suppose, when the initial shock of our arrival had sunk in, the sense of outrage and affront quickly surfaced and was made apparent to us. The middle-aged lady who occupied one of the houses nearest where we stood came out and commanded us, in a tone which wavered right on the edge of hysteria, to move on and get away from her home. We just looked at each other and laughed.

I suppose that woman thought that we were taunting her or that we had no respect for her, or both, but actually neither was true. It just felt like such a ridiculous demand to us, from beginning to end, that the most natural thing to do was laugh. It was ridiculous because the petitioner and the petitioned were from two different worlds and the former had assumed it permissible to stake a demand without any dialogue at all.

We had several visits from her before we eventually told her to fuck off, and her attitude really was a study in how a person ought *not* to conduct themselves in order to get what they want. If she had approached us on that first night and explained in calm, measured and respectful tones that she entertained legitimate fears, I know for certain that, laneway or no laneway, we would have moved to the opposite end of that street.

We had considered working the other end, the Baggot Street end of Waterloo Road, before we had settled on the entrance to the laneway close to that woman's home. The other end of the street was not much less viable as a working spot, because there was a large building with a short laneway leading to an underground car-park, which was always empty at night, but we had decided that the police spent too much time driving up and down Baggot Street and that we would be less exposed to their scrutiny at the opposite end of the road. But yes, I know that had that woman approached us with an acceptable degree of respect and laid out genuine concerns, and *certainly* if they had included fears for children, we would have moved on for her that first night. Had she spoken to us respectfully, we would have so appreciated having our human worth acknowledged that we would have done anything she asked, and done it gladly. Instead she spoke to us as if we were nothing, and that was her mistake. Prostituted women are routinely paid to be treated as if they are nothing, and I have noticed that (obviously as a consequence) they generally cultivate an attitude that aggressively rejects that treatment in any other situation that presents it.

People feel that street prostitution is the 'lowest of the low', that you can't descend any further down the ladder than to work the streets, as I did. But I discovered a surprising aspect to it and later, when I came to research international studies into prostitution, I found that the prevalence of violence in non-street prostitution and other areas of the sex industry is reportedly higher than in street prostitution. For example, one Seattle study found that women in strip clubs, massage parlours and pornography had less control over the conditions of their lives and seemingly faced greater risks of violence than women involved in street prostitution.[3] There are no surprises in that for me. My experience reflects that directly.

I was always aware while working in brothels or escorting that I had scarcely any control in the matter of which men I would or would not see. This was different from the situation of working on the streets, where I'd had the opportunity to see each client before I got in his car. In street prostitution, there is some minimised degree of selective choice. Oftentimes your choice will be influenced by other factors, such as how busy or slow a night it might be, how much money you need to make, how dreadful the weather is, etc.; but ultimately, you do have the opportunity to make an assessment of a man's demeanour and what this might mean for you. Not so in massage parlours or escorting. If you are working for yourself, you cannot adequately assess a man down a phone-line, and if you are working for someone else, you do not even have the chance to try.

For this reason the greatest autonomy to be found is in street prostitution. This is in contradiction to the most commonly held belief about prostitution, which depicts street-walking prostitutes as the most unfortunate of their ilk. They may be less fortunate in other ways, such as in the rates they are paid, but when it comes to self-governance, nowhere can match this area of prostitution.

This is one of the reasons why the Sexual Offences Act of 1993 was so traumatic for street-walking women. It robbed us of our autonomy, the little we had to begin with. Incredibly, the bill didn't seek to criminalise the act of prostitution itself, for either the male or female participants. What it did was criminalise the act of *soliciting* for the purposes of prostitution. Soliciting is the legal term for loitering with the intent to prostitute oneself or to seek to engage in prostitution. Therefore, the

3   Debra Boyer, Lynn Chapman, Brent Marshall, 'Survival Sex in King County: Helping Women Out', 1993.

act criminalised the participants of one section of prostitution only: the street-walkers. It targeted street-walking prostitutes and street-walking prostitutes alone. This had the obvious (and I believe, *intended*) consequence of driving prostitution indoors.

The consequence of this was many women, including myself, could no longer make a living on the streets. This caused an inordinate level of suffering. In my own case, I had to start having paid intercourse for the first time. I was seventeen years of age and had managed in prostitution without giving up this side of myself for over two years, but that was not possible any more. You cannot explain to a man down a telephone that you will do certain acts and not others, when he knows he can call the next number and get whatever he wants. It was possible for me on the streets, because I was slim and young and pretty and many men were content with oral sex or hand relief from me, but this was no longer possible. The Sexual Offences Act of 1993 robbed me and many others of the right to have some level of control over our already disempowered lives, while not only allowing brothel prostitution to persist, but encouraging it to expand.

For me, having to have sexual intercourse was the worst of the 'layers of negativity' I experienced in prostitution. I did it only sporadically for about four years, because I simply found the sense of violation too traumatic. Often, I would sit for hours in agencies hoping for a call from someone who wanted to be dominated or to be catered for in some other unusual request. I could not deal with intercourse, mentally or emotionally and I think this was compounded by the fact that I'd managed to avoid it for so long. There was such a sense of defeat in it and I could feel it driving me into a deep depression. Sometimes after sitting for hours I'd eventually agree to intercourse if nothing else had come through on the phone lines. As time went on I gathered transvestites and men who were into s&m and bondage as my regular clients; men whose penchants I found tolerable and who other women routinely referred to as 'total perverts'. This was for me, strange as it may sound to some, a *bona fide* way of disconnecting from the layers of negativity that suffocated me.

I was sixteen when I first arrived at a Leeson-Street brothel after having returned from spending five months between a juvenile detention centre and a foster home, where the courts had placed me for a probationary period. I'd been arrested from what the media termed a brothel in the early summer of 1992. It was actually the home of the girl I worked the streets with and we both occasionally serviced clients there. My arrest had made the front page of the *Irish Press*. The headline was 'SIXTEEN-YEAR-OLD TAKEN FROM BROTHEL'. I was just thankful the guards hadn't raided us a couple of months before, when I'd still been fifteen. I'd imagined there'd have been worse legal repercussions for me then, in that I'd have found myself under considerably closer scrutiny by the children's court, and I was probably right. It was beyond me by that time, after a year in prostitution, to imagine living my life any other way because I could see no alternative that would offer me any sort of security or independence, and I thought I was no good for anything else anyway. It is strange how the sense of institutionalisation sets in so quickly in prostitution. In this way, prostitution can be likened to the prison experience.

A weight of sadness settles on me when I think of the way I reacted when my foster parents invited me to stay after those court-appointed few months. They invited me to live there, to make a home there. To go to the local school. To have a life. I just knew, somewhere inside myself, that I couldn't do it.

The family had a hobby farm and I'd spent that summer collecting eggs from the henhouse and feeding milk at dawn to an orphaned black baby lamb. These things felt too pure for me, or rather, I felt too dirty for them. I felt that I couldn't stay, because I didn't belong there, and the thought of sitting alongside girls my own age in the local school made me imagine myself a drop of oil in a bowl of water. I made arrangements in private to stay at the brothel in Leeson Street, which I knew of because I'd done a few indoor jobs for the pimp who ran it just before I got arrested. I said I was going to stay with a friend of mine, which wasn't a million miles from the truth, because a friend from my hostel days was staying in the brothel also.

When I arrived on Leeson Street I felt, along with other things, at least a sense of belonging. I was used to being out at three and four in the morning. I was used to nobody telling me what time to come in or how much alcohol or drugs to take or not take; I was used to being unrestrained in certain senses. That feeling of unrestraint was the feeling of home to me, and it was the only home I knew.

The brothel had steel steps leading down to the basement entrance and there was a sign on the wall depicting an old-fashioned tripod camera with a black cat whose tail curled round one of the leg stands. I can't remember what colour the door was, but I remember the dull thud of my heart when I knocked on it.

The pimp was far from the most odious person I ever met in prostitution, but it still would be difficult to speak of him in non-offensive terms. He was, in short, an arsehole. He was somebody who had stumbled upon prostitution and saw it as a way to make easy money. He was an upper-middle-class man in his late twenties, complete with Dublin-4 accent, who hadn't a shred of the harsh life experience common to the women and young girls he endeavoured to exploit. He was simply ill-prepared for the world he had immersed himself in and I resented him dreadfully. If I sound embittered, it's because I am. If there's one thing more degrading for a woman than selling her body to a man, it's selling her body to one man for the benefit of another.

There were several different elements to his operation. One of the main ones was stripping. He organised strippers countrywide and in a very short time I was one of the most in-demand strippers on his books. Not because I was a good dancer (I wasn't) but because of my youth and physicality. Myself and others packed out hallways from Dublin to Tipperary for him on a weekly basis. Speaking of Tipperary, I remember one particular show a few of us did in Cashel: driving into that place was the mother of all shocks. The streets were absolutely plastered with huge posters advertising our arrival in neon green, pink and orange, so we knew we were in for a lively night. The pub was like a converted barn inside and that was very apt given the men in it behaved like a herd of animals. To watch their carry-on you'd think they'd never seen a pair of

breasts or a woman's arse in their lives. This was typical behaviour countrywide, by the way, and certainly not confined to the men of Cashel.

I had similar feelings towards the stripping as I had towards the
prostitution. It seemed like there was a trade-off in swapping one for
the other for the night—it was a case of more eyes on you versus fewer
hands. That's not to say that sometimes you wouldn't have to contend
with both, because sometimes you would; some men took great pleasure
in grabbing us and mauling us and humiliating us publicly to the maximum possible extent. I knew one girl who had a man's fingers shoved
inside her vagina in the middle of a show. She ran from the floor screaming and in tears. Needless to say, the man who was supposedly paid to
protect us was nowhere to be seen when these sort of things happened.

A lot of people, including women, view stripping as some sort of
harmless fun. It isn't. It isn't harmless or fun when your heart is thumping
out of your chest in the middle of a crowd of fifty or sixty drunken men,
all roaring vulgarities and obscenities, and you're there, slowly peeling
off the only layers that exist between you and them—your clothes. It is
thoroughly psychically invasive.

When I think back to the evening I arrived on Leeson Street, in the
autumn of 1992, my mind keeps pulling me back to that first moment
I looked at the picture of the cat winding its tail round the leg of the
tripod, because it sent a ripple of negative energy through me that I
didn't understand. The image, I later came to find, signified the nature
of what went on there. It was a pornographic studio.

I can't remember how many men photographed me there, and I actually don't want to know. The set-up was that a man would arrive with his
own camera and a blank roll of film. He'd pay a set amount, I think it was
ninety pounds, and when he was done photographing whichever girl
he'd selected, he'd do whatever else he wanted to her, for an additional
fee. He'd then give the roll of film to the pimp, who had it processed,
God knows where. Someone was in on the operation obviously, because
this was in the days before digital cameras. The photographs had to be
processed somewhere, and most of the girls in them were under-age.

I remember one man in particular because he didn't seem interested in taking explicit photographs; this was unusual. He told me to pose any way I wanted and never instructed that I take my clothes off. I remember sitting balanced in the window ledge, with my head resting against the wall and my chin tilted up and closing my eyes as though I was deep in thought, and suddenly I *was* deep in thought, and I was imagining that I was a model; that it had all worked out in the modelling agency and I was just doing a day's work. The click of his camera brought me back. He told me that it would be a very beautiful photograph. I felt injured; violated in a new way. He had caught something of the real me on his roll of film. That was a new sort of lesson in never letting your guard down.

Some women have no problem with pornography. Well, I do. I know from having been photographed in sexually explicit poses that there is a lot more going on behind those glossy graphic images than most people take the time to consider. It is a demeaning exploitative business that is hugely damaging to women, both within and without the industry.

In the on-going effort to sanitise pornography we are told that it is 'sexually empowering' and a form of 'sexual self-determination'. For me, this was no truer of being photographed naked and posing than it was true of being fucked naked and posing. I worked alongside a half-a-dozen girls at that time, all in their mid- to late-teens. Some I'd known from the hostels and others I'd been introduced to by girls I'd known from the hostels. What we did in that freezing-cold seedy basement was the same thing we did out on the streets; we took the only thing worth taking out of our circumstances, the opportunity to put roofs over our heads and food in our mouths. This was the only 'empowerment' evident in our lives. One seventeen-year-old girl I worked with (a survivor of child sexual abuse) had left her flat, newly pregnant, because her landlord kept trying to have sex with her. She reasoned that if she was going to be sexually harassed by older men, she may as well get paid for it. It was a reasoning many of us arrived at.

The consistent reality of being exploited by men in more socially powerful positions could not be abated and since we could not escape it we 'chose' to frame the terms of that exploitation as financial, since those were the only terms open to us that could have been of any practical benefit. The attempt to frame prostitution as 'sexual self-determination' simply doesn't hold up, because our decisions were not sexual, they were economic. The sexual element was endured, not enjoyed, and if we had been in any position to exercise true self-determination, our pimp would have had an empty brothel and our clients a whole pile of blank rolls of film.

Because I've been on the other side of the camera, I honestly wouldn't and couldn't have a relationship with someone who had a current porn habit. For any woman who finds porn distasteful I would consider it good advice not to allow anyone convince her otherwise. Sometimes honouring who we are as people necessitates framing the boundaries of what we're prepared to accept. I have experienced the damage and degradation of stripping and pornography. These are not harmless industries. They are not, by the way, distinct industries: they are part of the same one big prostitution *machine*; a mechanism which actively reduces the worth of women and does so by placing their commodification both at its apex and at its core.

Chapter 9 ~

THE INTERPLAY OF
DEPRAVITY

*(We) know more about sexuality today. We may be no
better at controlling or humanising it, but we do understand how fragile and complex it is, and how mysteri-
ously prone to disorder and disease . . . In spite of the
claims made by sexual utopians in the 1960s, sex is never
value-free, never without its human and emotional consequences.*

RICHARD HOLLOWAY, *ANGER, SEX, DOUBT AND DEATH*

One thing I have not heard prostitutes or former prostitutes publicly discuss is the inevitable interplay of depravity that exists
between prostitutes and their clients, but it is absolutely central to the job. It is as much a part of prostitution as chalk once was to
the teaching profession and just as essential to the performance of their
'work'.

The interplay of depravity between a prostitute and her client takes
on a dizzying array of forms and an infinite number of nuances. These
work in combination with each other in a busy spirit of production, and
they never produce anything but depravity in a new and different form.
Depravity here is self-propagating.

One of the ways this depravity manifests itself is in the strange interaction between a 'mistress' (or 'madam', as I sometimes insisted on
being called) and her 'slave', which is in fact a sort of co-dependency
of depravity, in that each relies on the behaviour and responses of the
other to bring about perverted interactions which are required to cause

arousal for one and payment for the other. I worked as a dominatrix for a good portion of my prostitution life, so I am experienced in the ways that men and women relate in this area of prostitution and the reasons why they must, and what is to be gained for both by doing so. This is complex; there are more psychological layers here than an objective observer might suppose.

What you do when dealing with less common requests as a prostitute (and most particularly with a sexually submissive client) is to ascertain as closely as possible exactly what it is this man *wants*, and also what he *needs*, because these two requirements are very important and also often very distinct, though he may be unaware of the duality of his requirements. You figure out both what's missing; what the actual lack is and also what he *perceives* that lack to be, because as I said, the man may be confused on that point; and consequently you make it your job to fill both vacancies. There is no point satisfying either one or the other, you must satisfy both. In this way, you generate repeat business. You cannot be slipshod in your approach here: to satisfy a want and neglect a need is to create a situation whereby a man will have a niggling underlying sense of frustration and discontent and you will see him for a short time before he moves on to somebody else. To satisfy a need and neglect a want is to ensure he will visit you for a time-frame that is considerably shorter, as his wants are more apparent to him than his needs; you must first identify both and then satisfy both, and in this way, you guarantee your own fiscal return.

These wants and needs cover a spectrum that is truly vast and ranges from the obvious sexual proclivities to emotional and even surprisingly practical types of facilitation that would be considered far outside the usual remit of what's expected from a prostitute. It is mildly amusing to me to imagine how this process would be referred to in another sector: 'client satisfaction' or 'customer relations' perhaps. You employ these methods, of course, only when you're dealing with a man whose repeat business would be particularly acceptable to you. The only times I ever employed this approach were when a man was a transvestite or a submissive. It is not a method to be used wholesale. It would be of no practical widespread use because there are many instances where you would not wish to see a man on a repetitive basis, regardless of how much it might enrich the financial side of your life.

The interplay of depravity here, as it relates to the prostitute's contribution, is in the wilful manoeuvring necessary to mirror the requests and requirements of a psychologically fragile male mind. Manipulation is quite necessary. In fact, with this type of man, it is mandatory; the ability to carry it out is simply a requirement of the job. This is not evidence of some sort of prostitutes' autonomy. It is evidence that this type of client must recognise in his 'mistress' the actions of a master manipulator. There is one reason for this: it arouses him. It is not, truly, at its core, about the woman being in control; it is about the man's need to perceive her to be.

In my own life, I have worked with a plethora of men who exhibited these tendencies. For example I had one particular client, I'll call him Donald. He saw me regularly for about three years. I met him when I was still on the streets, at seventeen, and he continued to come to me for a few years after that. Donald was the very epitome of the client who wants to be dominated. He appeared to revere and worship women to truly bizarre proportions and spending time with Donald was a study in the converse dynamics of power in prostitution, because, although it might have looked as if I was in control to the casual observer, since he was controlling the purse-strings, the ultimate power was always his own. There is a lot of sense in the old adage: 'He who pays the piper calls the tune', but neither he nor I would have ever dreamt of making reference to that. To do so would have been to destroy the fabric of the rapport between us, which would have cost me money and him his erection.

Donald venerated women in a negative and unhealthy way. He did not simply treasure them; he dignified them by debasing himself. The same was true to one degree or other of all the men I met who liked to be dominated, but Donald took this sexual proclivity to the highest degree. He begged and nagged to be used in every manner imaginable, from having his time and effort taken for granted to being kicked, whipped and beaten.

He would call me up regularly in the evenings and beg to take me to dinner, and even the first time this happened, without ever having to be instructed, I instinctively understood that his particular penchant would not be satisfied unless I gave him clearly to understand that this was a very great chore for me; that suffering his company for an hour or two was an imposition and an insufferable inconvenience. We had many conversations that went similar to this:

Me: 'How dare you? How dare you impose your worthless self on me, as if I had nothing better to do with my time than look at your simpering face? Well? Well? How dare you?'

Donald: (stuttering and incoherent with nerves) 'I'm sorry, Madam, I mean, Mistress, I mean Madam.'

Me: 'You know, or *ought* to know, BETTER by now than to call me Mistress. I'm not some marriage-wrecking floozy!'

Donald: 'Madam, Madam, I'm so sorry, Madam.'

Me: 'You haven't answered my question. I am waiting, and you know how I hate to wait.'

Donald: 'I'm sorry, Madam, I've forgotten the question.'

Me: 'Well that's no surprise, you being the fool that you are. The *question* was HOW DARE YOU presume I've nothing better to do than grace you with my company?'

Donald: 'Oh I'm so sorry, Madam, I'm so sorry. I am only calling because I thought you might be hungry and need someone to take care of you and feed you, Madam. I would hate to think of you hungry or needing anything you hadn't got, Madam.'

Me: 'I never need anything I haven't got my dear, because I have half-a-dozen fools like yourself ready to rush around and fetch it for me. Where are you?'

Donald: 'I'm parked across the road, Madam.'

Me: 'Lucky for you.'

Donald: 'Oh, you know, I never keep you waiting.'

Me: 'You never keep me waiting, *what*?'

Donald: 'Sorry? Excuse me, Madam?'

Me: 'You never keep me waiting WHAT?'

Donald: 'I'm sorry madam, I don't understand.'

Me: 'Well that's hardly surprising, given the moron that you are. I don't know why I bother trying to train you. You really are an incorrigible fool and a total waste of my time; you do know that, don't you?'

Donald: 'Yes, Madam, oh, I know, Madam. Thank you for putting up with me, Madam.'

Me: 'Well it's more than you deserve. I was chastising you because you forgot to call me Madam when you reminded me that you never keep me waiting. Do not show yourself remiss in that department again. And now I can feel my heart softening towards you because you are across the road and I will not be kept waiting; you are a good boy in that department at least. You may take your madam to dinner. I will be out when I'm out, and you, needless to say, will wait until I am ready.'

Donald: 'Oh of course, Madam, and thank you, Madam, thank you.'

So this is an example of the interplay of depravity here; the way he debased himself by requesting to be spoken to like that, and the consequential and interrelated way I debased myself because it is not in my nature to speak to people like that. Donald's behaviour was simply wormlike. His perversion was in the desire to be treated as less than human. It was a desire that was depraved in its nature, and in facilitating it, I myself behaved in a manner that was depraved.

This interchange is also an example of the prostitute's acquired skill of discernment; the way in which I had to abuse him thoroughly and then throw him a few words of comfort, before finally debasing him again. Donald *wanted* to be debased, but he *needed* to be comforted. Once this has been established, there is also the important matter of degree. How must the client's needs and wants be balanced, and when? This is the psychological tightrope a dominatrix walks in her working life, and she makes up for a lack of training by instinct and experience. The balance is always a delicate one, sometimes as delicate as steadying the head of a needle on a thread of spider's silk, and you wouldn't always get it right. I got the balance right with Donald, which was why he visited me for years.

Forms of word-play similar to those above ran in constant streams between us each and every time we met. Of course, these conversations were theatrically extreme, over-the-top and ridiculous, but you can't afford to care about the ridiculous here; not if you care about getting paid.

There is a lot of mental concentration required with a client like Donald. I was very aware of the ways he would try to provoke me and I played along with him always. In cases like the above, he often wouldn't have forgotten the question, or to call me 'Madam'; he would be looking for a good verbal tongue-lashing and it was my job to pick up on his cues so as to know exactly when and how to give it to him.

Clearly Donald was a very confused and damaged man and it was a therapist he needed, not a prostitute. I can see here clearly an example of the negativity prostitutes are capable of emitting as well as receiving. There was something that should have been movingly pitiable about the sick 'this is a safe place to get hurt' sense of security that he exhibited with me. This is another essence of the interplay of depravity here: it is in both parties knowing they are doing each other a disservice and neither having the benevolence to care.

Donald had been seeing prostitutes for years before he met me, nevertheless, the longer I saw him, the more deeply entrenched in his 'character' he became. I believe that his prostitution experiences began to live inside him and to contort and deform his nature. Some might say that it is strange to think of prostitution as a living thing, but if by your definition of 'alive' you simply mean something that progresses and grows, then this experience could be said to be alive. Prostitution lives and grows, not just on a level that's global or cultural from country to country, but on a micro level; in each life it touches, it develops and evolves. I have seen the evolution of prostitution everywhere I have seen prostitution and I have never seen an example of this growth and development that was in the positive. The interplay of depravity does not allow for that. It does not produce anything incongruent with its own character.

In the case of Donald it is obvious how he was damaged by this interplay—but only because we live in a patriarchal world, where witnessing the submissive degradation of men is experienced as jarring, but in reality it is as depraved for men to abuse women in any of the innumerable ways they do in other areas of prostitution, and the damage should be just as obvious.

You might think that, by way of us all being people, we might see something of ourselves in the lives of our clients. Some family-based practice, for example, that called to mind our own. We did not. We saw precious little to remind us of humanity in the private lives of our clients. There are no such links in prostitution. The closest a prostitute will get to understanding anything of her client's family life is by noticing a baby seat in the back of his car or feeling the cold metal of his wedding ring pressed against the inner walls of her vagina. All prostitutes have had this latter experience, as I have, and all street-walking women have had the former one, as I also have, many times. The mutual derision between prostitutes and their clients is starkly expressed in this experience recorded by journalist and political activist Julie Bindel:

> 'I visit Europe's oldest tolerance zone, often described by UK advocates of legalisation as an example of best practice. Unlike the zones that have been shut due to criminal activity, this one, I'm told, runs like clockwork. At the Marco Polo police station in Utrecht, half an hour's drive from Amsterdam, I meet Officer Jan Schoenmaker, responsible for policing the zone. In April, he was part of a delegation that visited Liverpool at the request of the local council, which is keen to set up its own tolerance zone . . . Schoenmaker translates some graffiti on the wall. 'Dear kerb crawlers, we hate you men. We want to get as much money from you as possible.' A response scrawled opposite reads, 'Fucking whores, you must be fucked until you drop on the ground. We fuck and suck you until your cunt is very sore. Thank you.'
> JULIE BINDEL
> *THE GUARDIAN*, SATURDAY 15 MAY 2004

Prostitutes and their clients exist at the coalface of human contempt, and they remain there, too disinterested in each other's discomfort even to throw the other a cursory glance.

The exchange of money is often a moment of tension or embarrassment in prostitution. Clients themselves sometimes treat with revulsion the act of paying a prostitute. This is especially common in dealings between individual men and women who've spent years together engaged in the exchange. One man I had been seeing for a long time liked to indulge in the idiocy of hiding the money under the pillow and looking the other way while I put it in my handbag. Of course I'd accommodate that, or any other absurdity he could come up with, as long as all the money was present and correct.

Also it should be noted that some men eroticise the point of payment and do so in a way designed to reinforce both the woman's subservience and the man's seniority. Some men would simply tug on the money gently as they were handing it over, so that I would have to expend a little more deliberation and energy in the taking of it. This would always result in eye-contact and a knowing smile from him before he would loosen his grip. Some men are rather more flamboyant. I once spent the evening in the company of a man who paid me one hundred pounds for the privilege. The privilege was all his. He paid me in five pound notes, one every twenty minutes or so, as openly and indiscreetly as possible, and with an audience. I endured the humiliation. I was sixteen years old at the time. Had I met the same man later in my prostitution life, I would have told him where to shove his fivers.

But yes, some men were uncomfortable with the moment of payment. Sometimes it became more complicated than that, and I suspect the deeper a man's sense of revulsion, the more difficult it became for him to appraise the situation honestly. Some men would, over a prolonged period of time, indulge the fantasy that I was there as much from a personal desire born of sincere affection as anything to do with money and they would make their position obvious by inviting me for drinks or other preludes to the sexual act. I hadn't any problem with that as long as I could trust my physical safety with them enough to take a drink in their company (which was unusual) and as long as they were paying me for my time, but to do so in a purely social sense, as was sometimes suggested, was blatant nonsense. I was not in the business of playing 'let's pretend' when it came to the reasons I was there, or at least that's not what I had signed up for, but the truth is, in prostitution, you often haven't any idea what you've signed up for until you're right in the thick of it, and besides, what you've signed up for changes as rapidly and regularly as it takes to get from one man to the next.

It was a talking point among us women that some men would try to distance themselves from the reality of what they were doing, so sometimes you would go for a drink and watch while they slipped money under your saucer or your beer-mat. Some men needed to do that and needed to be indulged in doing that, and it would not take a visitation from Sigmund Freud to figure out that they conjured up the charade because they found the truth of the situation so much less palatable. So we accommodated them in circumnavigating the truth; indulged the fiction of contorting this experience out of shape; played along with the denial element where necessary, but it was always a strange and discomforting experience. The truth is that sometimes this charade was necessary because the reality was that this moment, the exchange of money, was so symbolic of the interplay of depravity in prostitution that sometimes clients themselves found it distasteful and difficult to deal with.

Of course there is something sad about that, and of course a client who rejects his reality presents as a pitiable person; someone who, through his own fantastical enactments, has made it apparent that what he really wants is a relationship. These men ought to see that their desires will almost always be unreciprocated by the women they are paying, so they are wasting their time going to brothels in the first place. The bottom line is this: there is no sexual equality or mutual respect in the basic structure of prostitution and anyone who hopes to find a relationship there is on a fruitless search that is sure to end in disappointment.

Where a prostitute plays along with these sorts of whims, some people might conclude that she is no different to the second-hand car salesman who omits to mention problems with the clutch, or the banker who points his client towards a savings scheme which is more in the interests of the bank. Some people would charge her with duplicity and fraudulence but excuse her by maintaining that, after all, there are many professions which operate on the capitalist ethos that as long as it is conducted in the name of business, we are all entitled to screw each other. But people who buy used cars don't ask to be lied to and people who frequent banks don't solicit expensive charades either; but the clients of many prostitutes do, and this is exactly what they do, and they know what they are doing, and they pay to be accommodated in doing it. When a prostitute plays along with this charade, it is for the purposes of the punter's own solicited benefit. If a prostitute is to be castigated for doing this then she is to be castigated for giving the man exactly what he's asked for, and paid for.

There are layers of reality here, as in all of life, and another reality is that as the game is played, longer and longer over time, some of the imagined facets become real, or as close to real as is possible in this unnatural relational situation. She knows that, though her affection is not sincere, he wishes it were to the degree that he must have some genuine affection for her and so it is reasonable to assume he will never hurt her. A new and hesitant degree of trust has been established and her anxieties are somewhat assuaged. The upshot of this is that the usual tension of her environment lifts temporarily in his presence and this, experienced enough times with the same man, deepens her sense of security in his company. Eventually her anxieties are near-eradicated; she *knows* that she is safe from violence here, in this place, with this man, at least. In comparison to her other clients, it offers her something edging closer to respite, so she is relieved to see him when he calls. Sometimes, she will discuss small things but real things, and because of the very rarity of her divulgences he will treat each of them like treasures of enormous value. For a prostitute who holds herself at the degree of emotional distance that I did, these fractured and flawed moments of connection are as emotionally close as a client will ever get. This does not mean that she does not resent him. She does, and she always will, and that's why he will never get any closer.

There were a very small number of regular clients of mine for whom I would have felt something that mimicked distress had something desperately tragic happened to them, but those men numbered two or three out of God knows how many, and the distress I'd have felt would not have been the natural and wounding pain felt for a loved one; it would have been a misrepresentation, diluted and disjointed, like a forgery, a clumsy counterfeit of feeling.

What I have always taken from this is that the normal human bonds of emotion cannot grow in a woman for a man who pays her for sex. It is not, in my opinion, a peculiarity of prostitution that some clients can and do form a deep emotional fondness for some of the women they pay (or at least for the people they believe those women to be). It is something that further confirms to me the nature of the offence. When human feeling runs in one direction only, there is a reason for that.

The interplay of depravity in prostitution cannot be discussed without focusing somewhat on the unusual sexual practices in prostitution. It is remarkable how warped some people's sense of their own sexuality can be. I'll record an experience here. It was not one of mine, thank God, and to be honest I can scarcely imagine I'd have had the stomach for it, but here it is: a woman I know who worked in prostitution in Canada met a man whose penchant was for women's menstrual blood. He explained to her the origins of this: apparently when he was a young boy he'd been using the bathroom in his home and for some reason he decided to rummage through the bathroom bin. He came across one of his mother's used tampons. It was soaked in menstrual blood. He smelled it and found the strange, strong pungent smell intoxicating in the sexual sense and then he went ahead and did the thing that was to affect his sexual life forever: he sucked all the blood from it. From that day forward he entertained the sexual desire to experience the smell and taste of menstrual blood.

Menstrual blood, as any woman could tell you, is thicker, darker, and more pungent than the blood that leaks from the veins. The man was sexually entranced. His penchant led him to a lifetime of visiting prostitutes because he felt, for obvious reasons, that he could not share such a desire with the women he met in his personal life. And this really is one of the cornerstones that support the sex trade—the male insistence on offloading onto another class of women perversions they cannot reasonably expect to present to the women in their lives. Here, women are very distinctly divided into the respectable and the contemptible, the decent and the disreputable, the revered and the reviled.

In my friend's case, they would organise their meetings to happen only when she was in the heaviest part of her period, this man and my old colleague, and she'd wear a tampon for at least a day before their meeting so that it was absolutely soaked in blood. He was always adamant that it needed to be 'thoroughly soaked'. Then they would meet, she'd remove the tampon and he'd relive his childhood experience.

The particular interplay of depravity between my former colleague and her Canadian client was this: she assisted him in debasing himself by facilitating his continuance of a foul and disgusting habit which would hold him at an emotional distance from every woman he ever met, and he assisted her in debasing herself by presenting this station to her which he would never dare present to any other woman.

The interplay of depravity in prostitution is exactly that: interplay, because it runs in two directions which affect, reflect and merge with each other. It is required and delivered, sought and satiated, presented and accepted. Depravity is a master of its own renewal and regeneration and just as certain bacteria multiply best in the damp, it finds prostitution a most hospitable environment.

Because I worked as a dominatrix and with transvestites, I would have been privy to more 'traditional' perversion than women who refused to see such people, but another anomaly I ought to mention first: the ratio of street prostitutes who refused to involve themselves with unusual sexual practices was far higher than that of women who worked in the massage-parlour, brothel or escorting ends of the business. And another inconsistency which might surprise people: not all transvestites were interested in unusual sexual practices, beyond the obvious sexual pleasure which they all got from dressing as women, though a high number of them, I noticed, enjoyed experiencing women as a domineering force and more than a few of them experienced 'golden showers' as pleasurable.

One particular transvestite I knew well would order champagne from room service, only to have me urinate into one of the champagne glasses—I would enjoy a glass of Moët and he would enjoy that instead. He would then bring his glass into the bathroom and would lie on his back in the bath, sipping all the while, while I'd stand, one foot on either side of the bath, and urinate all over him; his genitals, his chest, his face, and when I'd reach there he'd open his mouth and drink more of the same. You'd need a strong stomach in this business.

Some people may find all that horrifying and certainly I did not find it pleasurable, but still, the truth is I encountered less perversion within prostitution from the adherents to unusual sexual practices than I ever did from those who would be considered 'straightforward' or 'ordinary' clients, as I have said. It is clear to me that there is something worse, something deeper, something much more fundamentally wrong about a man shoving his penis into a woman and enjoying her powerlessness than there is about a man who lies back in a bath in suspenders and make-up, sipping her urine as if it were wine.

The man I am referring to here was a gentle-natured person and someone who I often chatted with over a meal somewhere or a drink beforehand in the hotel bar. I always spent the night with this man and was paid for my time so we would always meet like that, either for a meal or a drink, depending on whether or not we were doing any cocaine together that night. Cocaine decimates the appetite and would have made enjoying a meal impossible. Also, it wouldn't have been realistic to have the meal first; the urge for cocaine is too strong to take second place to a beef Stroganoff. I had progressed to snorting cocaine at that point and would procure it for certain punters, making a mark-up on it, so that I was profiting from the drug transaction as well as whatever bizarre fantasies I was helping these men indulge.

All transvestites have a favourite female name they wish to be called while dressed and what happens between the transvestite client and the prostitute he regularly visits is that a peculiar sort of bond is formed based on her intimate knowledge of his female persona, which he keeps expertly hidden from the rest of the world. She is, in a very real sense, the only person who knows his name.

For the prostitute's part, her transvestite client is a man who will almost certainly never want sexual intercourse from her. (Of course I do not contend that this has never happened anywhere; only that I have never come across it or heard of another woman come across it.) Because of that I was always far more comfortable in the company of transvestites. It was always my experience that a transvestite's primary sexual thrill is to indulge the experience of femininity and of being appreciated as a woman.[4] Some transvestites sought additional thrills, but this was always the primary one. I met many transvestites in prostitution and I believe the reason I never met one who was interested in having sexual intercourse was because that would have cast him in a clearly masculine role. Men in prostitution, never, in my experience, seek to do anything which runs counter to the fantasy they are indulging. Transvestites are no different in that respect.

Often our transvestite clients would bring us gifts, like jewellery or expensive perfume. Many of them had taste in women's clothes that far surpassed those of some actual women I have known and often they would bring us clothes as gifts. I had one client who, if I admired something he was wearing, would invariably turn up the next time we met with the same garment in my size.

I noticed that while some of these men had gregarious personalities generally, they all did so while dressed. You would see before your eyes the shyness slip away with the application of each layer of make-up, the putting-on of stockings and heels. The transformation obviously wasn't restricted to the physical and was in many ways more emphasised by the attitude that emerged. There was a new confidence there, a new happiness and sense of freedom and, strange as it may sound or difficult as it may be to imagine, the truth is that transvestites were, singularly, the most tolerable company I ever encountered among my clients.

As true as that is, the barriers you hold between your private self and prostitution are just too strong and too necessary to allow an authentic friendship to form. I spent five years being visited by a particular transvestite who was a basically decent person, but who just could not bring himself to involve the woman in his life in his fantasies to the degree that he felt they needed to be indulged. I found it necessary at times to distance myself from him on a personal level, as he continually issued me with invitations for holidays and trips outside the remit of prostitution that, of course, had to be declined. It was difficult to find ways to do this without having to directly assert that we could never make genuine

---

4   There is not always a sexual edge to this thrill, the psychologists tell us, but of course in the remit of prostitution it was those who did indulge a sexual thrill who presented themselves to us.

friends of each other. I would never have said that to him because I simply didn't want to be cruel. There was so little of humanity to be found in prostitution; the tiny speck I saw was fragile and I didn't want to hurt it. However, I knew I could never accept those invitations. It was a slightly saddening understanding, but there were no surprises there. It was just further mundane and depressing evidence, as though it were needed, of the polluting nature of prostitution on human interpersonal relations.

Chapter 10

THE MYTH OF THE HIGH-CLASS HOOKER

*[F]rom the perspective of a woman in prostitution or a
woman who has been in prostitution—the distinctions
other people make between whether the event took place
in the Plaza Hotel or somewhere more inelegant are not
the distinctions that matter. These are irreconcilable
perceptions, with irreconcilable premises. Of course the
circumstances must matter, you say. No, they do not,
because we are talking about the use of the mouth,
the vagina, and the rectum. The circumstances don't
mitigate or modify what prostitution is.*

ANDREA DWORKIN, *LIFE AND DEATH*

Because I've worked in every area of prostitution, I can say that no area has a monopoly on degradation and no area is free of it. The perception exists that street-walking prostitutes are unique among their kind in that they are the only women in the business who suffer daily degradation. They certainly suffer the consequences of being regarded as the lowest of the low, but it would be very wrong to assume that degradation is restricted to the red-light zones. There are no such restrictions in prostitution. Contrary to this misinformation, it is just as possible and just as customary to be humiliated in a five-star hotel.

Some of the worst experiences I've had in prostitution took place in Ireland's most exclusive hotels. Indeed, sometimes when you are dealing with a particular type of man, with a particular type of mindset, you are far worse off finding yourself with him in environs of opulence: some wealthy men (not all, thank God) communicate to you that you ought to feel yourself privileged to be there, regardless of how immaculately and expensively dressed and made-up you may be.

The sense of the male being the dominant force in a money-for-sex exchange only ever comes close to fully disappearing in the case where a man expressly requests it in order to fulfil a desire to be dominated, and even in that case, as I've said, they still enjoy the control inherent to the status of the paying customer. Some men I've met in very expensive hotels or on call-outs[5] to extremely affluent houses were among the most difficult people a prostitute could meet. There was a sense of entitlement with those men that actually increased with every pound they paid you. The attitude was clear: 'I have paid you two hundred pounds—therefore I will do whatever I feel like doing to you and you will keep your mouth shut about it'. Of course, in some men this attitude was simply a reflection of their general arrogance and inhumanity; in the majority of men who treated me this way though, it was clear that they got off in the sexual sense on humiliating me, on making me feel powerless, on giving me to feel and understand that I was there for one reason and one reason only—so that my body would be used as a receptacle for their sperm.

After I began working indoors in 1993, I found that it was not safer as far as violence was concerned (though it was certainly safer in terms of avoiding arrest) but the degradation was just the same and often worse. I cannot think of anything less 'high class' than some of the experiences I had at the 'upper end' of the market. The truth is there is nothing classy about the exchange of money for sex and the environs where it takes place are powerless to influence that.

I often met men who would have assumed that I was an escort, because they met me under those circumstances, and that I only ever worked in that sphere of the business; what they didn't know was that I was often to be found on the streets or in massage parlours, and that they were paying me several times more than I'd been paid for the same service the day before. I met plenty of women who did this sort of 'double-jobbing', who worked different areas of the business at the same time. What I didn't come across often were women like myself

---

5   The term in the business whereby a prostitute visits a punter's home.

who worked *all* areas. Almost always, the women I met who worked in more than one area of prostitution worked either on the streets and in brothels, or in brothels and escort agencies. Working a crossover on the entire range of the scale, as I did, was unusual; so I believe that through simple diversity of experience I've got a fuller picture of prostitution than many of the women I've known.

The women themselves bought into the supposed hierarchical structure of prostitution, with prostitutes in escort agencies looking down their noses at street-walking women and those in massage parlours comforting themselves with the fact that at least they weren't out on the streets, at least they 'hadn't sunk that low'!

I knew one woman, a lovely girl, who worked her own one-woman escort agency out of an apartment on an upmarket avenue in Ballsbridge. Her advertising costs were three-hundred-and-fifty pounds a fortnight. Her rent was a thousand pounds a month. Her mobile phone bills were higher than her advertising costs. This was in 1993. (Mobile phones were brand new technology in Ireland at the time and were the preserve of businessmen, drug dealers and prostitutes.) She spent a fortune on taxis and on clothes and shoes befitting her 'escort' stature. She broke even some months and when she did, she refused to work in any other area of the business to supplement her escorting income. 'What are you doing on the streets?' she used to ask me. 'What are you doing in this fucking apartment?' I'd ask her in return. It seemed so pointless to me—for some periods of time she was whoring herself just to maintain a situation in which to whore herself. The whole idea was supposed to be about making a half-decent living, I'd say to her, for God's sake.

Still, she managed to save ten thousand pounds in the time she rented that apartment, but her money was earned in fits and spurts during peak-time periods and I could not understand how she tolerated the dead-end intervals. The problem was that she was paying the same overheads an apartment full of women would have split between them, but she was compulsive about her independence and the privacy of her space. I was the only other woman who ever worked in her apartment. I was the person she'd always call if a two-woman job was required, and I sometimes did some of her clients in her apartment as well, usually impossibility here is another example of the myths, or falsifications, of prostitution.

Many of the women who enter prostitution at its high end do so out of desperation, but many of the women who begin prostituting themselves on the streets do so out of destitution. There is a difference. For this reason, socially disadvantaged women like my younger self fill the streets and the brothels and middle- and upper-middle-class women fill the escort agencies. But the transition from one to the other is entirely possible and for all the comments claiming it not to be, I've yet to hear anyone posit what type of obstructions are in place to stop a woman 'working up the ladder', or how they contend these supposed barriers operate. Certainly women from the streets are not welcome to apply for positions in escort agencies, being seen to be in possession of the lower-class vaginas I've mentioned already, but any woman with a whit of sense will simply keep her mouth shut about that, as I did.

The obstruction here, if there is one, is in the *belief* of the myth of the high-class hooker. Buying into this erroneous belief is possibly the biggest obstacle to any woman exercising social mobility within the prostitution world.

As to social class among the prostituted, I met advantaged middle-class women in prostitution and I honestly couldn't understand them. I just couldn't get what they were doing in brothels at all. (I always referred to the apartments escort agencies are run from as brothels, because that's what they are. The only time I broke with that tradition was when I referred to them as whore-houses with the intent to rub some of the women who referred to what we were doing as 'escorting' up the wrong way.) My problem, my incomprehension, was in what they were doing in the business. It made no sense to me. They were privileged. They were educated, only to second level usually but even so, I am talking about well-to-do fee-paying private schools. They seemed to have had other viable choices open to them; they could have gone to university, they could have gone to work in daddy's business, but yet here they were in this awful place doing something they clearly hated and that obviously made them miserable. Why? Well, there is no universal answer to that. The answer varies from woman to woman.

during periods so busy that two men would be booked for the same time.

We were close friends and I'd sometimes walk from the red-light district to her apartment at the end of an evening's work. She didn't try to hide her distaste for my street-walking work and I couldn't have cared less. I knew that if she'd started out on the streets she'd have had an appreciation of the differences between the different forms of work and the pros and cons contained within each. As I've said, on the streets I was not at the mercy of someone I'd had no chance to sum up before I entered into a contract with. In indoor work you don't know who or what you're dealing with until the door has closed behind you, and by the time the door has closed behind you, it's too late. She was inexperienced in these different dynamics.

Business was brisker on the streets. You often had the opportunity to make your money and go. There was much less of the waiting around inherent to escort work, which I found uniquely depressing. It gave you too much time to think.

I approached my work differently from my friend in other ways, too. I had a mobile but had it blocked for outgoing calls. It was strictly used for clients to contact me. I bought that phone when the laws changed in 1993 and street-walking prostitutes began being hounded nightly by the police. I rented an apartment in Terenure for a short time and opened an escort agency of my own. I was seventeen at the time and I'm quite sure I was the youngest person advertising an escort agency in Ireland. It was a very simple thing to do and only required an apartment, a mobile phone and an advertisement in the back of *In Dublin* magazine, but when I had to deal with the reality of the ridiculous overheads, I soon got rid of the apartment and advertised for call-outs only. I worked mainly in the brothels and escort agencies of others from then on and did my own call-outs to homes and hotels. If I'd get a request for a call-in on my agency line I'd use a bedroom in the brothel of one of the women I was associating with at that time. I'd pay them a fee for the use of the room, which was common practice. I'd made money myself that way when I had my own apartment.

The consequences of the new laws took a lot of getting used to. An understood street rule had always been that the encounter was over when the client climaxed, but now we found ourselves alone in rooms with men who were paying by the hour and wanted every minute of their money's worth. I found this new form of prostitution *more* dangerous and *more* degrading, not less.

And so, because of all this, I developed a very à-la-carte approach to prostitution. I never bought into the nonsense that some forms of it were somehow 'better' in a social or moral sense than others. There was no true distinction that I could find there. Of course society would clearly tell you which was the most and least acceptable of these, but I had not been raised with an affinity to social structures or to compliance with social norms and I knew that such notions were nonsense here anyway. I measured the different forms of prostitution against each other in the only sane way I knew how, which was in terms of which was more dangerous, stressful or profitable. I found through experience that in terms of danger, stress and profit, each had their own pros and cons, but in terms of degradation, that was universal. It was to be found in differing degrees only with different men, not with different environments, and it was to be found everywhere.

One thing I never went in for in prostitution was calling myself an 'escort' or a 'call girl'. I find these terms derisory and ridiculous, 'call girl' particularly so. What this term seeks to do is to focus on the fact that a prostitute must call to your door and ignores entirely what goes on when it shuts behind her. It does not even seek to fraudulently repackage the prostitution experience, as the term 'escort' does, but rather discounts it entirely. These are lies, pure and simple. I never tried to sugar-coat what I did, no matter where I was working or how much I was getting paid for it. Similarly, while working as a stripper, I never referred to myself as a 'dancer', exotic or otherwise. I heard these terms at the time, both in the media and in the brothels, and when I heard them they always seemed to me to serve the same purpose, which was to seek to paint a deceptive veneer of respectability over what we did.

For the women involved to use terms like 'call girl' appeared particularly stupid to me, because to do that was to admit that you were not prepared to face yourself or others with the truth of your daily experience, and if you were not prepared to do that, was that not an admission

in itself? Did it not say something, and say it very clearly? I felt that the women who preferred to call themselves escorts and dancers were even less happy with their lot than the women who'd tell you they were strippers and whores and hated the whole business, because at least the women who weren't afraid to call a spade a spade weren't indulging in self-denial. At least they were not afraid to look the truth of their experience in the face. If you look at something and say you find it distasteful, your sense of disgust is probably less potent than that of the person who refuses to observe it at all.

As to the myth of the high-class hooker, this particular myth persists in the main (like most myths in prostitution) because it suits the men who pay for sex to believe it. Many like to assume that when they call an escort agency, a higher class of vagina will arrive at their door and, as an afterthought, that there'll be a higher class of woman attached to it. The notion of the high-class hooker is propagated by those who profit from it, because it is the simplest way to maximise the market. Women in escort prostitution buy into the notion that they are somehow better than their street-walking sisters because class-ism exists in all of life. Why should prostitution be any different?

There is a notion in and of the sex industry that you 'can't work up the ladder'. That is to say that it is not possible to begin working on the streets or in brothels and then move on to escort agencies. This notion is commonly held. It is commonly held nonsense. I know that because my 'career' followed exactly that supposedly impossible trajectory, and also because, though unusual, I was not alone.

Interestingly, I found that misconception usually held among those prostitutes who had only ever worked the 'high end' of the market. This is an important point to note because, of course, it means that the notion is held and circulated in the main by those who have no experience of having done what it is they are claiming it is not possible to do. Women who've always worked in the area of escorting wouldn't know how easy it is to enter that arena from 'below'; they've never had to make the career shift. It is possible. I've done it myself and I've seen it done. It is bizarrely easy, considering how 'impossible' it's widely perceived to be. In fact, it's as simple as making a phone call. The notion

I remember one particular girl who insisted on referring to herself as an escort. 'Ah, good for you,' I said to her. 'I'm a whore myself.'

She was blonde and in her early to mid-twenties. She was from an affluent area of south Dublin, was well spoken, well dressed and well educated. She was also a victim of childhood sexual abuse, regularly self-harmed and by the time I last saw her, had progressed from the level of recreational cocaine user to a chronic cocaine addict. That girl had every privilege in life, except the one that matters most to a woman: sexual serenity. She hadn't ever had that.

Not every middle- and upper-middle class woman who becomes involved in prostitution will have psychological issues that are so glaringly obvious, but I do not believe it is possible for a woman to wilfully involve herself in prostitution without there being some problem, sexual or otherwise, that precedes it. Everything I have ever seen in prostitution leads me to this conclusion. To know that women like the one I've just mentioned are commonly regarded as 'high class' amongst prostitutes just adds a new negative dimension to prostitution for me; it is the dimension of the preposterous and the absurd.

Most prostitutes are from backgrounds of dysfunction, just like I was, and relive the turbulence of their early years in prostitution, just like I did. It's important though, in examining the backgrounds of prostituted women, to remember that not all childhood dysfunction is as obvious as mine was. Not all young girls from emotionally unhealthy homes have greasy hair and tattered, dirty clothing. Many of the women I knew in prostitution had far more disturbing childhoods than I had; they just didn't have the outwardly obvious symbolism of my own. Many of them didn't have the visible symptoms that serve as sure-fire indicators that something's wrong at home. In many instances in their childhoods, no doubt their skin was spotless, as would have been their clothes and hair; it would have been only in the eyes that you would have gauged something of what was going on at home.

People who see prostitution as something which exists on a number of different, exclusive and distinct class-related levels are people who do not understand the interrelated nature of it, and some of the people ignorant of the shifting nature of prostitution are actually prostitutes and prostitutors[6] themselves. The evidence of this variable nature in prostitution is something which, looking back over my time in the business, is clear to me. When *In Dublin* magazine began publishing adverts for escort agencies in Dublin city in the early 1990s, many prostitutes and madams who had previously worked solely in the area of massage parlours reinvented themselves as 'escorts' and their operations as 'escort agencies'. This worked especially well in the early days of the economic boom, because many Irish people were seeing enormous stylish apartment blocks being built for the first time. The shift from brothel worker to escort prostitute really is and was that simple. (In fact, in this internet age, many will find it simpler still.) The reasoning behind the 'upgrading' of brothel workers all across the city was equally simple: at that time, a woman working in a massage parlour could charge somewhere in the region of forty to sixty pounds; a woman working in an escort agency could charge somewhere in the region of one hundred to one-hundred-and-fifty.

It is an economic reality in business that a customer is not disposed to paying more for a service than he has been used to paying, if there is no improvement or upgrade to that service. If a man walks into an escort agency and meets a woman he met in a massage parlour the week before, he will naturally feel disinclined to pay that woman several times what he paid the last time he met her; and if the transaction is completed before he recognises her, he is sure to feel cheated, and of course he would, since he has just paid three times the price for the same 'service' from the same 'service provider'. This is the only common-sense reality upon which the myth of the high-class hooker rests, and it is of no relevance for two reasons: the first is that an aggrieved client is always welcome to walk out the door. The second reason this rule of business is insignificant is because prostitution,

---

6 Wherever a woman is prostituted, there are also the men who prostitute her. There is a word to refer to them, in the context of their actions, but that word is not in common usage at the time of this writing. Therefore I would like people to pay attention to the term 'prostitutor' in the body of this text. It has been deliberately included here to refer to those men who have, until now, carried out a specific behaviour without having to bear the weight of the term that describes it.

because of its illicit nature, does not conform to most social rules or norms. Not being a legal profession, it is not regulated either, and it is unlike any other arena of industry in that the 'employers' (pimps and madams) make it up as they go along as far as their employees' (prostitutes') professional status is concerned. Their 'rank' or 'position' or 'standing' is something that has either been applied to them or they have applied to themselves. This elevated sense of status is applied, of course, with no legitimate qualifications to support it. For this reason, the notion of an exclusive 'high class' end of the market is a nonsense. I worked for two notorious Irish madams who both had decades of experience running 'low-end' massage parlours behind them before they moved into escorting in the early 1990s, like everyone else who had any financial savvy at that time in the Dublin prostitution world.

Prostitution can be a transitory experience; you can move around within it, but here is the catch: this only holds true for those women who believe that. The woman who believes that it is not possible to work in an escort agency because she is working on the streets will stay on the streets. The woman who believes that working in a massage parlour precludes her from working in an escort agency will stay in a massage parlour. The classist attitude in prostitution is very clear. The women who have only ever worked in escort agencies have no doubts that it would be *possible* for them to work in the lower end of the trade, but rarely do this, not only because there is less money to be made per client, but also because they scrupulously refuse to do so. It is not just about accepting less cash for the same 'service'; they feel that to work in these other areas of prostitution would in some way further diminish their dignity and would be somehow beneath them. I have heard a lot of sneering comments along those lines from women who market themselves as escorts, but what they are unaware of is that their bodies are routinely used far more thoroughly indoors than custom would deem acceptable to the women on the streets. If women's bodily ownership in prostitution was to be measured, escort agencies are where the least of it would be found.

The women I met in escorting who had come from brothels had a much more realistic grasp of the reality of prostitution than those who had worked exclusively in escort agencies. A sense of derision towards the myth of the high-class hooker was a commonality among them; they simply knew better than to buy into it.

People who depict prostitution as glamorous usually view prostitutes against the backdrop of expensive hotel foyers; they imagine prostitutes as entering or leaving five-star hotels wearing sharp designer suits and high heels, the look set off with vivid red lipstick. I've walked into more hotels more times than I could count wearing sharp suits, high heels and every shade of lipstick. None of that changed what was going on in my heart or in my mind and none of it made any difference to the bodily experience involved here; none of it was of any practical benefit to my mouth, breasts or vagina. What was going on was the very same thing that was going on when I was lifting my skirt in a backstreet alley. The nature of prostitution does not change with its surrounds. It does not morph into something else because your arse is rubbing against white linen as opposed to roughened concrete.

Chapter 11 ∿

PROSTITUTION'S SHAME, VIOLATION AND ABUSE

The practice of dissociation which prostituted women employ to protect their sense of self from violation is so similar to the dissociation employed by sexually abused children that it provides good evidence that the two experiences are similarly abusive.

SHEILA JEFFREYS, *THE IDEA OF PROSTITUTION*

I once had a client who used to wear a cotton ball strapped to his backside by way of a couple of strings fashioned together to fit him like a woman's thong. He took great pleasure out of pretending he was a poodle and wanted to be led around on a lead. This was no problem as far as I was concerned. He wasn't seeking to cause hurt with his odd fantasy. I brought him for 'walkies' round his apartment and instructed him to wear his 'tail' under his clothes for the pleasure I knew he'd get out of being my 'doggie' in public. Certainly this was a perversion by its dictionary definition, no doubt about that. But when I hear the word 'pervert' my mind does not call up men like this. Nor does it call up the men I've known who were aroused by household cleaning, admiring women's feet, dressing in women's clothes, or by the hundred-and-one other sexual penchants I've witnessed that would certainly be considered to fit the term 'perversion'.

You can't work shoulder-to-shoulder with human perversion for years without coming to understand something of its nature. Much of what is understood about human perversion is *felt*; it is understood on a sensory level. In sensing the true nature of perversion, I am no different from any of the prostitutes I've known. We talked about our disgust of their treatment of us openly, but even if we had not, I would have known that my interpretation of malignant perversion was shared by my fellow prostitutes and I would have known it for many reasons, one of the most obvious being that while they smilingly rolled their eyes and shook their heads at the mention of those sexually eccentric men they referred to as 'total perverts', their eyebrows furrowed and their vocal tones dropped when they spoke of the violators, who they flatly described as 'animals', 'filth' and 'scum'.

Nature intended us to procreate, to cause life itself through our love for each other; but the act of sexual violation expresses hate, through a malignant form of sexual dominance.

Not all sexual dominance is malignant. Men's physical strength has long been used to comfort and arouse their women. Any heterosexual woman who's ever had a romantic relationship has had the powerfully arousing experience of being held in the strength of her lover's arms before lovemaking and the wonderfully comforting experience of being held in them afterwards. The urge of sexual violators is to use this physically dominant position in the opposite way in order to create feelings which are the opposite too.

To work as a prostitute is to exist in an ever-present atmosphere of sexual violation. Men always violate in prostitution and in my experience the majority of them are aware of it, but it also remains true for those who would not like to believe so or are unaware of it. It is not possible for a man to use a prostitute without indulging in violation. The men who violate in prostitution fall into three basic types: there are men who simply prefer to believe that violation does not come into it, that it does not exist here; then there are those who know it exists but cannot or will not incorporate that knowledge into their behaviour; and then there are those who know full-well that violation exists and who derive a great deal of sexual pleasure from it. This last kind, whether they know it or not, are identifiable to prostitutes because of a sense of themselves which they emit and which is perfectly expressed by a quote from Japanese scientist and author Masaru Emoto: 'A person who loves others will send out a frequency of love, but from a person who acts out evil will come a dark and evil frequency.'[7]

People who indulge a wilful propensity towards sexual violation do indeed emit 'a dark and evil frequency'. When you come into regular contact with this frequency, you come to recognise it and to sense it. That capacity for recognition has never left me. To this day I can pick up on it in a person, even in a crowded room. It is a useful skill; it operates in more than one way. Some women have trouble gauging the nature of a man's intentions, but I can always tell, for example, whether a man has civilised intentions and has just said something foolish, or whether there is something more sinister lurking in his objectives. Prostitutes are exposed, over and over, to the soul-deadening vibration of sexual violation and they develop the ability to identify it, as part of the human capacity for self-preservation. This is a fortunate fact for prostituted women. I am sure it has saved many of us from violence and death. I know there were times it saved me.

I can trace my first understanding of sexual violation to my pre-prostitution life, in a memory from childhood. When I was nine years old, walking through Cabra West on my way to collect my younger sisters from school, I was passing the railings of the Precious Blood church when a drunken middle-aged man who had been walking towards me leaned down and said to me: 'I'd love to take you to bed'. I didn't know what sex was, beyond an instinctual understanding that there was some type of romantic secret intimacy between grown-ups, and I clearly remember thinking: 'There's something wrong with that man; I'm only nine'.

I passed him quickly. I was fearful and nervous. I felt violated and repulsed. I can still remember the smell of drink on his breath; but what I remember most, what stays with me to this moment with thought-defining clarity is the overwhelming sense of *wrongness* to what he was suggesting.

That was the first of three incidences of adult male paedophiles making their intentions clear to me as a child. It was the only one that was not physical, but I concentrate on that one here because I think there is

7   From *The Hidden Messages in Water*, Masaru Emoto, 2004.

a lot to be explored in what happened that day. There was a lot going on behind his action and my reaction. I feel it represents a recurring theme that, I suspect, has been going on as long as humans have been living.

There clearly is, for many people, a particular and powerful thrill in the act of sexual violation. For paedophiles, this thrill is found in the act of despoilment; in corrupting the uncorrupted, polluting the unpolluted. It is the sexual equivalent of picking a lovely young bloom and pissing on it. This is the nature of violation. It is the physical expression of an absolute lack of love. It is clearly a contemptible and despicable urge; yet for some it thrills, it affords sexual pleasure.

My mental response on that day, that immediate instinctual understanding that there was 'something wrong with that man' proves to me that there is something in humans that recognises the unnaturalness of sexual perversion regardless of whether they have ever come in contact with it. This capacity expresses itself in a sense of revulsion. It was operating so strongly in me that I was filled with it, even though I didn't have a fully formed idea of what sex was.

The way that paedophile communicated his urges proves to me that he was exactly aware of the inappropriate nature of what he was suggesting and that he experienced a very dark and negative arousal by way of it. His speech was low-toned, deliberately imparted so as not to be overheard, and laced with leering and lechery. I do not for one moment think that sexual predators regard their actions as natural; I think that they know exactly how unnatural they are, and that it is that unnaturalness they are getting off on. It is the sense of taboo, the 'something wrong' that excites them.

I remember a comment made to me by a young man, a stranger, years ago while I was in my late teens. I wasn't working that night, was in a different part of the city from where I either lived or worked, so he had no way of knowing I was a prostitute. He tried to speak to me on a darkened street and I sensed immediately that he wanted to violate me. I wouldn't entertain him, walked away quickly, and he was clearly affronted by this. 'Do you want to get raped?' he sneered after me. Of course, that was taking verbalisation several steps beyond vulgarity and into the realms of the overtly threatening and because of that, and many other things besides, I have learned this: you do not have to put your hands on someone to violate them sexually. You can, with your eyes or your motions or your words, destroy a person's sense of sexual safety. You do not need to be or have ever been a prostitute to understand this. What woman hasn't had the experience of being made to feel deeply sexually uncomfortable by a lewd comment or a leering lecherous look?

Our sexual serenity is a fragile, delicate and multi-faceted thing which isn't just damaged by touch: it is damaged by expressed thoughts, urges and intentions, and when this happens, what has occurred is a violation of the sexual spirit. This is the true level of sexual vulnerability and an accurate yardstick by which to measure the tsunami of sexual violation a prostitute must process.

For me, prostitution is the only sphere of life with which I am familiar where a person is routinely assumed to be without human feeling. In prostitution, you are treated like a blow-up sex doll come to life, with no purpose but to bend over and take it, literally. There are three general mindsets common to the men who use women in prostitution. The view of the prostituted as non-humans is the first of these and it is unnervingly common. It would be impossible to put an exact figure on these things, but I would guess it is an attitude present in at least thirty per cent of a prostitute's clients. I say so because this is roughly the ratio of men who looked at me in stupefied astonishment when I objected to being roughly manhandled; their expressions communicating the slow-dawning realisation that this was in fact a human being they were mauling.

The second scenario, where a man is conscious of your humanity but wilfully chooses to ignore it, is probably the most commonly held attitude to be found amongst the men who use prostitutes. I would say it accounts for around forty per cent. This has been my experience. For these men, their blinkered attitude is necessary. It allows them to do what they do.

The final thirty or so per cent are those who reduce themselves spiritually by indulging their desire to reduce the humanity of women. They are the vilest of all prostitutes' clients, and they make up a disturbingly sizeable minority.

So violation happens here in one of three ways: when the violator is not conscious of the humanity of the person he intends to violate; when the violator consciously chooses to ignore the humanity of the person he intends to violate; or when he is fully engaged with the existence of that humanity and takes pleasure from reducing its relevance to nothing.

Prostitutes are routinely violated in all of these ways and in each of them the significance of their humanity is eradicated. But this *last* way is the most potently damaging element in the prostitute's experience of violation and in the experience of violation generally. It is the voice that communicates with actions. It says: 'You are nothing'.

One evening, several years ago, and in a state of inebriation, one of my sisters said to me: 'Did you ever get raped or abused, or anything like that? You know you can talk about things like that to me'.

If a gag is applied to a prostitute (and I surely know that it is), when I see the image of a gagged woman in my mind's eye, I see that society has taken one end of the gag and the prostitute has taken the other and they have conspired together to tie the knot. It was still firmly affixed the day my sister asked me if I had ever been raped (though I was several years out of prostitution at that point) so I could not freely express the first thought that came to my mind, which was: 'Every day'.

I remember one particular experience in a Limerick apartment in the summer of '94. I was eighteen at the time. The man who'd paid me was on top of me, missionary position, thrusting violently. His face was somewhere between red and purple, split also between anger and elation. He was doing his best to hurt me, and it worked. I tried to move a little, to manoeuvre myself so that it'd hurt a bit less. He realised what I was doing immediately and held me fast to the bed in the same position while he kept going, even harder. He dragged out of my hair, my throat, my breasts, then orgasmed in a frenzy of hatred and afterwards got dressed, threw me a look of pure contempt, and walked, wordless, out the door. That was one time, but there were many such times, and there is no need to record them all here.

Drawing parallels between 'conventional' sexual abuse and violation and the sexual abuse and violation of prostitution is something many people would be wary of. It's a sense of caution born of the fear of ridicule. I can't afford to shy away from ridicule here; it would prevent me from telling the truth. The traditional view of abuse victims is one of people who in no way solicit their abuse, and yet we women related our experiences to each other, over and over, in the language of the abused. In discussing the sexual acts imposed upon our bodies we used expressions like: 'disgusting', 'horrible', 'stomach-turning', 'revolting' and 'sickening'. In referring to particularly abusive clients we commonly used expressions such as: 'bastard', 'scumbag', 'dirty pig' and 'filthy animal'. I have heard these words from innumerable women; but in all this descriptive terminology one word I seldom heard spoken was the word 'abuse', and I know why. It was because of a secondary dynamic that actually compounded our abuse. It was this, and it was the most heartbreaking: being, by way of our 'profession', unable to lay claim to our experiences of having been abused.

What you are actually doing when you prostitute yourself is sanctioning and accepting payment for the sexual abuse of your own body. You go through all the negative feelings associated with sexual abuse, but in the sanctioning of it you have effectively gagged yourself. You have literally sold your rights of expression; it is a twin prostitution really, and its second component is at least as damaging as the first.

Having to internalise and conceal the routine occurrence of abuse in one's own life is also a form of abuse; enforced silence is abusive, and how could it not be? Let's take sex out of the equation for a moment and imagine: if a whipping is the torture imposed and a gag applied to keep the victim silent, does the whip sting the skin any less? And if a woman says: 'Here, whip me for money' and hands over the whip and stays still for her whipping, does that sting the skin any less? And if she feels (because the world tells her) that she cannot, in talking about it afterwards, lay claim to having been assaulted since she accepted money for that assault, does that make her assailant, who paid money for the joy of hurting her, any less abusive?

The prostituted woman lives with the silence of how she is wronged every day. Modern societal views have applied her gag and a resulting psychological damage among prostitutes is not only commonplace, but inevitable. It is accepted among prostitutes, usually without question, as just another layer in an emotionally arduous life.

We didn't often collectively examine to any great depth the reality of our circumstances. We didn't get into protracted discussions about the psychology of it, but we did discuss the *feeling* of having been abused, without labelling it as such. What we didn't discuss were the mental consequences of that abuse. Our daily reality was this: we had enough to be dealing with in trying to stay alive with none of our bones getting broken and none of our mental screws coming loose. We did talk, as I've said, of course, and we did share our situations and our thoughts on our situations, but my very deepest thoughts, I kept mainly to myself. There were parts of prostitution that were just too painful to dissect openly, so there's nothing to say the prostitutes I knew weren't doing the same thing. And yet we talked incessantly and discussed most aspects of our daily lives, working and otherwise, and in all that talking I never, ever, came across a woman for whom selling her body caused her to be happy. Some of the *consequences* of having sold our bodies, the financial relief and the other forms of practical relief that came with that, were welcome; but that, as anyone with half a whit of sense knows, is not the same thing.

It is a game of computation, prostitution. Is it better to have sex with this man in the dark, whose face I scarcely look at, who I won't remember tomorrow; or is it better to accrue rent arrears or fall short of the money I need for my child's communion? This game of 'weighing up' is exactly what brings most women to the streets and to the brothels and yet, those who exploit their desperation are often presumed by society to be innocent of abuse. But exploitation *is* abusive, and in almost any other situation I can think of, it is unquestioningly regarded as such—is that not so?

I remember watching Oprah Winfrey discuss her sexual abuse on her TV show several years ago. I was stunned by her candour. The gist

of what she said was that the thing people often didn't realise about sexual abuse was that it didn't always feel bad, it sometimes felt good, and
that when it did, that compounded the psychologically abusive nature of
sexual abuse because it induced much guilt, shame, and confusion. She
used her own experiences as an example of this, which really was something I found impressive: that such a public figure would be prepared
to open this intensely private aspect of her past for the sake of communicating a message she knew needed to be heard—and it *did* need to
be heard. One abuse victim I knew at the time was moved to tears on
hearing what was said repeated to her.

That day, after listening to Oprah, I thought about the message in her
words and considered again the clouded and obscured nature of sexual
abuse within prostitution. That voice of shame that whispers in the ear
of some abuse victims: 'You can't say you were abused because you got
enjoyment from it', is not dissimilar to the voice of blame that tells every
prostitute: 'You can't say you were abused because you got paid for it'.

In my early days of prostitution, in my early teens, before I learned
to deaden any display of emotion while with a client, I met men who
positively revelled in the obviousness of my unwillingness. Was that not
abuse? And later, when I had learned not to show my disinclinations,
but just to present myself as unnaturally dead and cold as a shop-front
mannequin, did their abuse morph into something else? People are
entitled to make up their own minds, but remembering those men and
those times, there is nothing clearer to me than the abusive nature of
their urges.

I once had a conversation with a non-prostituted friend of mine who
had been sexually abused as a child. I told her how when I'd been fifteen
I'd always told the men who used me how old I was, because I found it
had the effect of causing them to become very aroused, therefore getting
them off quicker, therefore getting me out of there quicker. I said this
to my friend and she said to me: 'Do you not realise that was sexual
abuse? Those men knew how old you were and far from being horrified,
they were actually turned on by it and exploited your poverty in order
to exploit your body and you were fifteen years old at the time—that's
abuse.' I had this conversation the best part of ten years ago, before I had

been in a place to fully label my experience as sexually abusive, although I had *always* felt that, like most prostituted women, I was afraid of the ridicule involved in assigning it its own name.

There are several images of the prostituted woman that society is used to. One is of the teenage addict being used sexually in a needle-strewn alleyway. A converse stereotype is of the thirty-something escort; a woman poised, self-possessed, professional; a woman in control. Prostitution is neither one nor the other of these extremes. The truth is that prostitution is a composite experience and these are only two of its parts. It is a blend of both, and many others besides, and the degree to which humiliation and power are experienced in prostitution (either generally or in any specific area of it) can never be calculated as an average, because we can never compile witness testimony to calculate the degree of it: it is different in every single act of prostitution that has ever taken place.

What I am certain of is that the sexual humiliation of prostitutes is not simply underrated by many non-prostitutes (both men and women alike) but rather is unappreciated entirely; because it has not been experienced by them, it is simply not understood. It is understandable that it may not be appreciated on a quantitative level, but it is heartrending to know that it may not be recognised as existing at all. To anyone of that school of thought I would just say this: humiliation on a sexual level does not contain itself within the sphere of the sexual; it leaks out all over a life, most particularly so if it is repetitive and ritualistic. Drug and alcohol addiction, the annihilation of confidence, the shattering of self-worth, physical self-harm, suicidal ideation; all of these are well-recognised as the 'fruits' of sexual abuse. All of these I have seen in abundance in prostitution.

Regardless of what anybody says, it is clear to me that when a person needs to practise and perfect a state of mental lock-down (as prostitutes so commonly do) in order to stand the sexual acts they are enduring, that person is being abused.

There will be prostitutes out there who will not like the sound of this. I am certain of that. I am certain of it because I would not have liked the sound of it myself while I was in prostitution. I'm sure also that there'll be some former prostitutes who'll not appreciate it either. There is a fantasy some women in prostitution indulge in: that they are exceptionally strong, in control of all of this, *far* above being abused. I know this because I once indulged in it myself, or tried to, and I would not have liked having it pointed out to me that I was being abused while it was happening. It would have been too close to the bone and, moreover, it would have made the myth of my own 'control' much more difficult to believe. That myth is important to the working prostitute. It enables her to continue to function within the sphere of life she is in. It is very saddening for me to remember myself and the women I worked with tentatively trying to communicate our experiences of being abused to each other on the one hand, while actively participating in the myth that we were in control on the other.

So when my sister asked me that question, I had great trouble honestly answering her. Rape, here, is seen as a clouded issue. If rape describes the violently enforced entry of a penis into the vagina or anus, then no, I have never been raped. If it describes the violently enforced entry of the fingers or any other object into the vagina or anus then yes, I have been raped many times. If it can describe a situation where a prostitute has sex for money and is robbed afterwards, on those occasions I was also raped. But I wasn't sure how to answer that question. Like most people, I didn't know where the parameters lay.

Should I have told her that I was sexually assaulted each of the numerous times I had fingers and objects forced inside me against my will and outside of the agreed contractual exchange? Or any of the other innumerable liberties strangers had taken with my body for their own pleasure? Did they constitute sexual assault? I had already been paid. Those men wanted some extra 'fun' for their money. It was more than I had signed up for. It was more than I had been paid for. It hurt like sexual assault. It damaged like sexual assault. It degraded like sexual assault. It *was* sexual assault. I know what happened to me, but in the eyes of society and in the eyes of the law, where are the parameters here? But if I'd insisted on that much and said that, yes, I'd been sexually assaulted each of those times, there was a voice in my head that told me I'd have been leaving out the biggest part of the picture, which was that sexual exploitation *was* sexual assault. I drew a breath, gathered myself, and explained that prostitution *was* sexual abuse—*paid* sexual abuse. This truth had been incubating in me for a long time but this was the first time I had clearly expressed it to another person. It was an important conversation. I felt a loosening of the gag.

There are those who would say I was not sexually molested because I had been paid that day in Limerick in the summer of '94; but I do not believe that sexual assault can be explained and described along those clear, uncomplicated and, I believe, incorrect socially defined lines. The parallels between the sexual abuse inherent to prostitution and the sexual abuse found elsewhere are too blatant to ignore. Probably the most basic of them is this: as a prostitute, you do not get to frame the boundaries of your own sexual experience. Such luxuries are not possible for the woman who has commodified her own body. Such luxuries are redundant when you have been paid for.

An important point to remember is that prostitutes accept money *before* each experience; therefore they do not and cannot know exactly what it is they are accepting money for. You make your arrangement with each man, but you very often have to deal with a situation far removed from anything you agreed upon. Besides any of this, I felt the same sickening nausea and rising panic that is inherent to conventional sexual abuse in each prostitution experience I ever had, *and I felt that regardless of whether or not a man stayed within the agreed sexual boundaries.*

There were days when, God forgive me, I wished I had been a 'bona fide' abuse victim. At least then I would have been allowed to lay claim to my own feelings. There are few lonelier, emptier, more desolate feelings than looking, after a particularly abusive client has left, at the hush money he has paid for your silence over what would be considered rape in any other circumstances.

Prostitution and rape are commonly distinguished by the logical fact that to buy something and to steal something are two different things; but when we consider that the sex bought in prostitution is the same type of sex stolen in rape, sex that is, as Kathleen Barry puts it: '. . . disembodied, enacted on the bodies of women who, for the men, do not exist as human beings, and the men are always in control'—it is then that we understand how deeply traumatising it is for the woman whose body is so used. When we understand that the sex paid for in prostitution shares so many of its characteristics with the sex stolen in rape, it makes sense that so many prostituted women make clear parallels between the two experiences. One woman described her experience of the sex of prostitution very succinctly when she referred to it as: 'Paid rape'.[8] Canadian campaigner Trisha Baptie, who was first prostituted as a child, describes it as 'pay-as-you-go rape'. Another woman described it as 'like signing a contract to be raped' and I wrote an article for the *Irish Examiner* in 2012 where I described prostitution as 'being raped for a living'. That was first said to me by another former prostitute. Many of us describe our feelings towards the sex of prostitution in these ways.

I have found it to be especially common that prostituted women with prior experience of rape and sexual assault make this same link. A woman I knew, who had been sexually molested by her stepfather at thirteen, was one of many women I knew who made that same association. She never used the word 'rape' to describe her understanding and she never needed to; her actions did the talking for her.

She and I were close, we were friends, and she told me about the particulars of her abuse and how it affected her. Her stepfather had always taken the opportunity to abuse her during the day, when her mother was routinely out of the house, working. Unsurprisingly, she came to associate daytime sex with degradation, humiliation and trauma. She had a long-term partner most of the years I knew her and she confided in me that she would only ever have sex with him at night. She could not bear to be touched intimately by him during the day. This was the cause of some conflict at first but he came to understand that she was resolute about it and to accept that she would never be sexually available to him during the day.

On the other hand, in her working life, she could function as a prostitute during daylight hours. She worked Dublin's twenty-four-hour street from the late morning till the late afternoon and did call-outs to homes and hotels in daylight hours. She experienced prostitution as sexual abuse,

---

8 'Violence Against Women', Vol. 10, No. 10, October 2004.

and sexual abuse had to be kept in its place. This was how she functioned. This was how she separated herself from her abusive daily reality.

That she equated prostitution with sexual abuse was pathetically clear.

Recently, while speaking to a close friend about my experiences of prostitution abuse and about how I was forbidden from accurately naming them, I broke down sobbing and immediately apologised for my tears. She asked me what I was apologising for. I was apologising for the expression of my own feelings, as though I had no right to them, or certainly no right to express them. The indoctrination of prostitution is very strong. It instils a sense of shame and culpability in a woman to the point where she cannot feel free to lay claim to her own feelings, any feelings, and this remains true in the psyche of a woman who has ever been prostituted. It is necessary to struggle against this indoctrination. This entire book has been constructed in that struggle; and I will keep on struggling until I have managed to break fully free, and if I never manage to do that, then I will never stop struggling.

Many of the women who come to prostitution from a position of having been sexually abused in childhood or adolescence have an internalised view of themselves as sex objects. For this reason, for those women, the leap from one world to the next is tragically less monumental. There is, however, still a leap involved, because the experience of prostitution is exactly like no other, though the survivors of childhood sexual abuse in prostitution have documented the similarities involved. In some ways, and for some women, prostitution will understandably be experienced as the more positive of the two. As my friend who preferred to work during the day time described it to me: 'I may as well have been charging for it as having my stepfather take it for free.'

In her, and I suspect in many women like her, there was an appreciation of the contrast between her prostitution and pre-prostitution life, because at least in prostitution she had the pathetic degree of self-governance that allowed her to put a price on her own body, before experiencing its being used like an irrelevant rag. A woman could understandably interpret this as a step away from total powerlessness. Such a woman will soon learn though that self-governance exists in such a diluted form in prostitution that there really only exists the shadow of it, and that it is only detectable when measured against a situation where it does not exist at all.

Many adults who have been molested as children report their abusers as having bestowed gifts, sweets, outings, cash and other treats to buy cooperation and instil a false sense of culpability in the abused child. This tactic is especially effective in the child of an impoverished household. There is perhaps nothing as pitiable as the image of the child who has become so inured to being abused that he or she would actually solicit that abuse for material benefits, but prostitution is exactly that sad scenario played out by adults. The truth is *prostitution is the commercialisation of sexual abuse.*

The commercialisation of sexual abuse has created an arena within which this abuse can rage unhindered, precisely because it is unacknowledged and for the very reason that it is unnamed. This book strives to call attention to its true nature, and to assign it its true name.

Of course, one of the abiding feelings that comes with abuse and violation is a pervasive feeling of shame. It blankets everything, shrouds the prostitute in a cloak of it. I know that because for the years I was in prostitution I carried shame with me every day. When I think about that I am reminded of the line from an Annie Lennox song: 'Take this overcoat of shame; it never did belong to me'. If shame was in fact an overcoat that'd be grand; we'd all have the option of taking it off. Ridding oneself of this negative feeling is not that quick or that simple.

About two months after I started working in prostitution I was taken to a sheltered spot in the Phoenix Park in a large builders' van. I am almost certain it was a dark maroon colour, but my mind asks me if it wasn't navy. This bothers me for some reason. It bothers me that I am not certain of the colour, and I feel inclined to ask myself why this troubles me. I think it's because I want to take that memory and truly examine it, to fully understand it and present what it means, and I want every part of that to be accurate, although I know this detail is thoroughly irrelevant.

What I have no problem remembering is the view from inside the van. In other circumstances I would have appreciated it as very picturesque. The man sitting to my right had pulled the van in tight beside some low-hanging trees, so that their leaves hung down like fronds and framed the windscreen, as if we were looking into a picture. The ground was mucky and I remember noticing the track marks of the wheels. The sky was that crisp clear blue of Ireland in late autumn; the promise of good weather that might be snatched away at any moment. Nature was everywhere and I could hear birds.

The man was overweight and had a large beer belly and a lot of stubble. He turned to me and something happened that totally took me by surprise; it had never happened before. He recognised me. He asked where I was from, yet it was not a question. He identified my family and the road I'd grown up on. I felt something inside me uncoil and relax. It wasn't going to happen now. He'd known my dad and my dad had killed himself about a year and a half before. This made things impossible. He would have to turn the van around.

He didn't.

He grabbed me by the back of the head and mashed his lips against mine. His fingers locked into the muscles at the nape of my neck so that I couldn't turn my head. Instinct made me try to pull away. He tightened his grip. When he'd eventually had enough of kissing me he let me go. He looked like a clown with my red lipstick spread all over his face. My own face hurt from the roughness of his stubble. He took out some money and then he took out his prick and I did what I had to do. A quick glimpse of the woods first through the passenger window; I never even thought of running. I knew I'd never have made it further than the trees.

The worst part of that, of course, for me, was that he'd known my father. The best part of it, for him, was that he knew who I was. As soon as he'd recognised me, he experienced a powerful arousal. That 'did it' for him. It was something to do with one-upmanship and dominance and contempt and power. It was a sexualised sort of evil.

That day I experienced, in a very potent way, how sexuality could channel evil; how people could get off on it; how an essentially evil act could be the *source* of sexual excitement. That my body was the receptacle of that evil arousal was more damaging than I can express. When

I think of it, I am powerfully reminded of what that paedophile said to me walking past the gates of the Precious Blood church. For me, that day in the Phoenix Park, there was a depth of shame that would be difficult to articulate. I felt like the whole universe had so filled up with shame that I would never be able to experience any other feeling ever again. I went straight back down the street and kept on selling myself though, because not to do so would have been to acknowledge the enormity of what had happened, and ignoring it was the only way I could protect myself. My studied avoidance did nothing, however, to protect me from the shame. It continued to follow me, because that is what the shame of prostitution does.

Shame is the psychological cancer of prostitution; a woman develops this internal illness by way of her proximity to it in the same way the men who worked with asbestos on building sites once did. Site workers don't need to fear developing cancer from what they come into daily contact with any more. The world knows better about asbestos now. It is no longer acceptable, thank God. The world is just as enlightened, on a soul level, about prostitution, but does not act upon it because the sexual pleasure it affords men is deemed more important than the duty to treat women equally in humanity. So what we need is a consciousness of enlightenment; we need the acceptance of what prostitution is to reside in the forefronts of our minds, as well as in the deep recesses of our souls. We have a long way to go before we get there.

Non-prostituted women, many of them, have been schooled to accept prostitution along with pornography as something they dare not oppose as offensive for fear of being labelled frigid-minded prudes. However adept the world has become at ignoring it, none of these social constructs is capable of eradicating the truth about prostitution and pornography as experienced by its participants. No amount of society looking the other way will ever erase the shame at the heart of sexual exploitation.

Because shame is such an ever-present and abiding feeling among prostitutes and former prostitutes alike, the process of letting go of it is of paramount importance. What prostitutes must know is that there is no escaping the damaging ravages of shame while the source of it is ever-present in their lives; and what we former prostitutes must remember is that it is how we react to the feeling that dictates whether it will improve or corrode our lives.

There really are almost no other ways of earning a living I can think of which would induce such personal shame. When a person is treated dishonourably on a routine basis the natural human response is to lose touch with our innate internal sense of honour; shame is simply an inevitable response to these circumstances. The sense of self-respect is removed and it does not leave an empty void; it clears a space which is filled with shame.

There is a sense of 'otherness' that is inevitably caused in a person by their involvement in prostitution. It is compounded by the attitudes of other people, by the social shunning that is inherent to the prostitution experience. A prostitute will almost never announce her profession to a new acquaintance and in the rare case that she does, she will do so in an attempt at defiance.

Shame in prostitution has many sources. Firstly, for me, there was a sense of shame associated with the fact that I was not growing or evolving or bettering myself or my life in any way; in fact, quite the opposite. I felt like a failure and I knew I looked like one. I felt that I had failed in life before I'd even begun and that caused me to feel uniquely pathetic, and, of course, ashamed.

I knew that my physical privacy and natural modesty were obliterated and would never be taken seriously again. That did not continue to be true, but it was certainly true for me at the time and it was the cause of a very great deal of pain and shame.

I knew that people generally looked on me with disdain; that was part of my daily existence. I made a friend during my mid-teens who was not involved in prostitution. Her mother found out what I did, instructed her to have nothing to do with me, and our friendship ended right there. I found that understandable, but that did nothing to negate the hurt or shame. No matter how much we'd like not to make outside opinions our own, the truth is nobody wants to be thought badly of by everyone they meet.

By my late teens I was busy cultivating a dangerous drug habit. I'd had my first lines of cocaine at fifteen, but did not develop a cocaine habit until I was nineteen. The years in between had been spent smoking cannabis and taking ecstasy, the most popular drug of the early- to mid-1990s. I was only an occasional user of cocaine during those years, but in 1995, my use of the drug really took off and I was hopelessly addicted not long after my nineteenth birthday.

When I look back now I see that everything about the way I behaved back then was designed to buffer me from the reality I was living; yet sometimes, despite these tactics, reality would get a look in. I remember distinctly one bright sunny day, I was nineteen at the time and standing at a southside Dart station looking in over the city. I was struggling in my mind about my life, about my position in the world, and I remember thinking about how I was nineteen and this was supposed to be young, but I felt like an elderly woman. I felt weary from the weight of my own life.

I could see the whole of Dublin Bay and the air was crisp and clear. Boats came and went, tiny ones and large ones. Cars drove past the station, and trains drove through it, and smoke rose from the chimneys in Ringsend. There was such a sense of the whole world turning and me not having any part of it; and I wondered, right there on the platform, would I ever have any part of it, and was there any place for me in the world. It was one of the strongest aches I've ever felt in my heart, because I was so sure the likeliest answer was 'No'.

Chapter 12 ⌐

THE VIOLENCE INHERENT TO PROSTITUTION

Brothel owners and advocates of escort prostitution are well aware of the dangers of these kinds of prostitution, although they rarely admit it publicly. For example, an organization in South Africa that advocates decriminalization of prostitution, Sex Workers' Education and Advocacy Taskforce (SWEAT), addressed the dangers of escort prostitution by distributing a list of safety tips for women. These included the recommendation that while undressing, the prostitute should accidentally kick a shoe under the bed, and while retrieving it, should check for knives, handcuffs, or rope. The SWEAT flyer also noted that fluffing up the pillows on the bed would permit searching there for weapons.—A brothel owner in the Netherlands complained about an ordinance requiring that brothels have pillows in the rooms: "You don't want a pillow in the [brothel's] room. It's a murder weapon." (Daley, 2001,m p1).

MELISSA FARLEY, *BAD FOR THE BODY, BAD FOR*
THE HEART

P rostitutes encounter violence as a matter of routine. I know this as a generality and I know it was true for me too. My own first experience of real violence occurred a few weeks after I'd begun working on Benburb Street. I got into a stranger's car and was taken to an apartment somewhere in the Islandbridge area, about five minutes' drive away. I'd informed him before I got into the car, as always, that I did hand-relief and oral, but not intercourse. This was agreed upon and the usual fee settled. When we got to the apartment the man experienced a change of mind and decided he'd be having intercourse with me whether I liked it or not. I wasn't having any of it. Being raped was not something I could have coped with. He became angry and attempted to pull me down onto the bed; I struggled away from him. He then leaned over the side of the bed and slid something out from underneath it. It was a long hunting-style rifle.

When I saw the gun I became hysterical. I started to scream. I understood that he obviously meant business if he was going to the extreme measure of pulling out a shotgun. I understood too, for the first time, how dangerous he was as an individual. I had never seen a gun before.

I ran out of the room and he chased me. I made it to the top of the stairs before he grabbed me. I thought that if I managed to make it down those stairs and to the hall door at the end of them, I'd be free. It never crossed my mind that I was dressed only in my underwear.

He dragged me back towards the bedroom. I struggled like a crazy person and strained with all my bodyweight against getting dragged back in there, but he was far too strong for me. I was fifteen years old and weighed not more than a hundred-and-fifteen pounds; he was in his late forties and at least twice my weight. He got me back in the bedroom in no time. I could see that he was flustered. I think he thought that when he pulled out that gun, it was all going to go his way, with no questions asked. He kept telling me to stop screaming and when I saw him put his gun away, I thought it might be a good time to shut up. He took out his penis and told me to suck it. I did what I was told.

He started getting dressed and I think he was still experiencing some level of shock because he'd just had a near-naked teenager almost run straight out his front door screaming into the street. That wouldn't have looked good; particularly not with a firearm in the house.

As soon as I saw him getting dressed I followed suit. For some reason, he insisted on dropping me back onto the street, probably to ensure I was well away from his apartment building and out of his neighbourhood; and while there was a sense of relief in getting out of that building, there was also a sense of low-level panic at being with him in his car, which he could have driven anywhere had he chosen to. Still, it wasn't as bad as the apartment. At least I could see people out the car window. I was thinking at least I could try to catch somebody's attention if he decided to drive me off somewhere remote to hurt me.

That wasn't necessary. He dropped me on the quays near the bridge that crosses the Liffey at Parkgate Street, a couple of minutes' walk from Benburb Street, and before I got out of the car he let me know what he thought of me. Apparently I was: 'A very silly girl'.

I got out of his car and walked over the bridge, but the fun and games didn't stop there. I was shaking with nerves and as I approached the end of the bridge, I spotted an off-licence across the road. The thought that a few cans of cider would calm me down flashed through my mind and I literally broke into a run to get to the other side of the road. I hadn't looked left or right and didn't even see the car until I'd already been flung over its bonnet and was lying in the middle of the road. All I remember was a flash of red—the colour of the car, not my blood, fortunately. I was bruised and scratched and my nerves were in shreds, but my body was in one piece and I was, generally speaking, okay. I remember thinking that it had been the craziest day in terms of bizarre and horrible incidents and indulging the childish fear that bad luck came in threes.

The man who knocked me down pulled his car over to the side of the road. A well-intentioned passer-by tried to intervene and told the driver he'd had no business moving his car and the guards ought to be called. I was in no mood for the gardaí, told the driver I was OK and, to my shame, told the passer-by to fuck off. Then I hobbled on home. I forgot all about the cider.

Later that day, I was so bruised and sore I got the number ten bus to the Mater Hospital. I learned a couple of lessons that day. One: you never can tell what's coming at you when you accompany a strange man to his apartment, and two: if you ever need to go to a hospital, make sure you go in an ambulance.

Violence is every bit as inherent to prostitution as any other element of negativity contained within it. If anything is more pervasive than violence itself it is the threat of it. The threat of violence is something

I encountered far more regularly than physical violence itself. For every time I was slapped, punched or dragged around by the hair I was threatened with those actions, subtly or overtly, countless times. There always seemed in prostitution to be a sense of navigating your way through the negativity—of making your way from one end of the night to the other with the end-goal always being to come out in one piece.

The physical act of violence is by no means the only thing that happens in prostitution to induce high degrees of terror. I'm reminded of one man in particular who picked me up and brought me to the Phoenix Park a couple of months after I'd started working on Benburb Street. He had a jolly middle-aged-man sort of attitude and, bizarrely, reminded me a little bit of Santa Claus, with his white beard and protruding belly. He drove me to the foot of the Papal Cross, and that was where his demeanour changed entirely. It became apparent immediately that this man was mentally unhinged, as he sat there telling me that he was Jesus Christ and pointing up at the cross, saying that he'd died on it for me.

He wanted to have intercourse and tried to bully me into it, which was par for the course at that stage, but his line of reasoning was very unique in that he raged that he was the son of God and so how dare I refuse him? I was struck speechless by this lunacy and hadn't the first idea how to defend myself against it. He threatened to kill me and told me he would dump my body in the Dublin mountains. The man was so unhinged that he was not in control of his own actions, and it was horrifying to know that whatever happened in that car would not only be beyond my control, but beyond his also. He forced me into sex acts and robbed me, but still, I got out of that car in the sure knowledge that I was lucky, because I got out of it with my life.

That man did not hit me nor need to hit me to put me in a state of terror. The past experience of violence acts as a guarantee of the legitimacy of all present and future threats. The woman knows from experience that the threat is not idle or unlikely, but the opposite; entirely probable, believable, and to be taken with utmost seriousness. The threat of violence, therefore, is an act of psychological abuse; some conclude just as mentally damaging as physical violence itself. In the lives of prostitutes (and unlike the actual act of violence), the anticipatory fear of violence is without end. It cannot conclude because it is not an actual event. It does not present clearly defined stages; it exists perpetually, far beyond the violent event that first sparked it into existence and the others that punctuated your prostitution experience to continually authenticate your fearful expectation of being hurt. This state of fearful expectation is broken only by violent events themselves, which, as they continue to occur, reinforce the prostitute's sense of anticipation. You now understand that violence is certain to occur. You don't worry that it will, you worry *when* it will; and watchfulness is broken only in the moments you experience what you'd been watching for.

The more pliable a woman is, the more she is willing to have her body used and abused according to the whims of her client, the less likely she is to encounter physical violence. This, I believe, explains why some women experienced higher levels of violence than others. If I'd ever met a woman in prostitution who claimed not to have encountered violence (and I never did), I'd have had to assume that she had zero boundaries. But most of us, regardless of what we do for a living, are repelled by the immediate reality of having our bodies molested; and we react to that, because we are humans, and punters react violently to our reactions, because they do not correlate with the fantasies they are paying to indulge.

Prostitution inured me to violence to such an extent that these days I don't even get particularly panicked while getting attacked. I came face to face with this discovery a few years back after having been attacked by a large group of drunken people when out one night. Dissecting my feelings afterwards, while describing the experience to a friend, caused me to discover that I had been scarcely at all fearful during the event. I relayed for her the way I'd been affected after the fact, on a psychological level, by having had to spend eight weeks with my hand in a splint in order to heal my severed tendons, as I'd been stabbed with a broken bottle in the hand and head. Luckily, my head-wounds were all sustained on the side of my head, several inches back from the hair line. I must admit to having vanity enough to be grateful that I had no visible scarring to the face. I think most people would feel that way.

The deepest part of the negativity in that whole experience for me was the state of depression I slid into while operating with one hand. I couldn't type. I couldn't clean my house. For the first week or so I couldn't even clean myself; my sister had to wash me in the bath. Having my mobility impaired was so depressing. It got me very down, but that was honestly the only thing that stood out to me as awful in the whole experience. The beating felt like nothing. It still does.

Punches, kicks and lacerations are not a major problem for the woman who knows what is happening and what the outcome is going to be. It's a natural human thing, isn't it, to not be unduly stressed when we know what the outcome is going to be and that it is not going to be fatal? Of course you actually *don't* know what the outcome is going to be here (you could very easily die of a broken neck or excessive bleeding etc.) but because violence has happened so many times before and ended in the same way each time (recuperating in a state of lingering but transitory pain) I *thought* I knew, and behaved as such. This is an example of how inured to violence prostitutes become and an example also of how the experience of prostitution continues to affect the psyche of those who've ever been involved in it.

Some prostitutes, unfortunately, lowered their already debased circumstances by physically attacking each other. Thankfully I never involved myself in meting out that practice (personally I felt we'd enough to be dealing with), but I was a victim of it more than once. I was slapped, threatened and had my hair torn out a number of times on Benburb Street and Burlington Road by women much older than I was, who wanted to run me off the streets. Knowing as they did that I was in my early teens, I honestly don't see how they could justify that. In any case, it didn't have the desired effect. All it did was make me embittered and angry and hardened to it.

As a prostitute, you would almost always avoid a man with drink on him, but you would sometimes make exceptions to that rule if you knew the man, or if he was not too drunk.

Drunks were a regular exasperation. This was unavoidable if you arrived at a home or hotel and a man was drunk when you got there, but you had only to make the mistake of getting into a drunken stranger's car once and, if the experience was bad enough, you'd be very reluctant to get into another. For starters, it's a very disconcerting experience to be driven by somebody under the influence of alcohol, and of course, the more alcohol involved, the more disconcerting the experience.

Assuming you arrive at your location in one piece, you can almost always be sure of a row over money, with the man either forgetting or choosing to forget the agreed-upon fee. Should this matter be amicably resolved (and it usually won't), he will almost invariably have trouble either achieving or maintaining an erection, and you, as the women paid to ensure that he does, will certainly be assigned the blame when he does not.

At this or any other point, you may find yourself being attacked by an angry drunk in a car which has been locked from the inside. I have had this experience more than once, but one particular night stands out in my mind. I was only sixteen and still fairly naïve. He pulled the car so tight alongside a stone wall that there was no way for me to get out. I knew instinctively, the moment he did that, in a laneway not narrow enough to necessitate it, that I was in for a rough time.

I heard the click of the electric lock and something inside me flipped over. We turned to look at each other and what passed between our eyes was simply the acknowledgement of this new situation, this altered state of affairs.

He told me that a blow-job wouldn't do, he wanted to have sex with me. I told him I wouldn't do it. He grabbed me by the hair at the back of my head and smashed my face into the dashboard. I'd had that experience before. His fingers were still tightly entwined in the roots of my hair; I pulled my head around to the right, far enough for our eyes to meet again. I asked him, in my coolest most sensual voice: 'Now, how am I supposed to suck your cock if you're carrying on like that?' He stared in my eyes for a few moments while he processed this idea, apparently it aroused him, because he pulled down the zip of his trousers and let his erect prick bob out. He kept the same grip while he guided my head down onto his penis and held it there until he came. For a long while after that I wondered why he didn't rape me, but I was only sixteen then. Later I would understand why. He didn't need to demean me that way because he'd gotten all he needed from watching me demean myself.

Every night on the game is a learning experience. What I learned that night was to lean close enough in the car window to smell their breath, and to always use a laneway with hedges.

Talk about trying to reduce the levels of violence in prostitution is pointless and inane. If physical violence was never encountered in prostitution, if nobody had ever raised a hand against a woman in the history of prostitution, violence would still be inescapable for prostituted women, because prostitution *is* violence against women. My views of violence in prostitution are very much aligned with those of the women who penned this piece:

> 'We, the survivors of prostitution and trafficking gathered at this press conference today, declare that prostitution is violence against women. Women in prostitution do not wake up one day and "choose" to be prostitutes. It is chosen for us by poverty, past sexual abuse, the pimps who take advantage of our vulnerabilities, and the men who buy us for the sex of prostitution.'
> MANIFESTO, COALITION AGAINST TRAFFICKING IN WOMEN CONFERENCE, 2005

We could never have removed ourselves from the most fundamental form of violence inherent to prostitution, at least not while we continued to work as prostitutes, but we did our best to evade other kinds of violence. As far as physical violence from clients was concerned, I was always very cautious about avoiding that, but cautiousness can only get you so far in this game; there is only so much violence that can be avoided. However, I did go out of my way never to put myself in situations which screamed of danger from the off, such as meeting more than one man at a time. I knew one girl, a close friend of mine, who did not have such reservations. She worked in escorting at the same time I did and one evening a call came in on the agency phone line, which was diverted to her mobile.

It was a request for two girls to go to a well-known southside hotel. I begged and pleaded with her not to go to the hotel where a number of men were waiting for her—twelve of them. They were celebrating the outcome of a sporting event and were looking forward to having a good time. She was celebrating nothing but was looking forward to the twelve hundred pounds she was expecting to come home with. She asked me to go with her. We would earn six hundred pounds each, she reasoned. I declined.

I think I have made as easy a peace as is possible with the knowledge that as long as the world continues to accept prostitution, women like she and I will always be judged. It is an uneasy peace, but it is a peace; and I believe it is possible for me because I know people do not understand what it is they are judging us for. That night my friend was to perform a strip show and then service the men individually in a separate room; at least this was the arrangement they came to on the phone. It didn't work out that way. And I am sure the reader will understand what I mean when I say I never met the girl who left that night again, although I spent several years in touch with the one who arrived back the next morning.

Chapter 13 ∼

|SURVIVAL STRATEGIES

Hoigard and Finstad (1992) describe how women use "ingenious" strategies to survive prostitution: shutting off their feelings, thinking about other things, holding back on bodily reserves which are not for sale, hurrying the buyer by feigning sexual excitement to cut down on time. Others, such as Barry (1995), see the illusion of choice as an important survival tool and a means of holding on to some degree of human dignity . . . Survival strategies work sometimes, but not all of the time, and not forever. These survival strategies come with a price and there are long-term consequences for physical, mental and sexual health as the survival strategies become internalised.

'THE NEXT STEP INITIATIVE', *RUHAMA RESEARCH REPORT ON BARRIERS AFFECTING WOMEN IN PROSTITUTION, IRELAND, 2005*

When I was in prostitution, we would often discuss the tactics we employed to mentally endure the process. I remember one particular discussion where a few of us shared what measures we put in place while actually in the act, in order to make it halfway mentally sufferable. It was a small group but the coping strategies were vast in their diversity. One woman fantasised about killing her clients; another about the colour of Smarties. She had a little tune she used to hum in her head. It sounded like a child's nursery rhyme and the words went like this: 'Smarties, Smarties, red and yellow Smarties; Smarties, Smarties, brown and purple Smarties' and on and on till she could think of no more colours and she'd return to red and yellow again.

I laughed as I imagined that infernal mental rhyming going on and on and I told her I didn't think I'd be able to stand it.

Clearly, there are ways for women to psychologically minimise the impact of the prostitution experience, such as separation, disengagement and outright denial. The overall network of survival strategies employed by the prostituted comprises strategies both physical and mental and they include anger, self-deception, substance abuse, the rejection of truth, defiance and other attempts at control. These tactics evolve from a deep-run refusal to submerge fully in the prostitution experience. I liken these women to the drowning woman who, though she hasn't a hope in hell, cannot help, by reflex and instinct, but struggle against the tug of the tide.

As for myself, I employed the oldest trick in the book, common to prostitutes and victims of other forms of repetitive sexual abuse—I pretended it wasn't happening. A primary survival tactic was simply to deny the reality of the situation, especially in any sort of public capacity. I once gave an interview to a reporter in which I did just that. I was about seventeen at the time. A friend and I had been collecting the free condoms handed out at a local clinic and one of the health workers there told us a reporter was interested in speaking to some of us, so I said I wouldn't mind talking to her. A couple of days later a few of us met her in a Baggot Street bar. She focused on me, I think, because I was very much the youngest of the group and she probably found that shocking. She asked me why I did it, and I belligerently told her: 'For the money', communicating with my eyes and tone that it was a stupid question and inferring that she must be stupid for having asked it.

She wanted to know if I didn't care what people thought, and I responded that I, 'Couldn't give a shite'. She asked me then if I *really* didn't care, or if it was just a front, a way of protecting myself? I looked her straight in the eye and confidently lied: 'No, I *really* don't care'.

I remember her face and her eyes and how I saw budding in them the surprising new understanding that some women were quite content working as prostitutes and attached no sense of stigma to themselves; but she was wrong; she'd been duped. I can understand why some women lie to themselves and others about what prostitution truly entails; I've done it myself, and the comment that reporter made all those years ago was accurate; I *was* protecting myself. I was protecting myself from her and her questions. I was protecting myself from the truth.

I think though, that I was wrong that day. I shouldn't have done that. I was too young to understand the responsibility I had to be honest, especially to somebody who would repeat my words in the media. I think it does a disservice to society and to humanity actually, to pretend that the act of prostitution is anything other than what it truly is: a degrading and exploitative exchange. Thoughts like this were far from my mind though, when I was busy protecting myself from the reality of prostitution.

My conduct with that reporter was a classic example of the prostitute's defence mechanisms of defiance and denial combined and it certainly was an example of a survival strategy. Surviving in prostitution is not possible for those who have a consistent, consciously held view of the self as vulnerable. It is necessary to lie to yourself here, and sometimes in lying to yourself, it is necessary to lie to others.

Anger and defiance are also closely related, and they often appear together in response to humiliating incidents. The most obvious ones I can think of would have been street-walking women vehemently returning the verbal abuse hurled at them from passing cars. The survival strategy here is in the attempt to protect dignity which is under attack. I find these saddening and pitiable memories, because I see them now for what they really were: attempts at preserving a wholesome sense of self and struggling to stay psychologically healthy in the most thwarting and hostile of circumstances.

Alcoholism and other substance-abuse problems were widespread, as I've said. As survival strategies go, they were probably the most obvious and certainly the most useless. Yes, they provided temporary oblivion, removed the women from their current reality, but of course, due to their nature, they worked only for a time and with a very serious payback.

A few years ago I called to the home of a woman I've known since we were both in our teens. She has been stabilised on methadone since her early twenties, but every now and again she will relapse and return to abusing heroin and benzodiazepines. I knocked on her door and when she opened it, she had the two biggest, most brutal-looking black eyes I'd

ever seen. They were every shade of black, blue, grey and green and were
so swollen they were closed into two tiny slits. I was shocked to see her.
She looked as though she had two golf balls shoved behind her eyelids.

She let me into her house and walked slowly up the stairs. I followed
behind asking what in the name of God had happened to her. Because
I hadn't been able to see into her eyes in the condition they were in, it
wasn't until I saw how slowly and clumsily she was walking that I realised she was stoned, *very* stoned. My heart sank. She had been doing so
well.

She sat cross-legged on her bedroom floor and started riffling in
slow-motion through a make-up bag, looking for concealer, it turned
out. She then took her blouse off and pulled on a skimpy-looking top.
I saw that her body was covered in huge horrible bruises. She started
applying her concealer so clumsily that at times she missed her black
eyes completely.

'Where are you going?' I asked.

'I'm going down the street,' she eventually slurred in response.

Every time I spoke, there was an interlude of at least ten seconds
between my words and hers; it took her that long to mentally process
what I was saying and to formulate a response. Her reply left me horrified. I couldn't believe she was going out to prostitute herself in that
condition. I couldn't believe, beyond anything else, that she would actually be capable of making any money. Though I'd often seen women
working the streets with black eyes and bruises, her injuries were in a
different category. She looked as though she'd been kicked by a horse.

Eventually I drew it out of her that she'd been beaten up by several
women outside the methadone clinic a week before, that she'd been
working every day since, and no, she'd had no problem making the hundred euro a day it cost to buy fifty benzodiazepines. She'd been working
for the money for drugs all week and today would be no different. There
was a lull in our conversation as I struggled with my feelings. She broke
the silence, eventually, by saying: 'You'd better hang up the phone now.
You'll use up all your credit'.

I said: 'I'm sitting on the end of your bed'.

There was nothing for it but to get into my car. I cried the whole drive home. It is a strange truth that, after everything I had been through myself, it was the experience of another woman, many years after I had left prostitution, that brought my opinion of prostitutors lower than it had ever been.

I recount my old friend's experience here because it is a potent example of how the survival strategies of prostitution can turn into monsters against which the women of prostitution will not even begin to struggle, because for many of them anything is preferable to prostituting themselves without that buffer between themselves and the men who use them—and men do continue to use them, even when they look like they've been kicked by a horse.

The attempt at control in which all prostitutes engage is one of the more common survival strategies of prostitution. The myth of control, the belief of control, is a separate issue, but is also a survival strategy. It is, however, a strategy which is constantly under erosion from the daily realities of prostituted women. It is possible to believe yourself in control when it is necessary that you believe it, but it is not possible to hold onto this belief when the circumstances of your daily existence work aggressively to contradict it.

I may have considered myself in control for days or weeks at a time, but this was brutally interrupted whenever I was beaten, sexually assaulted or robbed. It was more subtly interrupted on a frequent basis any time I found myself doing anything I didn't want to do, which was hourly, rather than daily; but the mind is a complex and stubborn thing and it believes what it needs to believe in order to navigate any difficult environment or circumstance. For this reason I silenced the more subtle contradictions to my self-held myth of control. I remember doing it, and doing it deliberately. 'Just get it over with', was the mental rebuke I used to silence my surfacing feelings of distress in any given situation. I couldn't afford to look at them; that would have been to acknowledge a loss of control.

It was necessary for us to believe that we were in control because to accept that the opposite was true would have been to internalise the full awfulness of our present situation, and the conditions of prostitution are damaging enough without a deep and thorough acknowledgement of their character. It is enough to feel them without accrediting them with the fullness of their destructive power. Ignoring them, shutting out the viciousness of their nature, is perhaps the prostitute's primary policy of defence; her principal survival strategy.

Since women enter prostitution in order to rectify a situation of financial hardship, it is very obvious to see where the belief of control comes in here. The prostitute is now able to feed her kids; she is able to pay her bills; she is able to meet her mortgage repayments. There is a sense of imposing order and a consequential sense of control here, and in this most basic of ways she has achieved control, but here is the crux, and it is a cruel one: only as long as she stays in prostitution can she maintain it. What many women (and I certainly include my younger self in this) fail to realise is that they have not, in fact, achieved control of their own finances: they have passed control of their finances into the hands of prostitution itself, so that although their financial problems are alleviated, those economic issues are no longer controlled by themselves: they are controlled by prostitution and they themselves, as women, are controlled by prostitution also. It is a straightforward swap: prostitution for poverty.

In order to rid yourself of the first you must invariably contend with the second. This is not financial freedom; it is not fiscal control. This is imprisonment in prostitution. It is a form of sexual slavery and it is the reality for the *vast* majority of prostitutes. Those who have had a very high level of education and have excellent job prospects are unlikely to be found in prostitution in the first place, at any of its levels; these women are so rare in prostitution that I have only ever read of them in the media and entertainment depictions of prostitution and in a tiny amount of prostitution literature (if you could call it that).

The truth is, at this base level, there is no personal control in prostitution, but there is a very great need to believe so, and there is a very great number of women who adhere stringently to that belief. Their delusions are utterly understandable to me, and they would be, since I once adhered to them so ardently myself.

I see now the control fantasy in the fullness of its frailty, and it is a pitiable and embarrassing thing to consider. The 'I'm the boss' attitude only every worked while I was loitering on a street corner or making my way through a hotel foyer. It dissolved like a Disprin when the car or bedroom door clicked shut behind me, and it didn't always even make it that far either. Very often, I would carry the full weight of the situation's reality with me and I would feel it constricting my insides like heavy coils of rope before I'd come anywhere close to taking my clothes off. 'Just get it over with,' I would say to myself.

'Just get it over with' is not the mantra of a woman in control.

We also used humour to make the situation more bearable and we also leaned on each other for practical and emotional support. In all of our survival strategies, I can now clearly see, there was the strong impulse to *extricate* ourselves from the situation. Whether it was in the psychological sense, by dissolving ourselves right out of there, or whether it was in physical ways, like spraying perfume on our nipples to prevent them being chewed and bitten, there was always that same sense of creating distance. It manifested itself in so many ways. This compulsion to remove ourselves from the fullness of the experience should not be surprising; it is a very human impulse to create distance between the self and a toxic environment.

My latter years of prostitution involved seeing a number of regular clients I'd built up over several years, as well as seeing new punters; my regulars included transvestites and men with inclinations towards being dominated, whom I had been very accommodating towards because I appreciated their passivity and timidity of manner. Although I hadn't identified it as such at the time, this was a *bona-fide* survival strategy.

I know if anyone had asked us what survival strategies we employed we would have mentioned the short knives some of us carried in secret compartments of our clothing, or we would have said that we relied on our senses to keep us safe, but I doubt many of us would have been able to identify that we lived our lives employing survival strategies subtly, by instinct. I really don't think I would have been able to point that out then.

It is important when reflecting on survival strategies to remember that they usually did not work in the longer term, and even where they did they worked only partly, so that they afforded some relief, but never total release. This is so because survival strategies help a woman to avoid mentally engaging with the process fully; they cannot assist her to avoid engaging with the process at all.

The truth, though, is that some days were harder than others. I'm remembering here the necessity of a very practical disconnection. One day a particularly horrible client visited our brothel in Limerick, where we worked sporadically for a couple of years in the mid-to-late-1990s. He was renowned for the disgusting unwashed state he'd always turn up in. A fouler man in terms of personal hygiene I have never met in my life, and that really is saying something.

He turned up this day and requested to see a new girl. I was the only one there he'd never met and I was horrified to be picked to deal with him as I'd heard so many horror stories about his indescribable filth. Nervous as I was, I couldn't have imagined how bad it was going to be. This man was so unclean I could smell him the moment I opened the bedroom door. When he peeled back his foreskin there was so much cheesy-smelling gunk under it I had to struggle not to vomit. I cannot remember how things panned out with that client, I have probably blanked it from my mind, but I remember one thing for sure: he was not satisfied with my performance. He made his protest in a manner that was impossible to miss: he shat all over the bathroom.

I opened the bathroom door some time after he'd gone and the mess he'd left was a sight to behold, just as he'd intended it to be. He'd shat all over the toilet seat (which was down) and all over the side of the bath and there was shit smeared on the side of the sink and toilet. He'd shat all over the floor. He'd shat, in fact, on every surface available except for the walls. There was so much shit it seemed he must have been relieving himself of a three-week constipation.

The message of this protest was, of course, that we were only fit for cleaning up his shit. It was sufficiently contemptuous in his view and very much in line with his perception of us prostituted women as lesser humans. Etiquette in prostitution would dictate that you would be expected to deal with, or at least help with, any mess or damage a client of yours had the nastiness to create, but there was no way on this earth I was cleaning up that man's shit. I closed the door, walked away, and point-blank refused to deal with it.

There were other times I'd have to rely on what I've come to think of as the 'unplugging technique'. This was necessary because there were times when you could be halfway mentally present and then there were times you'd have to plug yourself out of the situation just like a phone charger being plugged out of a socket. An example of this would be the times one particular regular client of the brothel visited. This man was as ugly as they come and he had a face the colour and likeness of a big beef tomato. As he'd peel off his clothes, he'd be ogling me and making the most inane and skin-crawling comments, often referring to the genitalia, like: 'Let's share a banana split—you have the banana and I'll have the split!' The overwhelming natural response a woman must contain in these situations is: 'Oh would you ever just go and FUCK OFF!' Sometimes you'd be close to choking on the unsaid words. That's when you'd unplug yourself. I did a lot of that.

Chapter 14 ~

DISSOCIATION AND THE SEPARATION OF SELF

International research shows how women in prostitution have worked out an ingenious, complex system of creating and maintaining boundaries to protect the 'real self' from being invaded and destroyed by prostitution . . . Dissociation, the psychological process of banishing traumatic events from consciousness, is an emotional shutting down used by women in prostitution in common with women being raped, battered and among prisoners of war who are being tortured.

'THE NEXT STEP INITIATIVE', *RUHAMA RESEARCH
REPORT ON BARRIERS AFFECTING WOMEN IN
PROSTITUTION, IRELAND, 2005*

The age-old practice of using an alias is an example of how prostituted women have always actively sought to separate themselves from what they do. Women who use an alias (as all prostitutes do) literally do what they do under another name; this is dissociation at its most practical level.

For women in prostitution, dissociation is a necessary but dangerous thing. Just like the woman in an abusive marriage who continually tells herself that it 'really isn't that bad', the woman in prostitution also breaks away from the reality of her situation, with disastrous consequences for her mental and emotional health. Continually denying any painful lived reality inevitably causes a person to become separated from their own self. As a woman feels her psyche being abused she will protect against that and she will use the act of dissociation as a tool to do that. As she fails (and she will always fail, because it is not possible to dissociate fully from an influence you continue to be exposed to) the degree of her ability to dissociate from prostitution directly reflects the degree to which she has become separated from herself.

She is cut by either side of a two-edged sword. She is, in other words, psychologically polluted by prostitution to the exact extent which she manages to disconnect from it. But if she were not to disconnect from prostitution she would be equally polluted by her proximity to it; she would just find herself polluted in a more presently painful way. (Dissociation just puts these issues on the long finger.)

Here is the essence of the paradox: to dissociate is to break away from and to turn away from, so the disconnection which is so crucial for maintaining her own peace of mind is itself a pollutant because it forces her to deny to herself the reality of her own experience. Dissociation is essential here; the prostituted cannot maintain her identity or sanity without it, but the cruel double-bind is that, on a psychological level, dissociation is a betrayal of the self. She's damned if she does and damned if she doesn't, on the deepest of levels.

Every time a prostitute numbs her inner self against the feel of unwanted hands on her body she both employs dissociation and suffers the separation of self.

Sometimes when I would be with a client who overtly got off on violation, if I knew that protest was pointless and very liable to lead to a beating, I would allow my body and mind to go limp. This was my own form of protest, the only one possible here. Since there was no getting out of the situation I would not struggle against being roughly manhandled; I would not partake in the mental push/pull friction necessary for him to enjoy his game of tug-of-war. I would drop the rope from my end. He would still have his climax, but I knew its potency had been diluted. There was no pleasure in this for me; just the small payoff of dissociation that sat alongside the payback of my further disconnecting from my own truth. Without exception, the man would be belligerent and cantankerous afterwards, and sometimes aggressive. There was always the understanding on his part that I hadn't played ball, and the attitude that he'd been somehow short-changed because of it. He hadn't wanted my acquiescence; he'd needed my objection.

It bears repeating here that a prostitute has no rights to set the boundaries of her sexual experience, no right to object, and no right even to *not* object when that is not in line with her client's requirements. Her body is there to accommodate the sexual experience of another, no matter what anguish it causes her, regardless what it demands of her, and regardless how damaging and degrading she may find it to be. The sort of retreat I've described is received as passive aggressive and very often a woman will be punished for it. We would often be flung out of cars or spat on in hotel rooms after incidents like these.

There were different categories of violators, as there were distinctions in fetishists of other sorts. Some of the less overt violators would not need to physically feel a woman struggle against hands gripping her breasts so hard she thought they'd burst; some would gently stroke her breasts and feel her involuntary shrinking from their touch, and they'd get off on that, for some that would be enough. There is clearly a difference in magnitude, but for me it does not alter the nature of the offence.

I reacted to these situations always in the same way; I pretended they were not happening. Surely it is obvious that anything that forces a person to lie to themselves cannot be positive?

In prostitution, because you continually deny your own feelings, you come to have a very traumatic relationship with yourself and something in that causes the real self to become very obscure. There is a sincere danger in that, because when you have become obscure to yourself, you have lost the ability to ask yourself questions.

So then in prostitution you have on one hand this need to imagine yourself out of the situation and an unintentional distancing from the essence of yourself on the other. When a woman has negated her own feelings ritualistically there occurs in her an inevitable fracturing; in this way dissociation leads to a separation of the self. It is not the sole process by which this severance occurs, but it may just be the most important one. I say so because the breaking away from truth inherent to the process of dissociation is what makes prostitution possible for a woman in the first place.

A woman must first dissociate from her natural reluctance of prostitution before she can incorporate it into her life. This necessitates the initial act of disconnection from the self. The very first thing prostitution teaches a woman is this method of personal disconnection; the very first thing she will learn is how to hone it. But this is only reinforcement; the separation of self occurs *prior* to the first act and this, for the vast majority of women, is the only way prostitution is possible. It is in the moment when a woman first ignores her natural revulsion and forges ahead anyway that the separation of self begins. It begins with the disregard of her own feelings; and so the separation of self first manifests in the disparity between internal instinct and outward behaviour. It begins in the moment we deliberately divorce what we desire from what we do, and the prostituted are a long way from being the only women who do this.

Some non-prostituted women routinely force themselves into a state of shutdown in order to accommodate men's sexual demands, and many more women will have had that experience at least a few times in their lives. Some women will go to very great lengths in order to facilitate superfluous desires which are presented as critical sexual requirements. Many women who do these things do them not in an effort to please themselves, but in an effort to be pleasing, and they are strongly encouraged to do so by a mindset outside of themselves which imposes a straightforward choice between being 'sexually liberated' and 'puritanical'. There is no middle ground, apparently; and there is no acknowledgement of the true essence of sexual liberation, which does not in any sense accord with having your sexual behaviours dictated to you.

Many women who acquiesce to their bodies being used thus do so under the weight of insecurity issues so oppressing they cause them to crumble in the face of accusations such as 'frigid', 'closed-minded', 'unadventurous' and, God forbid, 'prudish'—labels which they process

as too unthinkable to bear. This is psychosexual bullying, and its consequences are lasting, and severe.

The quotes I include below are powerful testimony that women are
damaged by the sort of sex that sexually coercive situations produce,
and that they respond to that damage by shutting down via the same
system of dissociation that occurs in prostituted women. It is interesting
and important to note that this happens as a response to unwanted sex
even where no money has changed hands.

'What he wanted, besides having an affair, was to take nude photos
of me. I find it hard to explain to myself that I didn't think I could
say no even though I didn't want to do what he asked. This is painful to write about, but I do so because I want readers—especially
women—to know that even an essentially smart and good girl,
if she lacks self-esteem and believes a woman is supposed to "go
along"' will allow herself to get into some inexplicable situations. I
wish I could say this was the last one for me. I had a brief affair with
him, every moment of which I hated. Mostly I hated myself for my
betrayal of my body, and I felt terrible confusion about why I was
letting this happen.'

'In my public life, I am a strong, can-do woman. How is it then,
that behind closed doors, in my most intimate relations, I could
betray myself? The answer is this: If a woman has become disembodied from a lack of self-worth—I'm not good enough—or from
abuse, she will neglect her own voice of desire . . . this requires . . .
compartmentalizing—disconnecting head and heart, body and soul.'
JANE FONDA
MY LIFE SO FAR

'So the Ideal American Girl bought into every myth the guys could
fling at me—about Bloomsbury, sexual liberation, not being a puri-
tan; about keep-on-doing-what-you-don't-like-because-the-more-
you-do-it-the-more-you'll-like-it; about D. H. Lawrence's ideal

quartet (two women, two men, all possible sexual permutations). I never questioned whose needs and self-interest these models served. The first threesome . . . was followed by encores, and by foursomes, and by various numerical combinations with other people (always with Kenneth present)—ordeals my memory still can neither purge itself of nor fully grasp. I know I partly dissociated my consciousness in order to survive them, an attempt to compartmentalise and contain the experience of violation.'

ROBIN MORGAN
SATURDAY'S CHILD

In her book Fonda describes different instances of having been sexually coerced as a younger woman, including how she had regular threesomes with her husband and other women, which she had no desire to have, for the sexual benefit of her husband. She talks, just as Morgan does, about the damaging effects these experiences had on her psyche in terms that I could only compare to the impact of prostitution abuse, the two are so startlingly similar.

Sexual coercion is very easily employed, especially upon those who have been pre-schooled by previous experiences of abuse. It causes a crack in the structure of the self, which continued sexual coercion goes on to widen. When it does there follows a shattering of the self, the 'terrible confusion' Fonda speaks of, and the psychic fragmentation and disconnection so common to the findings of prostitution research.

Over time it becomes second-nature, this process of fragmentation, until it is almost unnoticeable to the prostituted woman, and maybe, many years after she has first employed it, she will finally learn to fully recognise it. I say this because it was true for me in prostitution and I saw it everywhere I looked, and because I wouldn't have known in my teens that the duplicity, loneliness and confusion I was experiencing and witnessing came about as a result of an unnatural separation of self.

One of the ways I protected myself in prostitution was to divide myself, to literally split myself into two characters; the authentic me, and the imaginary version. Of course, the former was reserved for the people who did not pay me for sex and the latter created in order to distance me from those who did. If a client asked me what my favourite fruit was (and I've been asked stranger questions than that) I would answer with any fruit I could think of, but I would never admit to my true preference for mangoes. If I was asked my favourite colour, I would attest to adore the first colour that came into my head, any colour, except green.

Sometimes a client would ask these questions in a deliberate attempt to get to know 'the real you', and in those cases you would be very much aware of his intentions and very much on your guard against them, protecting your identity by swathing it in a tissue of omissions and outright lies. At other times he would ask these probing questions for purely practical reasons, such as if he had the intention of buying you a piece of jewellery, but even if I actually preferred a bracelet with green gemstones, I would always lie about my genuine preference because keeping that to myself was more precious than any jewels he could give me.

I have never in my life met, nor even heard rumour of, a prostitute who was generally content to allow her clients into every facet of her private life. Some women I met were a good deal more comfortable with that than I was, a tiny minority even forming relationships with their clients, but even in those cases, from what I saw and heard, there always remained some measure of concealment. A prostitute generally removes herself from her lifestyle mentally, since she cannot remove herself from it physically, and this is a trait that is utterly inherent to the behaviour of prostitutes. This extreme reluctance to merge the truth of her identity with her client's perception of it is actually the strongest evidence of a woman's rejection of her own participation in prostitution.

Of course, however successful a prostitute is in her attempts to conceal her authentic identity from her clients (dissociation) that same authentic sense of self is altered by her participation in prostitution (separation of self). This happens both because she is influenced mentally and emotionally by what she does and therefore alters her own self-image accordingly, but also because perceptions of her held by those outside of the sphere of her world are altered dramatically by learning of her involvement in it. Knowing the latter (and usually through bitter experience), most prostitutes will keep the facts of what they do to themselves. This is an attempt at avoiding those judgemental attitudes; it is also clear evidence that she expects to be judged.

It is a cruel and confusing conundrum for prostitutes, who must come to understand that the maintenance and protection of their own identity is supported by the lies they tell their clients, while the dignity of that same identity is defiled and diminished by the truths uncovered by those who are intimately familiar with it. She is left struggling to keep hold of whatever aspects of herself she believes worth holding onto, and whatever they may be, their validity is under constant attack. It is little wonder that so many prostitutes suffer with crippling issues of negative self-image and diminished self-esteem. These feelings, of course, do not disappear upon leaving prostitution. They linger long after it.

At times, since I got out of prostitution, I've asked myself, who am I any more? Am I still myself? What is there left of me now? That is another of the prices of prostitution, that incessant introspective questioning. In prostitution, you are not just selling a quick fuck up a laneway or a long, unmercifully lingering one in a hotel bed. When you take that money what you are really being paid for is the deepest and most unspoken part of the contract: a lifetime of looking inward and wondering who you are.

I am taking the long way back, because there is no short way; and it is sad to find myself on a journey that takes me in a direction I want to go, but which I know will never end. This is not melodrama; it is fact. How could it be possible to complete a journey when you do not know the landscape of your destination? How would you know when you'd arrived at the sense of self that would have existed had you never become a prostitute? How would you recognise that state of being, having never experienced it? You wouldn't, any more than you'd recognise a city you'd never been to, and anyway, it's probably just as well because you're never going to get there. The you that you are is the one that exists; you're never going to know the you that would have existed in some parallel universe you can't access.

What I *do* recognise (and this is a great blessing) are the little mile-

stones along the way that indicate further removal away from my prostitution 'self' and towards the self I should/might/would otherwise have
been. I haven't got there, but I move towards there, and there is clear
progress in the moving. They are not always dramatic, these milestones;
in fact the journey is usually marked by mundane and commonplace
things. One day you'll find yourself standing at a supermarket checkout
handing the cashier a store loyalty card and it'll hit you that you never
would have considered applying for one of those before; not because of
a lack of fiscal conscientiousness, but because as a prostitute you just
didn't *live* in that world.

Propriety, normalcy, participatory routines . . . I was scared of and
unfamiliar with these things, in equal measure, for the longest time. And
I was scared because I was unfamiliar and I continued to be unfamiliar
because my fear kept me at a distance, and my childhood sense of social
disconnectedness entirely supported the sense of otherness that made
it possible, even predictable, that I would remain in prostitution for
so long.

One question I asked of myself in prostitution (and it came back again
and again) was 'Who are you when nobody's looking?'

By 'nobody' I meant both the public and the punters alike, everybody.
I had no idea why I asked this of myself, but I believe today that it was
an instinctual grounding exercise; that it was something I asked myself
in order to hear the answer. I think it was an answer I needed to hear in
order to remind myself that I was a good person, because the 'who I was'
when nobody was looking rarely reflected anything negative. When I
was alone, I usually read literature or listened to calming music or bathed
in the light of scented candles. Often I'd do all three; play music down
low while soaking in a lavender oil bath with my favourite book in my
hands. I enjoyed being alone. I enjoyed being with myself. I realise today
I asked myself that because I liked who I was when no-one was looking.

The opposite of this is also true; I usually didn't like what I saw of
myself or how I felt when I was in company. When I was among people
who didn't know I was a prostitute, I felt negatively about myself because

I compared my prostitute-self with their non-prostitute-selves and felt dirty and worthless by comparison. When I was with other prostitutes I was sometimes happy, less often miserable, but quite often depressed by our common ground, and when I was with clients I seldom felt anything other than psychologically sick.

As the years went by and the separation of self became more solidified, the question remained the same but the tone with which I put it to myself changed. There was a sense of sadness to it, and a low-level urgency, a panicked sense of trying to recall. In those days, I would ask myself, 'Who *are* you when nobody's looking?' You begin to slip away from yourself in prostitution, especially if you throw drugs into the mix. I think towards the end that question was, in essence, a struggle against the natural separation of self which becomes so inherent to the working prostitute. It was asked in an effort to remember who I was.

This feeling, this woundedness from having experienced a fracture of the self, calls on the capacity to further separate and divide. The aim is positive. It seeks to safeguard a healthy self-perception; but it is damaging because it involves a further splintering. The aim is irrelevant, because its fulfilment causes a woman to become locked in a very great struggle. It is a perfectly balanced struggle, firstly because it is the most natural thing in the world to move to protect oneself from accepting a negative self-image.

We are not made to function healthily whilst feeling badly about ourselves. It is natural, normal, even necessary to struggle against that; to deny that others are justified in viewing us in the negative way that they do. But the tragedy is in the futility of the struggle, because while it is paramount for the prostitute to separate herself from the publicly accepted image of the prostitute, it is also impossible. Every police officer, every fire fighter, every teacher and tradesman and professional the world over will understand what it is to be regarded as a member of a collective staff group. At some point you understand that you cannot escape being perceived by others as they see you and you begin the secondary struggle, which is not to see yourself as they do; and it is a struggle because it does not feel logical to consistently deny the image of ourselves as we are universally perceived. It is an inward exertion, and because it can never be overcome, it can never end.

Sometimes the truth of my past and its contrast with the image of my present-day life reminds me of the little holographic pictures I would find in cereal packets as a child. Tilt it this way and you see one image; tilt it in the other direction and an entirely different picture will emerge. I feel this way about the transition from being a prostituted woman into being a non-prostituted woman.

I am not that woman any more, but she has not disappeared either. She is the other side of me and her re-emergence is only ever a dirty look or a whispered word away. It is beneficial to imagine her as a mirage, someone who never would have existed if life had not been tilted in a certain skewed way.

I remember standing in the dark one night in the car-park of a Galway hotel. I'd just finished a particularly demeaning job and was waiting for the taxi I'd called on my mobile phone. This great wind picked up and I had the eeriest sensation that it was blowing right through me. I felt very benumbed and very lonely and as if, strangely, I wasn't even there. Looking back on it, I felt as I imagine a ghost might feel.

Afterwards, I wondered why I'd felt so disconnected from myself in response to an experience I'd had many times. I both wondered and responded at the same time. It was one of those rare moments where the conscious meets the subconscious. I knew that I had beaten the feeling down each of the many times I'd almost previously felt it. I knew also that somewhere inside me I had always known this and needn't have wondered at all.

At times I have been asked of prostitution, 'What does it feel like?' The truth is I learned to operate a certain part of my psyche so that sometimes it didn't feel like much of anything at all. There is a switch governing the release or restraint of emotion with which most people are unfamiliar because it might have to come into play only a limited number of times, sporadically, over the course of their lives. But in prostitution the use of this on/off function in the governing of emotion is so pervasive that it is very unlikely a woman would not eventually become aware of it. It is not lost on the men who buy women in prostitution either. As one of them reported 'it's like she's not really there'.[9]

I believe it is thanks to this psychological mechanism that the ability to enjoy some degree of 'normal' sexual functioning within relationships remains intact for most prostitutes. If you were to be fully engaged, mentally and emotionally, in every act of prostitution over the course of several years, intimate relationships would no longer be possible. Conversely though (and this is much commented on among prostitutes who have taken part in Irish and international research) there are times when it is not possible to switch back on, even when you want to; times when, basically, the switch has become faulty and is no longer under your control. In this way, the prolonged practice of 'shutting off' sexually can have lasting negative implications for romantic relations.

Also at times, there is overload, and a situation or multitude of situations is too much to be managed by this emotional control switch; or at other times your control switch has been overused to the point where it no longer functions on automatic, you can temporarily be unable to restrain emotion and you then come to the painful awareness that you've been deliberately blocking yourself from experiencing trauma. These can be sad and scary times.

Many times I've heard prostitutes make comments along the lines of: 'It's just as well you do be miles away in your mind' and 'He was a horrible rough smelly fucker, but it was only my body in the bed, the rest of me was floating out the window into the clouds—you know yourself'. Remarks like these confirmed for me then that other prostitutes dealt with the job in the same way I did, but also I see now that the Dublin colloquialism 'You know yourself' was repeated so often that, as a group, we obviously expected a general understanding of the situation, and we

---

9   'Comparing Sex Buyers with Men Who Don't Buy Sex', Melissa Farley et al, 2009.

expected it because we didn't see what other way it could have been perceived to be.

We all practised dissociation; each of us found our own ways to remove ourselves from what we were doing. We all shut down in similar ways and for identical reasons and we all suffered the same price for it too. We were alienated from ourselves. It was a common, shared, collective experience, this separation of self.

Chapter 15 ～

THE MYTH OF THE HAPPY HOOKER

Even where research has shown different perspectives on prostitution, from demanding recognition on a par with other occupations to fighting prostitution, nowhere is the suggestion made that women enjoy prostitution.

'THE NEXT STEP INITIATIVE', RUHAMA RESEARCH REPORT ON BARRIERS AFFECTING WOMEN IN PROSTITUTION, IRELAND, 2005

Freedom is universally accepted as one of the fundamental necessities for contentment in human life. The myth of the happy hooker does not make logical sense, because the distinguishing feature of any free person is that their body is inviolable, while the distinguishing mark of the prostitute is that her body is not. Therefore, it is only common sense to conclude that a prostitute does not experience either life or her body as a free person does; in fact, quite the opposite. Are we to believe that women are generally 'happy' in this circumstance?

The quote that prefaces this chapter plainly states that in the research carried out into prostitution, no woman said she enjoyed it. Yet there are women who have publicly claimed that they found it enjoyable. I never met one of those women in prostitution. But the phenomenon is attractive, and has given rise to books and TV series which glamorise prostitution and abuse the young females of our society in much the same way as anorexic images on the covers of magazines. No doubt some young women become curious about prostituting themselves in the skewed

and unrealistic context these portrayals present, and no doubt some go
on to do it.

I have also read the opinions of some outside of prostitution who
view it as an expression of sexual liberation. That opinion indicates
either the inexperienced notions of a person wholly removed from the
reality of prostitution, or someone who has no idea what sexual liberation actually involves. The only thing prostitution ever liberated me
from was homelessness.

The idea is unfathomable to most women in prostitution, as the testimony of this French prostitute demonstrates: 'And don't think, either,
that prostitutes—because they're prostitutes—are liberated. Just the
opposite. Prostitution and sexual liberation have got nothing to do with
each other, they're exactly the opposite.'[10] In the seven years I spent as
a prostitute I met innumerable prostitutes and I have had friends in the
trade for more than half my lifetime, and I have *never* met a prostitute
who didn't wish she were doing something else.

In reading the interviews and writings of prostitutes and other former prostitutes something that strikes me as an increasingly common
theme (though still very much a minority among memoirs, thankfully)
is the attempt to make prostitution more acceptable or palatable for the
outsider. I don't know for certain why some women feel the need to do
that, but I could hazard a guess, and I'd be willing to bet it's accurate: I
think denial exists to a very large degree in the minds of most prostitutes
or former prostitutes who maintain that they find or found prostitution
even a reasonably tolerable profession. Denial is easy here; it's telling the
truth that's difficult.

I need to be honest; I have to be. This is not the place to hide or disguise my thoughts and feelings. I've made that mistake once already. I
will not repeat it here.

As to *why* some prostitutes colour their trade in unrealistic terms; that
will vary from woman to woman. Self-protection and denial are major
features in this; but as to their confidence in being believed, that is pretty
universal. Prostitutes know they can get away with describing their trade

10   Claude Jaget, *Prostitutes, Our Life*, Falling Wall Press, 1980.

in any way they choose because the world of prostitution is entirely incomprehensible to those who do not inhabit it, and they know this because they did not always inhabit it themselves. They, once upon a time, found it just as unfathomable as anybody else, and they have not forgotten that feeling, or missed the monumental shift that is the journey from incomprehension to thorough understanding which came through intimate acquaintance. Prostitutes know and remember their state of pre-prostitution naïveté because they have memories which function exactly like everyone else's.

However, despite the fact that prostitutes are aware of the scope for fabrication and despite the fact they'd be generally disinclined to volunteer details of their experience of the trade, most of them, I believe, would be more disposed towards being honest rather than dishonest if a direct question were put to them in a non-threatening manner and by a non-judgemental person. The issue, and the problem for those seeking answers from prostitutes, is that however non-threatening the question and however non-judgemental the asker may appear, the questions are, by their nature, invasive.

They are invasive because they are received as intrusive, as all questions asked of somebody who is reluctant to discuss the subject matter automatically are. It would be imprudent not to assume this while attempting to discuss her history with a prostitute and it would be unwise not to remain aware that her responses may be coloured by the sense of defensiveness she naturally feels. She has been assailed on all fronts, remember, for her involvement in the subject matter at hand. All of society has conspired to tell her how unworthy she is and she will be naturally timid and cautious and reluctant to open up. You would be likely to hear truths, but general truths; edited versions, removed from the personal, with the worst of her experiences deliberately omitted, so that she might avoid the feelings of humiliation and shame associated with reliving them.

I have heard the idea aired that women who are desperate enough to enter prostitution should 'make it a means to an end'. A means to an end . . . but what end? Here is the problem with that: there is no end, and even if there were, most prostitutes are in no position to chart where that end might be, never mind influence it.

My first instinct on hearing that was that I'd have liked to be able to reason this out, but even if I could have done, there are some conversations just not worth pursuing. I do not mean this in a disrespectful manner directed at that person. I mean it simply as I state it: you cannot argue the shape of an experience with someone who has not lived it. You can discuss it, you can examine it; you can offer your experience, listen to and consider the sometimes illuminating suggestions of someone looking at it with the fresh eyes of an outsider, but you cannot argue the structure of it. You cannot argue the composition of its nature, because the argument you're presented with will be naturally composed in its entirety of assumption and conjecture. This brings the debaters to an impossible impasse, but when I think of both positions I am reminded of an old Irish saying which translated to English reads: 'The wearer knows best where the shoe pinches'.

However, I did continue to think about what had been said afterwards, the assertion that prostitution could be 'a means to an end'. The suggestion played on my mind. There was a minimalism to it which was superficially plausible but just not practicable in prostitution. Its simplicity bothered me and I was annoyed about this evidence that there was such confident ignorance about prostitution in the world.

We have, most of us I'd imagine, come across in contemporary literature or film the image of the prostitute who 'works her way through college'. In Ireland, while I was in prostitution, those women amounted to such a tiny figure that I never met one myself. I would predict they present in higher numbers in countries where third-level education is very expensive. I can certainly say that had I lived that depiction of prostitution, had I prostituted my way through law school, for example, I would never have shared my classmates' sense of confidence and self-assurance upon graduating. What I would have felt instead was a lifelong fear of discovery and exposure; the fear of society judging me as a whore in a suit. The bottom line is this: it is impossible to make prostitution a means to an end because the changes that take place as a result of it alter the end in itself.

Sometimes we would offer each other suggestions as to how our daily lives might be made more tolerable along practical lines, but as for any sort of inner contentment, I very rarely heard prostitutes offer each other any advice of that sort. That does not surprise me as a prostitute's job being a miserable business was the accepted assessment of matters.

What I *have* encountered is more evidence attesting to the unhappiness of prostitutes than I can convey; and I have no doubt that when I have completed this book I will have failed to identify most of it, as much of it now, at the distance of more than a decade, has merged into a generalised sense of dejection made up of a mish-mash of miserable memories; but here is one offering: the practice of prevarication, the act of evading our circumstances that we would sometimes indulge.

When we would be working a shift in the brothel together, two or more of us, there was no better-loved practice than knocking off the phones, kicking off our heels and indulging in alcohol and Chinese food. You might want to do that in most jobs, you might think, and you'd be right, but there was something deliciously appealing about doing so in prostitution; it was not about taking leave of banality—it was about returning to being human.

So we would do that, but only very occasionally, for a number of reasons: firstly, often we hadn't the power to do so because we were caught in the trap of someone else's employ. Other times we would be visiting some other city and only had a set amount of days to make our money and go. Oftentimes, business would be very slow and we wouldn't have made enough money to take a night off, and that is another of the myths of prostitution: that the money is always plentiful enough to offset the degradation of the lifestyle. It isn't. Quite apart from the fact that no money on earth would compensate for the degradation and humiliation inherent to prostitution, for a variety of reasons (including seasonal, surprisingly) there are sometimes spells with not enough business to go round. The only thing that approaches the degradation and the psychic stress of a brothel full of clients is a brothel empty of them, filled as it is with the dismal atmosphere particular to a group of women waiting around for the opportunity to be used.

So we didn't very regularly take the disobedient pleasure of a night off, but when we did, the mood and tone changed to its absolute opposite. We were like undomesticated creatures that had escaped from the enslavement of an enforced captivity and spent the night as though revelling in our first moments back in the wild. This was something I experienced with too many different groups of women, all unknown to each other, in too many different locations and at too many different times for it to be shooed away as some kind of coincidence. It was no coincidence. When the same human behaviour is exhibited in very similar circumstances over and over again, there is a reason for that. The reason here is this: women in prostitution are unhappy.

This too I offer into evidence: the nights I shut down the brothel when I was alone; or at least it must have seemed shut to those trying to gain admittance, though I did not so much shut up shop as abandon my post. I didn't knock the phones off, as we always did when there was a conscious decision made to take a break from being prostitutes for one night. I suppose that disparity may hold some clue as to the meaning of my behaviour, because, as I remember, there never was a conscious decision made on my part. Just sometimes I would listen to the phone ringing and ringing and some part of me would refuse to answer it, and when that happened it was never a one-off thing; it would always continue for the night.

It would not have been possible to predict when this shift of mood would occur, but when it did it was absolute, sudden and total. I have sat behind a locked door, more than once, with a would-be client who'd arrived for his appointment knocking on the other side. It might suit the melodramatic to picture me crying, but I never was. I was thinking absolutely nothing; perhaps when the mind is concentrated in an effort not to think and feel there is simply no room for thoughts; I don't know. What I do know is that there was nothing but coldness and the sound of knocking and the blank pastel nothingness of the opposite wall.

This severance of the self from feeling is a prostitute's practised art. It allows for the 'acting' sometimes described as integral to a prostitute's work. Very often she carries this learned ability outside of the individual acts and applies it to her general attitude towards the work itself. This is necessary. It affords her the capacity to believe she feels nothing, as I believed on those days I sat in stony-cold silence to the reverberations of a would-be client's knocking.

I refused to allow it to invade my mind deeply enough to thoroughly chill me, that sound that so signified someone else's urge for an encounter I did not want to have. It was a monolith in my mind, and I couldn't afford to have its shadow cast over me. It was too big. It would have obscured me. So I had to silence the part of me that recognised its danger and enormity. But yet as much as I thought I could feel nothing, I must have felt something, because I knew that if I could have opened that portal between myself and feeling, the first thing I'd have felt, because it was the feeling nearest me, would have been this: I would have felt unhappy.

In everybody's life there will be that sound; that one sound, whatever it is, that slows their heart down and makes their soul take notice. That sound will be different for everybody. For me, it will always be the hollow-knuckled knocking on a wooden fire door.

There is, as a consequence of prostitution, an inevitable encircling of the self as we try to make the shapes fit the structure of what is left of our understanding of sexuality and of our selves. We do this by asking ourselves questions, and we answer the questions we ask, sometimes slowly, the information leaking in a measured drip drip; and yet those answers are rarely surprising, as if we really knew them all along and were not lacking knowledge, but acceptance. At other times awareness comes so quickly that the question and the answer seem almost to arrive together, so that we know they are related, a part of each other, intimately linked, rather than some sort of opposites.

But slowly or quickly, the enormity of this acceptance cannot but be painful. To realise that we have sold our own freedom is to arrive at an agonising understanding. I believe that, in some women, a natural evasion of this painful realisation goes a long way towards their supporting the myth of the happy hooker, and that in many more women the same natural evasion goes a long way towards their not contradicting it.

But we prostitutes never lied to each other when it came to the business of prostitution. We never tried to misrepresent the basic shape and nature of the experience with which we were all intimately familiar, so it is strange and quite nauseating for me to read accounts of prostitution by women who depict it as radically different from the experience myself and every other prostitute I ever met lived. One of the realities that make up this experience is that attractive men less often hire prostitutes and physically ugly men more often do. I would like to hear how these supposedly happy hookers reacted to the sense of physical and sexual revulsion so integral to the prostitution experience.

For example, I remember one particular man among many who was morbidly obese. When it came to sexual function, this man had two problems combined; or rather he presented two problems for the women he prostituted: he had a very small penis and a very large amount of fat concealing it. He asked me to give him hand-relief. I had to go burrowing through folds of fat to find his elusive penis, and when it was found (and it was eventually found) I was just thankful he hadn't requested a blow-job. I would have needed one of those umbrella-handle-shaped snorkelling devices wedged into the corner of my mouth. His flab wobbled like jelly as he shook with this rare excitement and his genitals stank as a result of never being exposed to the air. I had to breathe through my mouth because I couldn't stomach the smell, but the thought of drawing that stink into my lungs made me struggle not to vomit. How happy, I would like to know, are these 'happy hookers' in situations like this?

Sexual revulsion is a daily experience in prostitution. It is something that was acknowledged by us all as absolutely routine, and, tellingly, something I have noticed about the accounts of women who say they enjoyed prostitution is their absolute silence on the matter. What I would like to know is: what is it that is operating (or not operating) in them that makes them immune to the experience of sexual revulsion? They certainly encounter situations liable to provoke it daily. Sexual disgust is as usual to the prostitute as encountering coffee is to the waitress, so what is it that we are to believe makes them impervious to this central aspect of the job? Dissociation works to somewhat mentally remove a woman from these sort of physical realities, but it certainly does not work so thoroughly as to blind her to them.

The accounts of women who claim to have enjoyed prostitution do not explain any of this. They do not explain it since they do not mention it, and they do not mention it because they know it's beyond explanation.

Their reason for silence here is obvious: it would not be possible to depict prostitution as pleasurable or even moderately tolerable were the fullness of its ugliness laid bare. I actually find their silence on the matter a little heartening; though it in itself is disingenuous, *they* are not so disingenuous as to pretend such disgusting experiences could be painted as pleasurable. That does not mean I condone that they omit them (and I *know* they do not do so for lack of having encountered them), but I do take some small comfort from the fact that women who contend they enjoyed prostitution simultaneously do not present the experience as it is really lived. It is therefore not truly prostitution they are defending; it is an incomplete version of it.

I think a woman would have to be cut off from her own reality to the point of psychosis to consistently fail to recognise and react to something so odious and so central to her job description, and I do not contend that supposedly happy hookers are psychotics, not at all: they are not women who fail to *recognise* the true state of affairs, they are women who refuse to *acknowledge* it, and that is a different matter altogether.

The first step to being a happy hooker is, of course, consenting to be one. Consent to prostitution is viewed as a one-dimensional thing; in reality, it is anything but. Consent here is over-determined. I have never come across an example of prostitution in any woman's life that was not an attempt to get *out* of a situation rather than to get into one. In other words, the plethora of women I met over the years were attempting to remove themselves from financial problems; not simply entering prostitution because they'd developed a penchant for designer handbags.

The assumption of choice leads to the conclusion of consent, but choice and consent are erroneous concepts here. Their invalidity rests on the fact that a woman's compliance in prostitution is a response to circumstances beyond her control, and this produces an environment which prohibits even the possibility of true consent. There is a difference between consent and reluctant submission. As a lawyer and scholar Catharine MacKinnon says: '. . . when fear and despair produce acquiescence and acquiescence is taken to mean consent, consent is not a meaningful concept'.[11]

---

11 Catharine MacKinnon, *Women's Lives, Men's Laws* (Cambridge, Mass: Harvard University Press, 2005), pages 259–60; also Catharine MacKinnon, 'Liberalism and the Death of Feminism' in Dorchen Leidholdt and Janice G. Raymond, eds, *The Sexual Liberals and the Attack on Feminism* (New York: Teachers College Press, 1990), page 3.

One woman I met during the later years of my involvement in prostitution, in an escort agency, had entered prostitution in her mid-thirties because her marriage had broken down and her husband had left her with several children and a mortgage to worry about. He'd always been the provider while she'd stayed at home to raise the children. It was not destitution but the fear of destitution that drove that woman into prostitution. Her fears were very real. Were her choices?

I remember that woman very clearly because her story was so different to mine. In many ways, we really were at polar ends of the same spectrum. She had been married since her early twenties and, prior to prostitution, had not ever had sex outside of relationships. She hadn't ever had brief flings or one-night stands. She was actually in much worse psychological shape than I was; that was clear to see. She was new to the business when I met her and was timid and quiet in her manner but over time became more talkative, eager to form some sort of bond with the other women. She was clearly lonely, scared and overwhelmed by the situation she found herself in. In a display of the Pavlov's dogs syndrome I've felt myself and witnessed many times, she'd gulp and shudder when the doorbell sounded and visibly attempt to calm her nerves before she walked into the bedroom. It wasn't long before she figured out a few vodkas could assist her in that, and I can tell you true consent certainly did not exist when she lay down on that brothel's bed and opened her legs for man after man after man—men who, no doubt, very often convinced themselves that by fucking a woman who had expressed all-hallowed 'consent' this meant there was no possibility they could be abusing her.

I didn't work with that woman for very long. It was never my habit to stay too long in one place, but I can make a reasonable guess at what happened to her because I've so often witnessed the same scenario. I'd be willing to bet she stayed in prostitution, because she had no viable choice but to do so; and I'd be willing to bet that she, like so many before and after her, began to become desensitised to prostitution by simple dint of having to. At that point, when her hands and voice had stopped shaking and men found it easier to believe they were having consensual sex, did that make the sex more consensual? Of course it didn't. She'd just have gotten inured to it and, like the rest of us, more adept at concealing her vulnerability by hiding the non-consensual nature of the sex.

What the proponents of prostitution conveniently ignore is that lack of opportunity *is* lack of choice. I have seen this played out in so many lives that I fully understand there is no point talking about choice without identifying the presence or absence of *viable* choice, because when a woman cannot choose between two or more viable options, she can hardly be capable of truly consenting to the single 'choice' that she has. In other words, if a woman has no viable choice, she may as well have no choice at all.

The myth of the happy hooker rests on ignoring and disregarding the ambiguous nature of choice in prostitution. As long as any choice is reframed to have no relation to the context in which it's made, then we might be said to choose anything, and be happy about it.

Chapter 16 ∿

THE MYTH OF PROSTITUTES'
SEXUAL PLEASURE

Testimony of an erotic dancer: "Nobody—not myself,
not the other women—enjoys being pawed, poked, prod-
ded and fucked by men we wouldn't give the time
of day if we met them elsewhere."

PEGGY MORGAN, *LIVING ON THE EDGE*

I remember one evening, in the clinic where I used to drink coffee and collect condoms, a particular humorous remark made to a young prostitute by one of the older women. They were discussing an unexpected surge in trade the previous night and the younger woman mentioned how she'd gone home exhausted after it. 'Ah sure,' said the older woman, 'you probably enjoyed it!' The entire company, myself included, burst out laughing. The humour—for those it is lost on—was in the absurdity.

The truth of the matter is that the nature of prostitution flavours the sexual act as far too distasteful and too sleazy and too bound up with degradation to allow any kind of wholesale enjoyment. Of course this will fly in the face of the fantasists, but the reality of prostitution usually does. A woman's feelings here range between mild distaste and outright disgust and only in unique or very exceptional circumstances will her experience be any different. That is not to say these unique and exceptional experiences do not, once in a blue moon, occur. For some women, they do, and when they do, no-one is more surprised than the woman herself. I would know, because on two occasions those experiences happened to me.

When I was sixteen I was released from a court order, the purpose of which had been to keep me detained for my own protection. It did not have the required effect. The reason for this was clear, and I still wonder how the children's court could have been so foolish as to imagine that a few months of detention would have turned my life around when I was released back onto the streets with no viable alternative to prostitution. If they'd had any real dedication to helping me change my life, they would have detained me for a couple of years and made it a condition of my future parole that I complete some form of training, be it secretarial, hairdressing, etc., and I would have been assigned a parole officer and social worker who'd have ensured I was placed with an apprenticeship or in an entry-level office position. It wouldn't have been rocket science, it could have been done and I know I would have been capable of applying myself to it. Anyway, this did not happen; I was released after a few months and it was at this point I went to live in the brothel on Leeson Street I've previously described.

The first car that pulled up on my first night back on the streets was driven by a young man in his early to mid-twenties. He was attractive, not disrespectful in his manner and he was shy, quiet, not speaking to me much on the way to the laneway I used. When we arrived there I realised that I was aroused. I hadn't seen my then boyfriend for months and hadn't had any intimacy. I suddenly realised that I missed it; I missed being held and touched. I told him that I'd changed my mind, that I would do intercourse, so he slipped on a condom and it was all over in minutes. He pulled out his wallet and asked how much he owed me. It was the first time I'd ever done anything sexual without being paid first and I knew why: this was not a job.

Nothing would have felt more unnatural than taking money for something sexual that I'd *wanted* to happen. Also I had never had intercourse for money at that point, I had never sold myself in that way, and I didn't want to be able to say that I had. I told him not to worry about it. No doubt he knew something strange had happened but it was easy not to see his expression in the dark. He dropped me back down to the street and then I went to work for real.

What happened that night is not something that could be seen as prostitution. An act of prostitution had been intended on both sides but none had taken place. What happened actually transcended the prostitution experience: wilful intercourse with zero mental reservations is not prostitution, and could not, to my mind, be framed as such. My co-workers did not share my views. They roundly agreed that in not taking the money I was: 'A fuckin' eejit!'

The second of these experiences happened about three years after that. I was working in escort prostitution at the time. I called to the house of a man who had a beautiful face with a gentle relaxed smile and eyes as brown and shining as polished chestnuts. He welcomed me with a lovely soft English accent and poured me a glass of chilled white wine. I almost never drank on the job and certainly not with a new customer, but for a combination of reasons I broke the rules that night with that man.

Everything in his home was warm; the colours, the smells, the textures. It was all amber and mahogany and the scent of cinnamon. The vibe was very gentle, very neutral. I was relaxed and at my ease. That in itself was highly unusual. I have already described how a woman in prostitution knows when she needs to be alert: she also knows when she doesn't, but because the former situation is by far the most common, in a converse way, situations like this contain more surprise.

He had hired me for two hours and was obviously not rushed. Sitting on his sofa, I realised there was so little tension in me there was almost none; I was not worried about where this was going. I was not mentally bracing myself the way I always did. I was not constructing the wall, not fully. I wasn't given to suspect that I was going to need it. The bald truth was that there was something about this man and this environment that was soothing, relaxing, and seductive.

When we went to bed I found that I didn't mind his hands on me. The first indicator was that I didn't feel repulsed, as I always did. His hands were smooth but firm and slow in their movements. They were not invasive, not intrusive, and when he stroked me it was from the base of my neck to the curve of my calf; he seemed to adore my whole body with his hands. He did nothing to me physically to signify his domination, which was as unfamiliar as to frame the experience as unique in itself. When he gently parted my legs and entered me, I inadvertently let out a little gasp. Then he muttered in my ear: 'You don't have to pretend you like it'. That was when the nature of the experience changed.

This was a very well-mannered man. Apparently decent, he seemed thoughtful. Besides the obvious point of his purchasing me, he was not overtly disrespectful (it would not have been possible to feel arousal for him if he was) but as for the way he viewed me and my part in this experience: he thought I wouldn't like it. He thought he knew I wouldn't like it, and, like so many others before him, his arousal was dependent on the fact that I would not.

Immediately I understood this and felt my response shut down. The wall had sprung up. I felt very disconnected from my own body, as usual, but not for the usual reasons. This time I hadn't stepped out of my body; I had stayed inside it, and found that I wasn't welcome there.

It was very surreal, the rest of that sex. I was as far away from myself as I have ever been, and it was such a strange and deeply disconcerting feeling, lying there feeling all the sensations that would have been arousing had I been welcome to inhabit my own body. For those who talk of prostitution as work, know this: the core skill of a prostitute's 'work' is learning to stay outside of herself for her own sake.

So as for these two experiences: the first was not a sexually pleasurable experience within prostitution; it was a sexually pleasurable experience which had been taken out of the realms of prostitution, because sexual pleasure was not congruent with it. And as for the second: it could have been a sexually pleasurable experience had I not been reminded how surplus to requirements a woman in prostitution is. Her body is useful—the rest of her is irrelevant, and unwelcome. Only if a woman were a masochist, deeply aroused by her own degradation, would it be possible for her to frame this reality as arousing.

As for the overall dearth of a prostitute's sexual pleasure, I have not needed to wonder about that and even if I had I would have been reminded by the bouts of sexual dysfunction I have experienced while writing this book, particularly during periods when I was writing a lot and processing larger quantities of unwelcome memories every day.

The myth of prostitutes' sexual pleasure exists as one of several tactics which are used to sanitise and normalise the prostitution experience. The reasoning behind this is simple: if it is seen to be pleasurable for *some* women, then it couldn't be all that bad for women generally, could it? This is nonsense, and like most nonsense, it exists for a reason: framing prostitution as acceptable is that reason. It is not the only tactic used to this end, there are several.

The two unusual and isolated experiences I've recounted do not point to the existence of prostitutes' sexual pleasure. They attest to the opposite, because the first of the times I experienced pleasure from a man I met in this way, the experience had to be wholly contorted into its opposite before it was acceptable to me; and the second time I experienced pleasure it had to, necessarily, be rejected. In both cases, my pleasurable responses were incongruent with prostitution. Female pleasure does not belong in prostitution, and both male and female participants intuitively understand it has no place there.

Perhaps my two experiences will be malformed and misrepresented so as to serve as evidence for those who would prefer to see prostitution filtered through the prism of erotica, but a person who draws conclusions from logic will deduce that such a very tiny sampling does not colour any experience as a whole. The simple reality is that if you are heterosexual and you meet thousands of members of the opposite sex over a span of several years, you are likely to find at least a very tiny number of them sexually appealing. The fact that I felt this way towards two men out of thousands does not attest to any type of enjoyment in the prostitution experience; it attests to the opposite, because there were surely many more men among them who would have presented as appealing had I met them in any other way. It was the context in which I met them that negated their appeal. This is just more evidence of the way prostitution pollutes human interpersonal relations. The vast majority of men are immediately discounted as unappealing to prostituted women, because of the manner in which they are presented to them. It is only in exceptional and very unusual circumstances that something may happen to cause a woman to feel differently.

Women's actual responses to prostitution are sometimes recognised, inadvertently, by the proponents of prostitution:

'Descriptions of the psychological harm of prostitution sometimes come from its advocates. For example, the NZPC[12] wrote in an unpublished flyer that people in prostitution know they should take a break from prostitution: "when every client makes your skin crawl, when your jaw aches from clenching your teeth to prevent yourself spitting in the bastard's face . . . [or] when you can't stand what you see when you look in the mirror."' (NZPC flyer by Michelle, circa 1994)
MELISSA FARLEY
BAD FOR THE BODY, BAD FOR THE HEART

Women who need to be administered such advice are clearly not living a lifestyle liable to cause sexual arousal.

The myth of prostitutes' sexual pleasure is somewhat related to another social myth that goes something along the lines of 'women in prostitution desire to be rescued by a man'. Where this myth is entertained in prostitution, it is by men and not women. We are keenly aware that if we are to be rescued, the ones doing the rescuing can only be ourselves. This myth was exemplified by the film *Pretty Woman,* which sees the lead character rescued from prostitution by the love of a man. I do not find this film hugely offensive, although it caused a great deal of offence in prostitution circles. I feel the way I do because the film does not seek to colour the prostitution experience as generally enjoyable. Julia Roberts' character is clearly unhappy in prostitution and relates the fact in a tearful scene. I did think, though, that if the filmmakers wanted to depict the reality of prostitution, we should have seen Julia's character with more than one john. As for the fact that the prostitute here is depicted as falling in love with one of her clients: I do not contend the scenario is impossible, only

---

12 New Zealand Prostitutes' Collective.

that it is *highly* unlikely. It is possible to fall in love anywhere in life, but there are some areas where you will find an extreme dearth of love in the human experience. Prostitution is one of them.

I remember when I was fifteen and had been in prostitution just a couple of months, yet another forty-something man picked me up; this one in an ugly dark-green car. I remember that he looked at me with his eyes bugging out of his head and was practically salivating at the sight of me. We drove to a spot of his choosing (this was in the days before I learned better than to allow a man choose where we would go) and when he stopped the car he turned to me and poured out what was on his mind that had him so excited. He said that he had seen me on Blessington Street a year or so before and that he'd 'got a hard-on' looking at me. (The bed-and-breakfast accommodation I'd been housed in a year before had been on Blessington Street. I had been fourteen years old at the time.) He said, 'I couldn't believe my luck' at having found me on Benburb Street a year later. I sat in that car as he groped my breasts, pulled his prick and shoved his fingers into my vagina, and I willed myself to become numb as I tried to blank out what he was doing, along with memories of the year before, and thoughts of how naïve I'd been then, and of what a dirty fucking bastard he was to be behaving like this now and to have been thinking like that then.

I cannot number the experiences I've had, but I can very clearly put a shape on my responses to them. The bottom line is this: when a man, who has paid you twenty or two hundred euro for the pleasure of watching you squirm, twists your clitoris with the fingertips of one hand while simultaneously shoving his fingers up your vagina and biting and licking your nipples with his tongue and teeth, you will experience many things. You will struggle to block out many internal responses. Arousal will not be among them.

Chapter 17 ~

THE MYTH OF PROSTITUTES' CONTROL

Testimony of a sex buyer: "I guess the big thing is the control aspect of it. When you're with a prostitute, you have control of what happens. You get to have control over what you do, when, how, in what order, and I like that."
M FARLEY, E SCHUCKMAN, J M GOLDING, K HOUSER,
L JARRETT, P QUALLIOTINE, M DECKER, *COMPARING SEX BUYERS WITH MEN WHO DON'T BUY SEX*

On no level and in no area of prostitution did we have true and full control. Nor were we assumed by the men who paid us to have any or to be due any. The same line of thinking was held by the authorities.

At sixteen years of age I presented myself at Donnybrook garda station. I had been assaulted by a punter and went to the station with the intention of lodging a complaint; this was in 1992. I explained the circumstances to the young male garda at the front desk. He laughed at me. I left, and I never approached the gardaí again.

I had assumed, in my teenage naïveté, that since I had been assaulted, I was entitled to legal recourse. It was a demeaning and revealing shock to understand this garda's position, which was that it was either not possible for a prostitute to be assaulted or not relevant if she was. There was a sense of abandonment in this understanding, a sense of being socially disowned.

If prostitutes are not protected by society's laws, how can society expect prostitutes to be bound by them? There is a great deal of entwinement between the way a prostitute is treated by society and the way she relates to society in return. Prostitutes are disqualified and excluded by society's authority structures and encouraged to remove themselves further until they exist entirely outside of the remit of social control; the only exception to this is when the authorities step in to see to it that they are punished. We were afforded no protection in law, but we regularly found ourselves at the rough end of it. Not only had we no control, but we quickly learned to have no expectation of it either.

I had not been sexually molested the night I called to the garda station, just dragged around by the hair and slapped, as was almost customary, but I was sick of it at that point. I had gotten the registration of the car and was determined that this man would not be allowed to get away with venting his hatred upon me, but he was, of course; and that night in the garda station was just one of my earlier lessons in understanding that, and that it was also almost customary. In those times a prostitute had to have been murdered or at the very least taken to the edge of death before anyone in authority would take the time to recognise that a crime had taken place.

In recent years, though, the situation has alleviated at least. The police began working with Ruhama in the years after I left the streets and set up a panel to coordinate with the women in order that their complaints would be heard. This is a positive thing as far as I'm concerned, but I have no personal experience of it. The only experience I had of the gardaí in prostitution was of being harassed when I didn't need them around and ignored when I did. I don't know if the liaising body that was set up after I left the streets is still in existence, but I hope that it is for the sake of the women who still work there.

As I've already said, the only thing approaching control to be found anywhere in prostitution, in my experience, was either in the selection and rejection process on the streets or the behaviour of women who exclusively saw a number of regular clients they'd built up over the years. I was in the former position for my first two years or so and the latter position towards the end, so I can attest to that. However, these two scenarios offer only a modicum of control, and even so, the majority of prostitutes exist outside of both these circumstances.

Control is not only diminished for the prostituted woman within the confines of her working hours. On a practical level, the prostituted woman is unable to frame her experience of many facets of her life, including relationships, in the way a non-prostituted woman takes for granted. She has a much-reduced level of control over her future in that prostitution is very difficult to get out of; and she has no control whatever over the lingering effects of the past, in that all those who know of her involvement will view her through the skewed and negative prism of who they presume her to be. Nor has the prostitute any control over being consistently vilified as the central point of society's sexual ills. She has no control whatever of the public perception of her, besides of course concealing that she is a participant in this way of life that is so wholly and generally disrespected. This duplicitous concealment is the only weapon she can use to protect herself from the judgement and contempt inevitable for the women in her sphere of life.

Beyond any of this, her lack of control does not stop at the end of prostitution, if she reaches an end. I myself wrestled with a much-reduced level of control here, fourteen years after the fact, in that I felt I could not speak publicly as I wanted to, without the use of a pseudonym. My decision-making wrangle was strongly influenced by negative perceptions over which I had absolutely no choice or control. I'm glad I did the right thing by myself in the end. I'm glad I chose to write under my own name.

Prostitution is essentially an issue that centres on the misuse of power—male power. It is universally accepted that those in command of greater fiscal resources are in a dominant position over those who are not, and the reality of women's entry into prostitution due to financial hardship has been uncovered in prostitution research globally, in country after country after country, again and again and again. Therefore, it is obvious that there is exploitation here. The exploitation element is indisputable, and the most succinct description of exploitation? An abuse of power. Women are quite obviously not in control in this area. If they were, men would hardly be capable of abusing a power they didn't have.

The belief that prostitutes are in control has no basis in reality, but it has two practicable functions, related but distinct: to sanitise and excuse the economic and sexual abuse of women by men, and to obscure the core of prostitution's true nature: the commercialisation of sexual abuse.

Sometimes prostitutes themselves collude in the myth of prostitutes' control. I have already described how and why I have done this myself and how other women engage in it. So yes, we sometimes claimed that we were in control, and we said so to ourselves and to non-prostituted others; but I have noticed that we never said so to each other. Some lies are embarrassingly obvious; but we did make that claim elsewhere and we said so not because it was true, but because we had to. We said so because we needed to. We said so because the pretence of control was less painful and less shameful than the acceptance of sexual powerlessness. This doesn't prove that we weren't victimised: it proves that we didn't like being reminded of it.

For a long time, I was ashamed of my own collusion in the fantasy of prostitutes' control and angry with myself because of it, but I don't feel that way towards myself any more, or at least, I am trying not to. I understand today why I misrepresented my feelings and I know I ought to forgive myself for having obscured the truth in order to protect myself from it. Sexual abuse induces shame. That fact is universally recognised. To be ashamed privately is painful. To be ashamed publicly is torturous. The pretence of control conceals and assuages these shameful feelings. The nullification of public shame is the main aim of prostitutes' pretence at control. A lot of prostituted women do this and I understand their position utterly—but the bitter truth needs to be exposed if prostitution is to be accorded its true nature, and the truth here is this: prostitution is defined by a lack of control.

If prostitution were an arena of life in which women had control, we would hardly have had to endure the innumerable sexually abusive experiences which depended on the lack of it. These situations were breathed into life by our powerlessness and, more specifically, by men's decisions to capitalise on it. The countless clients who derived great pleasure from our lack of control were not mistaken in their interpretations of the situation. They were very well aware of our powerlessness and very much aroused by it. The only thing approaching positive I could say about them was that at least these perverts made an honest appraisal of the situation, though I very much doubt they would have publicly declared it. A great many of the men who use women in prostitution get off principally on the power element and it is not necessary for most of them to beat a woman in order to do this. There is no doubting the intensity of the sexual thrill men derive from the elevation of their power status in prostitution, although the majority of them will deny it. These denials attest to their reading of their own conduct as wrong, as is so often the case when a person deliberately omits the driving force behind their own actions.

This deliberate omission of prostitution's power-imbalanced nature is an extremely common fiction among the buyers of sex, but it is not the only one. There are a minority of men who use prostitutes who will espouse the belief that prostitutes are in control because they believe it (and among these I do not count those who simply *want* to believe it; they belong in the former camp).

Some men will cite examples to back up their certainties. Usually these will refer to the fact that most prostitutes try to impose physical boundaries on the sexual act. It is true that they do. I avoided vaginal intercourse for the first two years of my prostitution life and anal intercourse for all of it. That is very unusual. I met many women who would never perform anal sex; that was not at all unusual. One particular young woman I met in my first months on the streets would not perform oral sex, ever. She just could not stand to do it and she could not understand how I was of the opposite mindset. I clearly remember her wrinkling her nose up in disgust and shuddering when I told her that all of my jobs were either hand-relief or oral.

There was always something a prostitute was unwilling to do, some threshold over which she would not wilfully allow a client to go. These were our choices, or our attempts at choices, because we all suffered outright sexual molestation, which obviously in those instances nullified any choices we attempted to make. Often a man would molest a woman in exactly the way he knew she least wanted to be molested, to maximise his own sadistic pleasure, of course. It was not difficult for a man to ascertain this: in the 1990s, all he had to do was ask her what she was willing to do or not to do either on the street, over the phone, or when he was alone with her in a hotel or brothel's bedroom. These days it's even easier; he'll know her boundaries before he lays eyes on her, because it will say so on her profile page posted on the brothel's website.

So yes, some men who try to justify their use of prostitutes will use the fact that women say no to certain sex acts as evidence that it is the women who are in control here, but it is flawed evidence. It is either misguided on the part of a man or it is a clumsy attempt at lying.

I can say from my own experience and from witnessing the experiences of many others that prostitutes attempt to create boundaries on the sexual act based on personal sexual thresholds over which it is simply too sickening to go. This meant for me only that a penis in my mouth was less sickening, not that it was not sickening at all; and since we did (and we certainly did) accept for ourselves that which was sexually sickening, could we possibly be said to have been in control?

Accepting the sexually sickening on a reduced level is part of the lot of the working prostitute. I could not count the times I've heard this discussed in prostitution.

These boundaries exist as an attempt to create a barrier between the prostitute and the intolerable experience of having her body used in every way imaginable. It is a typical strategy used by prostitutes to remove themselves from the fullness of their reality; it is dissociation manifesting in a physical sense. To use this strategy as evidence of prostitutes' 'control' is to misunderstand and misrepresent the reason for the existence of these boundaries. We did not attempt to erect boundaries in prostitution because we were in control of it; we attempted to erect boundaries in order to be able to stand it. If you need to erect barriers between yourself and a situation in order to be able to stand it, that is a situation in which you are most assuredly *not* in control.

The argument has been made that prostitution ought to be condoned in response to prostituted women's right to 'self-determination'. This is a term we should pay close and careful attention to when used in this context. Self-determination is the process by which a person controls their own life, but there is a significant difference between controlling your finances and controlling the totality of your life.

There have been countless studies conducted globally that show women's desire to extricate themselves from prostitution, but to keep things closer to home, I will cite the Haughey and Bacik analysis, 'A Study of Prostitution in Dublin'.[13] In this study, twenty-nine out of thirty prostituted women stated that they 'would accept an alternative job with equal pay'. The authors of this study noted that the single interviewee who did not agree with that statement appeared to be under the influence of some substance at the time of the interview. That sounds about right to me, given everything I've seen in prostitution. The survival strategies of defiance and denial were most commonly practised by those who were so injured by prostitution as to have to block out their reality with alcohol and other mind-altering drugs, and I certainly number my younger self among them.

Let us suppose though that the thirtieth woman in this study was being honest, since we have only the interviewer's opinion to suggest otherwise. Even in that case, we still have clear evidence that the overwhelming majority of women interviewed would rather earn their money in some other way than prostituting themselves, if they possibly could. What this proves is that those women were practising *financial* determination in prostitution, only because they could not practise it in any other way. Financial determination is only one facet of self-determination.

Another popular pro-prostitution fantasy is that prostituted women ought to be able to use their bodies as they so choose; the problem with that theory is that it is *others* who use the bodies of prostituted women as *they* so choose. That is the intention and the purpose and the *function* of prostitution, and there isn't a whit of bodily autonomy within it.

It is saddening to me now to look back and see how we used to scramble for any little bit of control we could exert. It is saddening because it speaks so clearly of how little there was to be found, and of how much we wanted to find it. In describing this it would

---

13 Conducted with funding from the Department of Justice, Equality and Law Reform, Trinity College, June 2000.

be useful to look again at the most universally recognised, yet least understood of all areas of prostitution: street prostitution. Although street prostitution is unique among the differing forms of prostitution in that it is the only single area of the business in which a woman has the opportunity to exercise any level of control, very often the decisions we made would be influenced by factors we had no control over. Very often you would be cold, you would be wet, you would be tired, you would be bored, you would be depressed, and all of these factors would play a part in your decision whether or not to get into a punter's car. Sometimes, while shivering in the cold, I was influenced in getting into cars simply because I could feel the warmth emanating from the rolled-down drivers' window. Many times I got into cars against my better judgement because I had not made enough money. Surely when a woman must ritually forgo her own safety the lack of control is obvious?

On the issue of safety: many of the women who work exclusively indoors come to do so in the first place because they believe it to be safer and they continue to believe so because they have nothing to compare it to. Some of them at first believe the nonsense they are told when a pimp or madam assures them that their clients are 'screened', but their clients are not screened, and it is not even possible that they could be.

How exactly do they contend that their clients are screened? And screened for what exactly? The only way a man could be successfully screened for the benefit of the woman he was using would be if a full police background check were carried out to ensure he had no history of violence against women, and that, I can assure you, does *not* happen.

Certainly there are regulars to particular agencies and a pimp or madam can make an experience-based judgement as to what a particular client's behaviour is likely to be and also, they can authoritatively say that a particular man has no history of violence with *their* agency. This may be comforting to the prostitute, but there is no guarantee that this will not be the night he chooses to show himself in a very different light. Nor is there any guarantee that he does not have a history of violence in any other agency or in his personal life.

To arrive at the home or hotel room of a man you have never met with a fixed idea in your mind as to how he is liable to behave when you are alone is one of the most dangerous things a woman in prostitution can do, and most women figure that out for themselves very early on in their 'careers'.

The nature of punters' consumerism in prostitution is a transitory one. They will often ring a different agency each time they hire a prostitute. This is well-known in prostitution circles and I know it personally because I've come across the same men many times through different agencies. When a man has behaved violently he will not call the same agency again; he will call a different one. For this reason the most unpredictable men you can meet are those who have never called the agency before, and there are brand new clients like these to contend with every day of the week.

Unlike the street prostitute, who can call on all of her senses and faculties in the weighing-up of a decision, the brothel or escort prostitute is stripped of almost all of them if she is working for herself, and absolutely all of them if she is not. When I had to move indoors after the Sexual Offences Act of 1993, I found it tremendously frustrating and risky to continually be in the situation where I could not use my senses in order to filter the men who would and would not use my body. It was not long before this new situation proved itself to be as hazardous as I'd sensed it to be. I met many men in this way who I would not have entertained had I met them on the streets. I am not surprised to find that higher levels of violence as compared to street prostitution have been uncovered in 'strip clubs, massage brothels and pornography' by international research.[14]

The point to remember here is that the reason a woman working in a massage parlour or escort agency has no choice in the men who will use her is because it is simply not permissible for her to turn down potential clients and thus lose commission for her employer. My situation was somewhat different at times, including after 1993, when I began advertising an escort agency myself. In this situation I was able to attempt to

---

14 Debra Boyer, Lynn Chapman, Brent Marshall, 'Survival Sex in King County: Helping Women Out', 1993.

filter dangerous or undesirable individuals, but of course, as I've said, I was attempting to do this with a much minimised scope for garnering the details I needed in order to make even a reasonable guess. I had simply to rely on the attitude and tone of voice of the man on the other end of the phone.

I remember on one particular occasion a man asked: 'How much *is she*?' in a very smarmy and condescending tone. I knew immediately the type of man I'd have been dealing with had I been foolish enough to meet him, because I'd met the likes of him enough times before. I responded that, '*She* isn't actually for sale; she is renting her time by the hour', before hanging up the phone. Arseholes are everywhere in life. They're particularly prevalent in prostitution.

It was about between the years 1994 and 1996 that I worked for two well-known Irish madams. The thing that surprised me about working for one of these women was that her brothel was like a ghost town, mostly because of the high degree of coverage she got from the tabloid press, which maintained all through the 1990s that she was the most prolific madam Ireland had ever seen. That was media hype if ever I've seen it.

The other of these women was quite a kind person in my experience, contrary to media reports I later read, which branded her a horrible and ruthless woman to work for. I met her first on a dark winter's evening at the gates of Trinity College. She was operating her business from an apartment on South Great George's Street at the time. I can't remember who suggested the meeting point, but if it was me, I don't know what I was thinking. I felt so dejected standing there, surrounded by throngs of students on their way home from being educated in the country's most prestigious university, while I waited for the opportunity to sell myself. I told her that I didn't want to have full sexual intercourse and I will always remember her saying to me, in no uncertain terms: 'Nobody is going to try to make you do anything you don't want to do here, love'. This was an unusual practice in prostitution and it has stuck in my mind because of that. She later died a violent and horrible death, and I was sorry to hear of it.

But her words, well-intentioned though they were, gave me cause to reflect in later years on the contorted and convoluted notion of control within prostitution. Nobody was going to make me do anything I didn't want to do in that apartment; no *body*, but prostitution itself demanded I do things I didn't want to do every day.

Chapter 18

THE LOSSES OF PROSTITUTION

By an image we hold onto our lost treasures, but it is the wrenching loss that forms the image, composes, binds the bouquet.

COLETTE, *MES APPRENTISSAGES*

The overriding feeling when reflecting on the experience of prostitution is simply this: loss. Loss of innocence, loss of time, of opportunity, credibility, respectability, and the spiritually ruinous loss of connectedness to the self. I could go on and on, but the primary element is always loss. The battle continues forever against the loss of self-worth. There is no magical shift back to your former self on the day you leave prostitution. You do begin the task of reclaiming what is left of your former self, as I have said; but how much is really left? And how qualified are you now, permanently altered as you are, to identify it?

I cannot identify all that is left of me after the mental and emotional carnage of prostitution, but I do know that this book, this dissection of the prostitution experience, comes from a place inside me that rejects prostitution on a very deep level, both for myself and for other women; and so I know that whatever it was that drove me to write it is something that prostitution did not manage to destroy. How much is really left I do not know, but this much is left, enough to make this effort, and I am glad of that.

The general assessment is that prostitution involves a very private loss, which of course it does, but I do not know how well people consider the numerous other losses it disseminates. This is understandable to me as I doubt I would ever have had cause to consider them much had I not been prostituted myself. Because the business of prostitution creates and is then carried out in a highly depersonalised environment, the focus of the commodification has no option but to begin to accept the depersonalisation of her own self.

Loss connects all the negativities in prostitution. It is both the dominant ingredient and the binding agent; it makes up the basic flavour and brings together all the other components of this recipe.

The losses to the prostituted individual are limitless. They are limitless not only because they are innumerable but also because there is no cap, no ceiling, no time-frame limit on when they will cease intruding into a woman's life. There also are no socially accepted boundaries which a woman can erect between prostitution and herself. The common saying: 'Once a whore always a whore' makes reference to this. A woman may be a former prostitute of several years, like myself, who worries about the impact of her history on her child, or she may be a former prostitute decades older than me who worries about the teasing and bullying of her grandchildren. The losses here are of safety and security, dignity, reputation and social status. They are old losses and hold no surprises, but they are horrible losses to see projected onto our loved ones. It is both heart-wrenching and nauseating to see those we love tarred with shame by association here.

There is another loss I hesitated to include here; it is the loss of humanity. I hesitated to include it because I do not believe I was ever less than human in my life, but I certainly know I was treated as if I were. In prostitution, men dehumanise women and women dehumanise themselves in order to be able to perform the acts men require of them. This does not mean that women are made less than human; it means that they are treated as such and operate in an environment in which they must not only accept such treatment from others, but actively seek it and learn to deliver it to themselves. And yes, there is loss here: it is the loss of the belief in and the experience of your own humanity. And what is the loss of anything if not the loss of connectedness to it? In that sense, I lost my humanity. I lost my humanity in that I lost touch with it. While I never quite forgot about it, I pretended, because I was paid to pretend, that it was of no consequence. There are areas of life where it is necessary to buy into certain untruths. My environment told me my humanity didn't matter, and I needed to believe that. Why? —Because it is easier to detach from an irrelevance.

There is also the loss I've mentioned to prostituted women as a group. Sadly, and in a sense paradoxically, one of the biggest losses to prostituted women as a group is derived from the fact that they are a group. It is in the fact that they must acknowledge and accept that they are collectively removed from the rest of society, and behave as such, and comfort each other in the knowing of it.

For my own sake, I believe I was lucky to have the company of other prostituted women. They understood me. They didn't judge me. We couldn't judge each other; but our very connection as a group solidified our separation from the rest of society. Yes, certainly we would have been worse off had we been removed from society individually, but, in a physical sense at least, we were not, and our coming together as a group was a natural convergence. There were positives and negatives in this, and of the negatives, the principal ones were defined by loss. We shared a collective lack of social standing and a dearth of respect from the world. We understood this, intensely, painfully. This was particularly obvious to me during my street-walking years. Besides the men who'd come there to seek us out, I don't think any member of the public ever walked by us without a wary glance and a quickening of the step. Had any of them any idea what a normal casual 'Good evening girls', would have meant, I wonder?

To be excluded as part of a group may not sound as horrendous as being excluded as an individual, and if those two methods of exclusion worked independently of each other it would be true that it is not, but the truth for all those who are excluded as part of a group is that they are excluded as individuals also. They are debarred and expelled on both counts. This is not only true of prostitutes; it is true of the members of all socially excluded groups.

Prostitution clearly promotes the depersonalisation of sex, which can never be good news for women—any women. Prostitution has a ripple effect. It creates the illusory view in the minds of men that women are not human beings as men are, but simply the walking carrier of a product, and that they serve one principal function, whether or not they are paid for it, which is to be used as vessels for the sexual release of men. By this mechanism, they are effortlessly and imperceptibly relegated from the realms of the human. They are not considered people on a par with their male counterparts. How could they be, when their principal function is as something to be fucked?

Prostitution obscures women's humanity from society generally, but it also causes women specifically to lose sensitivity to their own humanity by way of tolerating the prostitution of others of their gender. When women tolerate prostitution they are actually tolerating the dehumanisation of their own gender in a broader and more encompassing sense.

Countries with male-majority governments are implementing the legalisation of prostitution with frightening rapidity throughout the western world. Where is the female revolt towards all this? There is no widespread female revolt because female sexuality has so long been viewed as a commodity that woman have begun to believe in the necessity of a separate class of women to provide it.

If a woman tolerates this treatment of her fellow women, if she accepts it under the banner of 'liberalism' or anything else, then she must also accept that she herself is only removed from prostitution by lack of the circumstances necessary to place her there. Should these circumstances ever occur, her body, too, would be just as welcome for mauling, sucking and fucking by the clients of the brothels and would be just as reviled by the men who are on the look-out for a wife. The acceptance of prostitution makes *all* women potential prostitutes in the public view since there are only two requirements for a woman to work in a brothel: one is that circumstance has placed her so (and who knows when that can happen, to any of us?) and the other is that she has a vagina, and all women are born meeting at least one of these requirements.

It bears repeating: if the commodification of women is to be accepted then all women fall under that potential remit. If a woman accepts prostitution in society, then she accepts this personal indenture, whether she knows it or not; and yes, that is a loss.

As with women, not only participation in prostitution but even tolerance of prostitution causes men to lose their sensitivity to feminine humanity. Tolerance of prostitution clearly cannot exist in any man until he has formed the view that the commodification of women is tolerable.

I think one of the major losses to men, possibly the largest of them all, is the casual attitude they are encouraged to develop towards sexual intimacy, which allows them to slip their penises into female flesh with as little consideration to the female involved as if they were satiating their urges on mute and immobile non-living things, and sadly, in many ways, this is just what prostitutes must train themselves to be. Mute and immobile, docile and non-complaining, prostituted women are programmed to behave like non-humans.

But how does this influence male-to-female interpersonal relations generally, given that these men are fathers, brothers, husbands, sons and partners to women themselves? Men also suffer loss to their own humanity here; huge, undocumented, unexamined loss.

When I was fifteen or sixteen and working on Benburb Street a man somewhere in his forties brought his teenage son down to the street to buy him his way out of his virginity. It was a gift, in this man's understanding. He stopped the car beside me and explained the situation. I wasn't selling intercourse anyway at the time and told him this. Probably because I was around his son's age, whereas all the other women were much older, he asked me would I give his son oral sex instead. I couldn't do it. There was something inexpressibly sick about what he was asking me to do. I couldn't have articulated what exactly about it bothered me so much since I gave blow-jobs to strangers every day; I just knew that I felt a very strong instinctual sense of revulsion, stronger than usual. I know today that it was this up-close-and-personal view of a father training his son to treat women like meat that made me so repulsed. I couldn't be a part of that, and I wasn't. I walked away. Thinking about that day now though, and thinking about the teenage boy in that car, I can't help but wonder about what sort of man he has become.

If the view of women a father passes on to his own son is that they are simply things to be bought and fucked, I have to wonder what sort of husbands boys like that will grow up to be? What sort of partners? What sort of fathers? This desensitisation of men towards sexual intimacy with women is itself a very great loss to them; I believe it stops them functioning in their relationships to anything like the fullest extent of their potential. If a man has been taught to think of women as less than human, then he has, as a consequence of this skewed indoctrination, lost a human being for a partner. If women are so devalued in his eyes, then he has been robbed of the company of a woman he can value.

It is not the only loss men suffer, however. Any man who's ever discovered the pain of finding the body of a woman he loves being treated as a receptacle for other men's sperm will know the pain I am referring to when I say that many men have been wounded by the existence of prostitution in this world. The same is true for any man who has formed an unhealthy reliance on prostitution as a sexual outlet. How can a man's self-esteem be anything but damaged by the understanding that the only way he can experience sexual intimacy is to buy it? How can his sense of self be subject to anything but loss in this circumstance?

A certain segment of society maintains that prostitution is all fine and dandy as long as it is populated only by those women who wish to frequent it. This view ignores the vast spectrum of realities which exist outside this fantasy. It also clearly infers that those women and girls who do not wish to prostitute themselves should simply ignore prostitution as an option and go on their way. But the fact is, when you are fifteen years old and destitute, too unskilled to work and too young to claim unemployment benefit, your body is all you have left to sell. That is the reason why prostitution and other areas of the sex industry are populated in the main by young women and girls from lower socio-economic groups. Combinations of the losses of prostitution are reflected here: they are the losses of opportunity, autonomy and viable choice.

Since the truth is that the women in prostitution are overwhelmingly made up of those who feel they have no other viable option, how can prostitution possibly be framed as an area of life that should only be populated by those who wish to frequent it? If prostitution were open only to those who sincerely wished without reservation to sell their own bodies, prostitution would be dealt such a hammer-blow it would all but disappear from the face of the earth.

There are simply too many forms of loss involved in an individual experience of prostitution to document. The losses of prostitution are another area that could easily make up a large volume on their own. As for my own losses, there is one loss that stands above all others and could be used an as umbrella term to describe the prostitution experience in its totality. In that sense the story of what happened to me could have been written much more concisely than it was. The summation of my experience of prostitution was simply this: *I lost myself.*

Because everywhere in prostitution there is inevitably loss, there are many ways of measuring it. It's measured for me most clearly, I think, in the way I lost the connection to the fluidity of my physicality. When I was a girl of fourteen and living in my first hostel we would all routinely get dressed up and go to the nightclub La Mirage, which was situated just minutes from where we lived in the centre of town. Probably because I was the youngest the older girls would have fun dressing me up and making me up and teaching me how to dance. Once I got the hang of it I enjoyed dancing and thought it was great fun. I remember a very blissful feeling that I now know came from the experience of fully owning and being present in my own body. Then I became a prostitute, and I never danced after that.

Today, at weddings or parties or celebrations of any kind, I make my excuses and sit at the table. Sometimes I invent dizziness or tiredness or sore ankles. Then I become embarrassed, and go to the bathroom, and then outside for a cigarette, and then up to the bar, whether my glass is empty or not. I'll order peanuts and crisps and bacon-fries. I am waiting. Waiting for others to stop doing the thing I can't.

How come I can have sex but not dance? Surely lovemaking should be the first thing to go? I don't know why. I can't give myself an answer I don't have. I only know that when I'm expected to dance, my body can't move. I freeze and lose touch with my physical self. Maybe my having worked as a stripper compounded it, but I had stopped dancing before that. The sexualised out-of-body 'dancing' of stripping was possible only because I did not have to connect to myself in order to do it.

So who knows? I don't. All I know is there is loss here, and that this is just one of the ways I can measure it. You cannot expect a woman to experience the commodification of her own body and suffer no physical consequences of that. It is beyond obvious that the degradation of the body will produce a negative effect that manifests in the body. Perhaps what we lose as a result of this is individual to all of us. Perhaps we experience loss in the body at the point where we most deeply connect to our own physicality. For me it was dancing. For another woman it might be sex, or the ability to physically give or receive affection. There is loss here—make no mistake about it—loss like a fracture, the deep and abiding kind; the kind that will never fully heal.

I think it is important to keep thinking about these things, but they are sometimes musings without conclusions, which can be mentally frustrating. At other times I can sense when I have arrived at an accurate understanding; I know the truth when I feel it. I cannot have been what most women could not have been, given time and place and the slow methodical drip-drip-dripping that is the wearing down of a particularly persuasive circumstance.

Whenever prostitution touches the point where the lives of a man and woman intersect there is a loss of civility and a deep and irreversible fracturing of human interpersonal connections. This is the case whether or not they come together to engage in a prostitution act. It was true of the three relationships I had while in prostitution, but none more so than the first of them, with the man who actually introduced me to it.

I have always known (and this is not an exercise in charitable thought but rather the recognition of a reality) that the ex-boyfriend who first brought me to Benburb Street is not a monster nor an evil person by nature, but simply somebody who was emotionally damaged enough to do such a thing. There is no excusing an act like that, but it is important to try to explain it, and excuses and explanations are not the same thing.

Really, how could such an act, the encouragement of a fifteen-year-old girl into prostitution, be carried out by somebody who could be considered mentally well with a healthily functioning sense of right from wrong? It couldn't, in my view; and how damaged must a person be in order to do that? The truth was, he was detached from the enormity of what he was suggesting because he'd been a rent boy himself. He, too, was operating from a position of loss.

I had heard rumours from friends of his that he had been a rent boy before we met and at the time I didn't believe them. (I also knew better than to put it to him.) He was a very masculine young man and the idea seemed far-fetched to me, but I see the truth of it now looking back because I can piece together the other parts of the puzzle that support it. He was homeless, as I've said, and the friend's house we were staying in turned out (when it's occupier arrived home after a few weeks in prison) to be the home of a gay man of around fifty years old who always called him by a name that was not his own. I guess my 'boyfriend' had had enough of what he was doing and in bringing me down to Benburb Street he was passing the baton from him to me.

I bumped into him in recent years and we had an uneasy association that lasted a few months. We each seemed to circle around the other, neither of us knowing how to deal with each other or what the present-day rules were. I didn't bring up the subject of Benburb Street; he did. He brought it up by way of denying, unprompted, that he'd ever had anything to do with that and tried to lay the responsibility at the door of the other homeless girl I mentioned in earlier chapters, who hadn't even been there on the day.

I looked at him as he repeated his denials. He was edgy, uncomfortable, rushing through the words in his hurry to get to the other side. His were the eyes of a man trapped and they made me think of how eyes might look if you looked into them behind the wrong side of prison bars; fearful, panicked, deeply unsettled; half full of the fear of the trap, half of the desire to escape.

I remembered, while looking at his face, the things he'd said that day on the way down to there; 'Don't do positions'. 'Don't let them near your tits'. And, absurdly, 'I'll give you the real McCoy when you get home'.

I didn't argue that day, many years after the fact, and I didn't respond either, to accept or reject his protestations. I simply told him: 'I'm not ready to talk about that now'. Instead I thought about his denials and eventually settled on the idea that I was glad he at least had enough shame now, after all these years, to deny culpability. And I am reminded here of a quote I've come across by Edmund Burke: 'While shame keeps its watch, virtue is not wholly extinguished in the heart'. I interpreted his denials as having made his shame apparent, and shame does not exist in a vacuum; it is not an unsupportable emotion; it cannot, in most cases, stand without a sense of guilt. Guilt and shame don't go hand in hand, but rather one obscures the other. If shame were a glove, I believe, guilt would be the hand inside it.

I took all this in while I was looking into his eyes and I saw a pleading in them, the wriggling away from blame. I had never seen that before, not in those eyes, but still, I didn't respond. Guilt and blame are old coals and, for the most part, the dust has settled on mine. His were still aflame, I perceived, while my own didn't seem worth raking over.

Do I forgive him? Not in the traditional sense of the word. He feels guilty, so much so that he cannot accept the share of blame logic apportions to him, and while he cannot accept his own responsibility he cannot ask for forgiveness, and so it follows that while he cannot ask for it, I cannot grant it in the conventional sense; but that does not mean there is no forgiveness here, and I do feel some sorrow on his behalf. His shame is different to mine. The weight of my shame relates to an inwardly directed injustice and I believe it is testament to the psychological wounding of my pre-prostitution life that I have always experienced that sort of shame as much more bearable than its opposite. That is to say, I have always felt it more endurable to let myself down than anyone else; but that is exactly the sort of unhealthy thinking that helped lead me into prostitution in the first place. I am learning the dangerousness of these thoughts in counselling today and doing my best to eradicate them. However, I know the feeling of having shamefully failed somebody else; I am acquainted with its heaviness, and I would not wish that weight on him, or on anyone.

There is an attitude I've come across that wonders, how can we forgive when there has been no apology? That an apology is a request for forgiveness and forgiveness the acceptance of an apology; that the two go hand-in-hand, one cannot be without the other, and that forgiveness cannot come without a total acceptance of responsibility and a strong sense of contrition by the offender.

This does not reflect my experience of life, so I can't believe it is true in all cases. Firstly, I think a genuine apology has no purpose other than to let the listener know that the speaker is sorry. There aren't (or ought not to be) any requests attached to it, not for forgiveness nor anything else. I've also come to understand that sometimes the 'strong sense of contrition by the offender' is expressed by the very violence with which they abdicate responsibility. Sometimes the lengths a person will go to in denying culpability directly reflect the measure of responsibility they charge themselves with in the privacy of their own mind. It is a cowardly way of dealing with the matter, for sure, but guilt and shame can make cowards of us all.

An attitude of contrition by the offender makes forgiveness easier, but who ever said forgiveness was supposed to be easy? Sometimes forgiveness takes a lot of introspection and the practical application of compassion, and maybe that's what's required in the absence of an apology.

Although I know forgiveness has happened here independent of either an apology or a request for it, I would be deeply moved if one day my former pimp asked me to forgive him, though I know he never will and it's kind of sad in a way, because unless he happens to read this book his refusal to accept culpability means he'll never know he was long-ago forgiven.

It's a strange cocktail of feeling to care for and despise someone at the same time, but I have done a lot of thinking over the many years that have passed since the days I felt that way and I have come to understand that if you say to somebody with your actions: 'It's okay to disrespect me', then you are not well placed to ask them with your words: 'Why was I disrespected?'[15] There is culpability here, and it exists on both sides. I had to come a long way within myself before I could accept (suffering

---

15 This truism cuts to the heart of prostitution: when you make yourself available for abuse it is so much the more difficult to identify your abuser as an abuser, and your abuse as abuse.

as I do from a particular human condition that affects us all—that need
to categorise as either guilty or blameless the participants in any volatile
situation) that I was culpable, I was blameworthy. I was guilty of betray-
ing myself, and that, I have come to understand, is every last bit as bad
as hurting someone else.

As for my ex-pimp and boyfriend, since the need for clearly identifying and separating the subjugators from the subjugated is so inherent to
the human psyche it will not surprise me, in fact I fully expect that some
people will be horrified to know there still exists between us a sort of sad
but abiding affection. To this day I would still offer him my help were
he in serious enough trouble to require it, and I know I could expect his
also. There is a strange caring still there. We are old friends who scarcely
ever see each other, who can scarcely look at each other, who share a
history too hurtful to talk about; too shameful to accept on his part and
too painful to dissect on mine. It should be clear that there is loss here;
complex, confusing, disturbing threads of loss.

Chapter 19 ～

MISCONCEPTIONS ABOUT PROSTITUTION

I want to bring us back to basics. Prostitution: what is it?
It is the use of a woman's body for sex by a man, he pays
money, he does what he wants. The minute you move
away from what it really is, you move away from pros-
titution into the world of ideas. You will feel better, you
will have a better time; it is more fun; there is plenty to
discuss, but you will be discussing ideas, not prostitution.
Prostitution is not an idea. It is the mouth, the vagina,
the rectum, penetrated usually by a penis, sometimes
hands, sometimes objects, by one man and then another
and then another and then another and then another.
That's what it is.

ANDREA DWORKIN,[16] *PROSTITUTION AND MALE*
SUPREMACY

There are a number of misconceptions about prostitution, some of which, such as the myths of prostitutes' control and pleasure, I have examined already. However, one question that has always bothered me is this: why is there so much hatred of prostitutes?

Prostitutes are in one of the least enviable positions in society. It does not make rational sense that they should be so despised. And yet, they are. I feel that this has to do with a misconception that prostitution is a feminine arena and that this is supported by the fact that females are the most visible, most documented, most discussed participants in this

---

16 Andrea Dworkin (1946–2005) was a feminist campaigner against pornography and prostitution. She had personal experience of homelessness and prostitution.

arena, because society consistently seeks to vilify the female in all matters of sexual misconduct. But the truth is, no matter what area of prostitution I worked in, there were always far more clients than prostitutes.

This is backed-up time and again by international research. In Thailand and Cambodia, studies show that between sixty and seventy-five
per cent of males use prostitutes. In Europe, figures range from an estimated ten per cent in Britain to eighteen per cent in Germany. In 2004,
it was reported at a conference on legalisation in Alba, Italy, that one
in six (or almost seventeen per cent) of Italian men were prostitutors.[17]
Nine million men were said to be using fifty-thousand prostitutes in that
country. This equates to nine hundred thousand men using five thousand women; to ninety thousand men using five hundred women; to
nine thousand men using fifty women, and to nine hundred men using
five women. The final figure adds up to this: one hundred and eighty
male prostitutors for every one prostituted female.

From my own Irish experience of prostitution, I would estimate the
ratio to be at least forty or fifty to one, perhaps far more, and there is no
shortage of prostitutes. Prostitution is a thoroughly male-dominated
trade. In fact, if it were not, it would not be a viable one in the first
place.

Imagine there were suddenly a single customer for each butcher,
baker and mechanic in the world—businesses would immediately begin
shutting down en masse. The same is true of prostitution. If it were not
entirely held buoyant by the sexual demands of men, brothels would
have no viability and no purpose and no reason to open their doors—or
to have any doors to begin with.

I will try to explain the gender dynamics of prostitution with an analogy: imagine the circles on a dartboard, and the prostituted to be contained within the bull's-eye, and those who use them to exist within the
far larger outer circles that surround it. The majority population of Western societies, who do not prostitute themselves or others, of course exist
outside both these boundaries. Because those within the central sphere
are viewed from the perspective of the men who use them, it is perhaps

17 (International Conference, 2004) 'Prostitution on Demand', Janice G Raymond.

somewhat natural for the clients here to view prostitution as a female arena. They are, each of them, seeking to use a female after all. In seeking to satiate their desires, they are not motivated to consider those within their own area of prostitution. They are so focused on their objective that they do not bother to consider the throngs of males around them. It has to be said that prostitutes collude in this. Many times I took great care and witnessed the same efforts in other women to ensure that punters did not pass each other in a brothel's halls. It was rightly assumed that this would make them uncomfortable—and perhaps their discomfort deserves closer inspection. What does that mean? What does that *say*? *Why* are prostitutors so discomforted by the sight of each other? Do they not like what they see of themselves reflected back to them?

Because men far outnumber the women they use in prostitution, there have to be reasons for their strangely blinkered perception of prostitution as a feminine arena. When I was working the streets there was no obscuring punters from one another. That was not possible. They came into view of each other in the most literal sense and dealt with that by simply discounting the presence of the other, silently driving past each other in the night and never making eye-contact nor commenting on each other, not even when we women would step straight from one car to the next.

So the punters were wilfully blind to all else besides what they were seeking, but what about society generally? What about those who exist outside the circles? Why do they so focus on the women in prostitution? This could be explained away by the fact that females are the most visible participants in prostitution, but in my opinion we must ask *why* the female participants are the most documented, most noted and most discussed of the participants here.

Largely, I believe, it is precisely *because the act of prostituting oneself is so inherently alien to humans* that people are fascinated by it, but this ignores the fact that any act of prostitution is an exchange; it is the payment of cash for what has been reduced to a service. In what other sphere of commerce does the sex of the sellers dictate the gender identity of the industry? In focusing primarily and almost exclusively on the women, what's disappeared is that those with direct involvement and responsibility for the existence of prostitution are overwhelmingly male. Detective Inspector Simon Häggström, of the Stockholm City Police Prostitution Unit, stated at a government conference in Dublin in October 2012 that in over 600 arrests he had never encountered a woman paying for sex. We are often reminded by prostitution enthusiasts that there are men and transgendered people in prostitution. Yes, there are, but who's buying them? The demand for prostitution has a gender, and that gender is male.

Some of the myths of prostitution are wildly illogical; others are just nonsense: there are some men who frame it in terms of telling us that they don't pay prostitutes for sex; they pay them to leave—as if any prostitute anywhere ever needed encouragement to get out the door!

This attitude denigrates all women, as it so clearly identifies their sexuality as all they have to offer. It says, with great resonance, 'we can treat women with contempt in this sphere of life, in a manner we could not treat all women, however much we might want to'.

Women are quick to decode this. I repeated this attitude to several women, including one of my best friends, a savvy straight-talking Scottish woman who has never worked in prostitution. She shot back immediately: 'What does that say about the rest of us'? She saw the implication for women directly, and why wouldn't she see it? How could she not? What else are non-prostituted women to take from this, other than that a man who says this would have *her* leave after a sexual encounter only for the fact that he was constrained by not having paid her?

The 'we pay them to leave' idiocy is just one of numerous fallacies that strive to obscure the reality of the cash-for-sex exchange. It is an oft-repeated myth of the pro-prostitution alliance that prostituted women do not sell their bodies, but rather their 'sexual skills'. They never tell us what these 'skills' are supposed to entail. So what are these skills supposed to be? Opening your legs? Moving your hips rhythmically in order to get him off? Any woman who's ever fucked in her life knows enough about men's bodies to do the basic job of a prostitute. And if she hasn't? If she has no sexual experience whatever? All the better, as far as the punter is concerned—he'll get a great kick out of putting paid to her sexual naïveté. 'Skill' here is redundant. It is simply surplus to requirements.

Only when a woman is an experienced dominatrix does a prostitute ever have to call on anything that could possibly be described as a 'skill', and it is considered skilful only because it takes practice and experience to understand these unusual sexual dynamics. These are not men who are simply looking to fuck a woman, as most men are.

There are two bald truths here: the first is that it doesn't take much skill to get a man off. Male sexuality does not require skilful coaxing to release itself in orgasm. You do not have to be a prostituted woman to know this. Just about every sexually active straight woman on the face of this earth could tell you it'd take a hell of a lot more skill to *stop* a man's orgasm than it would to release it. Secondly, the men who used us were not interested in our supposed 'sexual skills'—they were interested in using our bodies. They were interested in ejaculating in and on our bodies—that is, in and on *us*. Their behaviour was dominant, not passive. It was proactive, not receptive. Skill did not come into it, on their part or ours.

Another great misconception of prostituted women is that they are generally deficient and inferior mothers. This is true of drug-addled prostitutes, but it is true of drug-addled parents everywhere. In mothering as a prostitute, I preferred, not so much given the choice but rather taking it, to keep prostitution far outside the home by providing sex for strangers in cars and brothels and hotels, while keeping my child living in a respectable area, entirely outside the remit of my other life. This will come as a surprise to some. It certainly did to one woman in particular.

About four years ago I first went to see a psychotherapist. I had been a long time working on this book, but I found it difficult and painful. I foresaw these problems continuing and thought she might be able to assist me in guiding me through the more difficult emotional repercussions of writing it. I began to tell her why I was there and, as was necessary in doing so, covered the most basic points of my past.

Very soon in the therapeutic process she alighted on the fact that I had worked as a prostitute. She wanted to know: had I ever neglected my son? Had I ever left him home alone? Clearly this well-heeled, well-spoken woman had listened to the basic rudiments of my earlier years and made up her mind about the kind of mother I was likely to be. These ideas were both deeply offensive and a very long way from the facts. Naturally, and needless to say, our client/counsellor relationship was prematurely and permanently severed.

Most of the prostitutes I've ever known were mothers, and of those, many of them were prostitutes precisely *because* they were mothers. Many of them did what they did to cope with the constant year-round financial demands of childrearing, and of course, the more children a woman had the more tightly her children's welfare was entwined with her involvement in prostitution. Of the women who prostituted themselves with the main aim being to take care of their children, the majority were single mothers.

The reality of a woman's prostitution does not automatically make her a neglectful or abusive parent. Although any person living an emotionally unhealthy life is not best positioned for parenting, prostitutes certainly are not automatically neglectful or abusive towards their children. I've known women to stand out in the freezing cold and the driving rain until the early hours of a bitter and dreary morning frantically trying to earn the money to buy their children school shoes and uniforms and books, and I know for a fact they were there, because I was standing alongside them.

There were a small number of women who only appeared on the streets sporadically, a few times yearly, and always in the run-up to Christmas or Communion season or the new school year, and you could bet your life those women were mothers; that much would have been obvious even if they hadn't told us what brought them out, which they did. The other prostitutes weren't abusive towards them, because even though they didn't have a regular patch, we all understood what was going on, and for my part, I felt sorry for them, because they obviously hated prostitution so much they could only bring themselves to do it out of desperation for their kids. You wouldn't try to move women like that on if you had any decency or solidarity, and these qualities are more common among prostitutes than many people might suppose. They are borne, I think, in the shared understanding of what it is to struggle. Those mothers who prostituted themselves at Christmas and Communion time and the new school year made bigger sacrifices for their children than most parents can understand, and whatever other label people might ascribe to them on account of their activities, 'bad mother' would not be an accurate one.

When mothering as a prostitute, you feel in touch, embroiled in fact, in a great negativity and your child, on the other hand, is someone you know to be completely innocent; so you feel that you yourself are a buffer between your child and the world of prostitution. Of course you could logically be framed as the link between your child and prostitution, but you powerfully reject this. You feel that you are the thing that separates these two opposites. There is a great weight of responsibility in this and you take it very seriously. You will never, ever, bring a client into physical proximity to your child. It is your job to be a parent. It is also your job to be a prostitute. But in being both you have a third job: to keep the other two apart.

The importance of this is commonly accepted in prostitution. I've known prostitutes who'd gladly stab a client who approached them in the company of their children. This is why, for the vast majority of prostitutes I've known, it was so very hard to understand why some women introduced their daughters to the business, but very occasionally, some women did; I've seen it happen on one occasion myself. I met this woman a long time ago, when I was just starting out on Benburb Street. She would have been in her late forties and her daughter was thirteen years old. The girl looked her age, incidentally, and there was no shortage of men using her body. It was distinctly disturbing, watching her getting in and out of those cars. I was only fifteen at the time but even so, I clearly remember being horrified that her mother had taken her down that street with her. The woman clearly didn't have all her mental faculties. She seemed to have the intellectual age of someone younger than her daughter. Her speech was infantile and erratic. Yet what she'd done was shocking to me. It still is.

Another misconception of prostitution is the presumption of a general unwillingness among prostitutes to conform to society. But what exists here is not unwillingness; it is inability. I know many people would have assumed that I didn't hold an ordinary job because I didn't want one, and they'd have further deduced that I didn't want one because I was lazy and couldn't be bothered to work. That assumption couldn't be any further removed from the truth, but people tend to simplify and negative assumptions are also a human proclivity. We're all prone to them; I know I am.

The truth of the matter was that I desperately wanted a 'real job'. I wanted the social validation of a job. I wanted the authentic place in society I felt such a position would afford me. I desperately craved that sense of normalcy and legitimacy. In fact, I felt absolutely starved of it, but I could never tell anyone that, because to do so would have been to lay bare a lack I could only just manage to admit to myself. It is a silently devastating understanding, to know yourself as an outcast.

However, the most glaring misconceptions about prostitution come from the clients of prostitutes themselves. I once read the confession of an English TV script writer who'd spent nearly twenty thousand pounds on prostitutes in times past and had chosen to speak publicly about the experience. He described how he'd never had any confidence with women; how he'd been mocked as a teenager in his first attempts to meet females and how the pattern had continued throughout his twenties with his having been stood-up innumerable times. Also, whenever he did become close to a woman, he'd be told he was 'too nice' or that they 'didn't want to ruin the friendship'. Of course his confidence continued to plummet. Eventually, at thirty years of age, he came across an article in a magazine about the escort business and for the first time began to seriously consider paying for sex.

Now, twenty thousand pounds I can understand; what I couldn't understand was the fact that this man spent two days preparing for his first visit to a prostitute by going to the gym, having a session on a sunbed, having his hair cut, buying new clothes and reading all the papers so that he'd have something interesting to talk about.

He admitted (with shame, he said) that he had been using prostitutes for about a year while feeling that his time with them had been 'relatively harmless and mutually beneficial' before anything happened to cause him to think otherwise. The transformative incident came in the form of a comment from a prostitute who said that she was pleased he was there, because it meant she was now able to pay her gas bill.

'The words were like a slap in the face', he said. 'In a year of visiting escorts, this was the first incontrovertible evidence I'd heard that not every girl did escorting because they enjoyed it. Some of them were doing it because they had to . . . the truth is that up until that point, I had been genuinely convinced that all the girls I'd seen were selling their bodies entirely of their own free will.'

I was thinking: 'Sweet Jesus, that man was just on some other planet!' I also thought though, that as it is so very far outside the norm in prostitution, there was something endearing in his naïveté. I would expect that the prostitute he visited thought so too, at least before he put his penis inside her.

He made only one more visit after that, to another woman. He noticed she became tearful as she was undressing on the bed, so he excused himself and left. 'This, I realised, was my greatest fear,' he said. 'Not catching a sexually transmitted disease, but meeting a sex worker who didn't want to be a sex worker.'

What men of this mindset don't realise is that the women they pay who do not become tearful or make comments about their utility bills are inured enough to the nature of prostitution to make a well-educated guess about what a man needs, and they give it to him, as they have been paid to do. Men of the demeanour of the screenwriter above, who hold benign views about prostitution, will be dealt with in such a way as to ensure that his notions about prostitution remain intact. Why? Because of the oldest rule in commerce: you must cater to the consumer's needs.

Nonetheless, the man who wrote that article caused me to think about some of the gentler, more respectful men I met in prostitution. They were in the minority, but I did meet men in prostitution who would have been surprised and maybe a bit distressed to know how unhappy I was, how sickeningly awful I was caused to feel by their touch on my skin, how revolted I was by the proximity of their lustfulness, before they'd put a hand on me, even. I was never a consummate actress when it came to portraying the happy hooker, it was just a stretch of the truth too damn far, but, with this gentler sort of man (and a prostitute can always discern the nature of the man she's dealing with) the pretence was a good deal easier. For this reason, it is an unfortunate certainty that the men who'd be most receptive to the reality of the prostitution experience are the least likely to be made aware of it.

As much as a decent man might want to believe that prostitutes are not damaged by their visits, I'm sorry to say there is just no evidence I've seen anywhere to support that. As for my own self: I always used to find it depressing that however obviously decent a man might appear to be, he still clearly had not grasped that he had no business doing this to me and that he had no business supporting this industry that I shouldn't have been in either. It was an industry in which I met decent people and I met lonely people, but I was decent and lonely too, and I now know that what happens when two people engage in the sex-for-money exchange is that they largely ignore each other's humanity and put their own considerations in priority above that.

If I had to apply one term that most suited the majority of the men who ever paid to use my body, it would be this: wilfully oblivious. But prostitution has taught me this: life is not black and white. It is not made up of honourable men and perverts. As a species, the urge to violate is strong within us. It is up to us to be stronger than it is.

Of course, the liberalists will tell us that morality and prostitution do not even belong in the same sentence, and of course I will dismiss that for the nonsense that it is.

One thing I have found interesting is that, while adults seem more easily duped, young people who've never had any involvement in prostitution are often uncannily adept at decoding the simple wrongness at play here. Once, just months into my prostitution life, I was visiting people I knew in the city centre where word had gotten out among the residents of the adjoining council flats complex that I was a prostitute. While walking past the flats from my friends' house to a chipper, I was set upon by a group of local girls around my own age and beaten, not badly, but I was shaken, sore and disturbed. When they had finished and were walking away one of them turned and screamed back at me: 'Your body is your own and no one else's!'

I felt then that they did what they did because they found me objectionable, but I know now that they did it because they found prostitution objectionable, and that I was merely a representation of it. It is utterly understandable to me, in emotional terms, that those young girls would see an example of prostitution and be angry enough with it and object enough to it to lash out physically and hurt the person who represented it for them. It's not that I condone anyone attacking people, but I understand why they and any female would aggressively object to prostitution itself and I wouldn't hold it against them that they, as young girls, misdirected their anger. Prostitution *is* objectionable to females. I of all people know that.

The immorality of prostitution is often laid bare by the very tactics used to conceal it. Thankfully these are usually irrational enough as to be ridiculous, which makes them obvious and easy to identify. One of the most astonishingly illogical arguments in the modern pro-prostitution movement is the attempt to frame the 'right' to prostitute oneself as a feminist principle.

The practice of women being liable to seek, wholesale and as a feminist entitlement, the 'liberty' of laying themselves open to abuse of a sexual, physical, spiritual and psychological nature from men exists only in the minds of those who do not (or will not) grasp the basic premise of feminism, which is the liberation of women, followed by the promotion of female equality, sexual self-governance included. Sexual self-governance is only possible for anyone where they are not influenced to make decisions regarding their sexuality based on circumstances beyond their control. Quite clearly, the necessary conditions for authentic sexual autonomy do not exist in the prostitution experience. They do not exist in a cursory glance at it and they do not exist in the lived experience of it either.

The rights and entitlements of this pseudo-feminist theory do not relate to women and they certainly do not relate to feminism; they relate to the entitlement-driven and all-too-often priapic nature of male sexuality, so it should be blatantly obvious who this theory is designed to serve. Men's use of women in prostitution is an evidently significant issue of gender and unequal power relations, so it is amusing to me to consider what the original instigators of the women's movement would have felt about the 'rights' of women to be prostituted being framed as a feminist ideal!

Men who use women in prostitution strongly argue against the immorality of their exploitative behaviour and some will try to create distinctions between prostituted women in order to do that. Social scientists and many human rights groups accept these distinctions as if they were fact. These academics and human rights groups create a divide in their minds between those women who have been trafficked i.e. sold into sexual slavery by someone else, and those who have sold themselves into sexual slavery because of a lack of viable choice. In a moral sense, there is no distinction; and yes, this is a moral issue, as human rights issues always are.

The libertarians tell us that we are to exonerate prostitution of immorality. I think we ought to really think about what that means, because what it means is that we are to remove from our consciousness anything that tells us the purchase of human beings for sex does not conform to acceptable standards of human behaviour. What it means is that we are to accept that an estimated 40 million[18] women and girls are consumed in prostitution globally and not only are we to be okay with that, but we are to consider it altogether outside the issue of morality, so that there is nothing not to be okay with in the first place.

The idea that we are to exonerate prostitution of immorality is an idea that, as its objective, seeks us humans to behave as non-humans, and to accept being treated as non-humans, and not to betray any sign that we are bothered by it; not, in fact, even dare own there is anything to be bothered *by*. It is a peculiar, disturbing and creepy lesson, yet it is an interesting lesson for me to consider, because it seeks to teach me to remove myself from myself. It seeks to teach me to behave exactly as prostitution did.

Women in prostitution are mischaracterised as essentially immoral and have been for centuries. Added to that is the fiction that they generally find prostitution more tolerable than 'normal women' would, and this is used as evidence to back up the theory of their character deficiencies.

The truth is that prostituted women are not essentially immoral; and

18 According to south-east Asian charity, the Blind Project, www.theblindproject.com.

they have not made an easy and painless transition rooted in autonomy, as the decision to sell the flesh on one's bones never is.

It is prostitution itself which is corrupt and the women who are abused in it and by it are expected not only to bear the burden of its corruption on their bodies, but on their characters as well. This is a slur and an injustice, because the act of prostituting oneself has nothing to do with a woman's nature; it has to do with a woman's circumstance.

Finally, one of the most ridiculous pro-prostitution arguments I have ever heard concluded that because prostitution is the only area where women are routinely paid more than men, it is the only area where women reach and exceed equal gender parity. This ludicrous opinion disregards the reason for the relatively high rates of payment in prostitution, which exist because if they did not, women simply would not do it.

This is not some magical arena of life where men decide to treat women as economic equals; women in prostitution are paid in an hour what other women are paid in a week or a day because it is the only way of ensuring they will allow themselves to be used as human masturbation devices. Their higher pay does not reflect gender parity; it reflects the difficulty involved in earning it.

Chapter 20 ∽

LEGALISATION AND DECRIMINALISATION

Prostitution is an extreme form of gender discrimination.
Legalisation of this violence to women restricts women's
freedom and citizenship rights. If women are allowed to
become a legitimate commodity, they are consigned to a
second-class citizenship. Democracy is subverted.

DONNA HUGHES, *MAKING THE HARM VISIBLE*

That, in Ireland, is it illegal to operate a brothel but not illegal to frequent one is just another display of the depressingly patriarchal structure of our world. It is also something that has for a long time caused great resentment among Irish prostitutes.

I have mentioned already the clinic I would frequent in my early teens, which was local to the red-light district and open one evening a week for us to collect condoms and have a cup of tea or coffee. They also offered STD and pregnancy testing. There may have been counselling offered, I can't remember; I didn't avail of it if there was. I'd collect some condoms and have a cup of coffee to break up the night and I'd sit there drinking it and listening to the older women talk. They were all unpretentious street-walking working-class women, almost all of them from Dublin, and they were much savvier about the social politics of prostitution than I was and I found their conversations interesting. One particular woman, Martina, regularly raged against the fact that the clients who used us were breaking no laws, yet we, when arrested, were subject to regular court appearances and fines.

After the Sexual Offences Act of 1993, as before, men were cautioned and told to go on their merry way while women were hauled up before judges to be further demeaned in front of courtrooms packed with strangers. The first time this happened to me after the implementation of the new laws was also the last because I decided on the spot to move on to brothels and although I visited the streets sporadically for another couple of years, I never worked outdoors full-time again. I never had to show my face in court again on account of prostitution either.

There will always be those whose interests it will serve to apportion a higher percentage of responsibility to women for the business of prostitution, but the first law of economics tells us that no market can survive without demand. That law made itself very apparent in my prostitution life. What I did as a prostitute was to make myself available to men. I responded to their advances. I never once approached a man looking for business—never had to—and I never witnessed another woman do so either. I have heard that prostitution operates that way elsewhere in the world, but during my time in prostitution at least, that was not an Irish practice.

However obvious it was that men always initiated the exchange, we knew they would be afforded vastly different and far less judgemental treatment than us women and that was just a customary part of our world. It was a discriminatory situation and, for the most part, it still is.

As far as legislation towards decriminalisation is concerned, I hold the same views today that I held all through the 1990s when I was a working prostitute myself, and that view is no, I do not support that, because to support decriminalisation would be to support prostitution itself.

What I have always wholeheartedly endorsed is the criminalisation of the purchase of sex. To say what's good for the goose ought to be good for the gander is a very balanced line to take, but when a situation is not grounded in equality, it is not balanced in the first place. This makes it difficult to justify taking an equal all-across-the-board legislative approach to it. You cannot, with any sense of fairness, criminalise someone because they have been exploited.

I remember having heated debates with one particular prostitute, a friend of mine, about the legal status of prostitution. She felt that if what we were doing was legalised we'd be safer. Maybe we would, I responded, but any daughters we had would be at greater risk of becoming involved in prostitution if it were given the nod as acceptable by the State, and anyway, maybe we'd have been safer as far as black eyes were concerned, but no legislative power in the State or anywhere else could make us safe from the mental torment. We were both in our teens during that conversation.

I don't remember ever directly discussing with her (or with any prostitute) the intricacy of the negativity that surrounded us, how it damaged in so many different directions, so I cannot offer anyone else's view on that, but I do know from scratches of many different conversations that some prostituted women are further removed than others from the concept of prostitution as a deeply damaging practice; a practice in which we were unwitting conduits through whom negativity travelled outwards into the world as well as inwards into ourselves. I believe if a prostitute or former prostitute wants to see prostitution legalised, it is because she is inured both to the wrong of it and to her own personal injury from it.

I see now that I was mistaken when I conceded in my debate with my friend that 'maybe' legalisation would have made us physically safer. For all of my time in prostitution I worked, as all prostitutes in Ireland still do, in an atmosphere of illegality and I think I supposed that legality would have imposed some order on the prostitution experience. I supposed that the beatings would have come to an end, or been reduced, at least. I thought that legalisation may have led to a reduction in the general physical harm that was part of our daily lives. But I now perceive, in light of having access to international research which has been conducted since I left prostitution, that my suppositions were not at all true; in fact the truth is the reverse.

The notion that decriminalisation and legalisation serve to protect the women in the trade is another of the myths of prostitution, and a particularly dangerous one. Since legalisation, the human trafficking of females has exploded in Australia,[19] for example, and the five

---

19 M L Sullivan, and S Jeffreys, 'Legalisation: The Australian Experience', *Violence Against Women*, 8, 9 (September), pp 1140–1148, 2002.

hundred trafficked women documented working in Sydney almost a
decade ago was only an estimate then, and probably a very conserva-
tive one. Today's figures on trafficking make for disturbing reading. An
estimated 2.5 million people worldwide are in forced labour, according
to UN statistics, and of these, 1.2 million are children. A total of for-
ty-three per cent of victims of human trafficking are used for 'forced
sexual exploitation', and ninety-eight per cent of these victims are girls
and young women.[20]

In the case of Australia, the legalisation of prostitution in Victoria
caused such an escalation in the number of brothels that it quickly out-
stripped the system's ability to regulate them, and these brothels became
a hotbed of organised crime, trafficking, corruption and coercion. Far
from being some sort of safeguard, international research[21] shows that
in fact legalisation *facilitates* the trafficking of women and children for
prostitution.

Motorists in Victoria today are met with the sight of huge motorway
billboards advertising the services of brothels. Female business professionals are forced to work in an atmosphere where their male colleagues
conduct their out-of-office business meetings in brothels/strip clubs,
thereby putting women in a position where they must choose between
being excluded from the boys' club and enduring the debasement of
their own gender.

All legalisation has served to do in Australia, Germany and The Netherlands is paint a veneer of normalcy over prostitution, to familiarise it
in the public perception and to sanitise it in the legal sense, while the
human suffering of female adults and minors has escalated immeasur-
ably at the same time. Most of these women have no public voice and
wouldn't risk raising one anyway, for shame.

There are people who will argue that in countries where prostitution
has become legal, we have seen the eradication of pimps. This is not so.
What we have seen is the transformation of the role of pimping into one

20 'Human Trafficking, the Facts', UN Global Initiative to Fight Human Trafficking.
21 Kathleen Barry, *Female Sexual Slavery* (1979) and *The Prostitution of Sexuality* (1995).

co-ordinated by local government. The governments *are* the pimps in these countries.

For a long time, the only country I was aware of which had acted honourably in its legislature on this matter was Sweden. The Swedish attitude to prostitution is set out very clearly by Swedish legal expert and activist Gunilla Ekberg:

'In Sweden, it is understood that any society that claims to defend principles of legal, political, economic, and social equality for women and girls must reject the idea that women and children, mostly girls, are commodities that can be bought, sold, and sexually exploited by men. To do otherwise is to allow that a separate class of female human beings, especially women and girls who are economically and racially marginalised, is excluded from these measures, as well as from the universal protection of human dignity enshrined in the body of international human rights instruments developed during the past 50 years.'

GUNILLA EKBERG
THE SWEDISH LAW THAT PROHIBITS THE PURCHASE OF SEXUAL
SERVICES

Sweden introduced its ground-breaking legislation, which prohibits the purchase of sexual services, in 1999. But Sweden didn't simply prohibit the use of prostituted persons, but also decriminalized them and did so while enacting measures that assisted the women in the areas of training, education etc. It was an admirable piece of legislation. It was a full decade before any other country would follow suit.

I am reminded of Ireland's workplace smoking ban that was written into law in 2004. Within a couple of years, several countries across the western world introduced the same ban on their own soil. Workers' lungs, apparently, are placed far higher in terms of importance than women's lives. It is shameful, in my view, and depressingly telling that it took so long for another country to follow Sweden's example; however, it is heartening to see that it has begun to happen. On the first of January

2009, Norway became the second country after Sweden to criminalise the purchase of sexual services. Later that same year, Iceland became the third. Jóhanna Sigurdardóttir, Iceland's female Prime Minister, subsequently said: 'I guess the men of Iceland will just have to get used to the idea that women are not for sale'. At the time of writing, the Nordic Model is under discussion in Israel, Britain, Finland and France.

I am deeply gladdened that a campaign has begun in Ireland to criminalise the purchase of sex. The Turn Off The Red Light campaign calls for the basic tenants of the Swedish law to be enacted in Ireland, and it calls for the decriminalisation of prostituted women as part of a broader legislative framework. Before now, when decriminalisation has been suggested in Ireland, the focus has been entirely on decriminalising the commercial act itself, with no emphasis on women getting out of prostitution and no focus whatever on the male role. This can be described as 'stand-alone' or 'blanket' decriminalisation, and wherever it is suggested, I will always oppose it.

Decriminalisation of the sale of sex as presented in the Swedish context is one element of legislature that aims to eradicate prostitution and has clear benefits for the women involved; for this reason, it is legislation I would support and encourage others to support also.

The laws relating to prostitution were the most widely publicised of Sweden's 1999 legislative changes; they were far from the only ones. Many other areas relating to the safety of women were concentrated upon and improved. A new offence (Gross Violation of a Woman's Integrity) was introduced specifically to deal with instances where a woman had been habitually battered or molested by a husband or partner. Annual financial support for domestic violence shelters was increased. The National Centre for battered and raped women received additional support. Prison sentences for those found guilty of genital mutilation were doubled. The National Police Board was charged with ensuring that female trafficking be prevented and counteracted. Neglecting to report the awareness of certain sexual crimes was made punishable in law. The definition of rape was widened to include the enforced entry of objects besides the penis and provisions to combat sexual harassment in the workplace were made more rigorous.

It seems there exists in Sweden a far healthier attitude towards the rights of women than in Ireland and that is evidenced not only in Swedish legislation but in the relatively high degree of equality between the sexes there. Swedish women have an employment rate of seventy per cent. Women's representation in Swedish government stands at fifty per cent; in parliament forty per cent; in county councils forty-eight per cent.

Women's general aversion to prostitution is clearly evidenced by the Swedish government's response to it. It is no coincidence that one of the few Western countries to have near-equal participation of women in government was also the first Western country to outlaw the commercialisation of women's bodies.

Despite the relatively more evolved role of women in Swedish society and policy-making, it had been noted in the 1990s that the number of reported physical and sexual assaults against women there had increased markedly and the legislation of 1999 was a remedial response to that. However, anyone who assumes that Sweden neglects to focus on the sexual abuse of males is mistaken. Legislation was introduced in Sweden in 1984 to widen the definition of rape to include male-on-male rape and the rape of men committed by female perpetrators. Males are clearly equally protected in Swedish law and have been for a long time. The plethora of laws protecting women which were introduced in 1999 came about not because Sweden concerns itself more with the protection of its women, but because they were necessitated by the behaviour of some of its men.

I am not wholly enamoured with Swedish policy, however. At the time of writing, it seems to me that there is still a divide between the way prostituted and non-prostituted women are protected in law there. Prostitutes are not protected by the legislation on Gross Violation of a Woman's Integrity, unless they have been abused within a relationship, as this legislation is afforded only to those women who have been repeatedly abused within relationships. A woman who has been repeatedly abused within prostitution can expect to see the client who has used her receive a sentence of not more than twelve months, whereas the woman who has been repeatedly abused within a relationship can expect to see her abuser receive a sentence of not more than six years.

Added to that, the individual offences (beatings, rape, etc.) perpetrated against the non-prostituted woman are still subject to prosecution as stand-alone crimes separate from the gross-violation offence. This means that a man will be tried for having committed a particular illegal act against a non-prostituted woman and also be tried for the separate offence of having violated her integrity. By contrast, a man who has bought and used a prostitute is legally accountable only for having done so; he is not held accountable for the separate offence of violating her integrity.

For a long time I found it saddening to see that even in Sweden, where prostitutes were first protected more firmly than anywhere else in the Western world, they were still deemed unworthy of having their integrity respected in law on a par with non-prostituted women. I do not believe this situation has been fully resolved. As the 2010 Swedish Inquiry into the effects of the ban on prostitution states: 'One reason why priority is not given to sexual purchase offences is the low penal value of this type of offence'. The 'low penal value' referred to the very short sentences imposed for this crime, which at the time was not more than six months.[22]

Overall though, Sweden is the first country in my awareness to have approached true gender equality. It does this by all the means I have outlined including the one that is most personal to me: by 'marking its attitude towards prostitution as an undesirable social phenomenon and by punishing those men who continue to exploit and promote it'. There is a simple and invariable truth here: for prostitution to be reduced, demand must be suppressed.

Prostitution which is not suppressed can only expand, and, most particularly in countries where it is legalised, it will explode. A glaring example of this would be the presence of Pascha, a twelve-storey nine-thousand-square-metre brothel in Cologne, Germany, that services up to a thousand men a day. During the World Cup of 2006, an enormous poster of a near-naked woman was plastered down the side of the building, replete with the thirty national flags of all the countries that had

---

22 Committee of Inquiry to Evaluate the Ban against the Purchase of Sexual Services. Chancellor of Justice Anna Skarhed, formerly a Justice of the Supreme Court, headed the committee.

qualified for the World Cup—an international invite to all men expected to visit the city. Pascha offers cut-price rates for OAPs and the unemployed. In 2003, a Thai prostitute was stabbed to death there. In 2006, another woman was stabbed by a sex-buying man. She survived because security was alerted by a woman working in the adjoining room. In 2005, police raided the brothel and it was reported that firearms and cocaine were found. Four of the twenty-three prostitutes arrested were between fourteen and fifteen years old. The brothel faced no legal penalties for pimping underage girls. Is this the type of building you'd like to see in your city?

When prostitution is legally sanctioned in a country its female citizens can sometimes find themselves indirectly involved in prostitution, regardless of their personal feelings or their consent:

> 'Speciality brothels advertise services that cater to men with disabilities, and caretakers (mostly women) are now required to take disabled men to brothels and assist them engaging in sex acts.' (Sullivan and Jeffreys, 2001)
> JANICE G RAYMOND
> *PROSTITUTION ON DEMAND*

The normalising effect that legalisation has on prostitution is very clearly expressed by the attitude of Berlin brothel keeper Tatiana Ulyanova, who said of her 'right' to present prostitution as a job option to women: 'Why shouldn't I look for employees through the job centre when I pay my taxes just like anybody else?'

After prostitution was legalised in Germany, Hamburg lawyer Mechthild Garweg said of the legal structures in her country: 'There is now nothing in the law to stop women from being sent into the sex industry . . . The new regulations say that working in the sex industry is not immoral any more, and so jobs cannot be turned down without a risk to benefits.'

The powers that be in Germany must have recognised the legal limbo, as the issue ended up in the Bundessozialgericht (Federal Social Court of Germany) in 2009. The judges ruled that employment agencies would not be forced to source women for brothels, and stated: 'The law was made to protect the workers, not to promote the business'. This was a welcome outcome, and as far as I am aware no woman refusing work in a brothel did actually lose her social welfare benefits, but it is important to remember two things here: that unemployed German women should not have been subjected to the threat in the first place, and that they never would have had it not been for the legalisation of prostitution.

These types of situations and potential situations should not be surprising when we understand that legally sanctioning prostitution obscures boundaries in a manner that would have previously been unthinkable. As Garweg also said: 'They are already prepared to push women into jobs related to sexual services, but which don't count as prostitution.' She was referring to sexually exploitative jobs, such as those of phone sex operators, which is prostitution in all but the physical sense.

There is a shift created here by governmental policy towards a certain sort of world. We need to ask ourselves whether it is one we want our daughters growing up in, and whether it communicates a view of females we'd want to see promoted to our sons. We need to look at the *proven consequences* of the legalisation of prostitution and ask ourselves, in short, are we happy with the sort of world it creates? And is it one we want to live in?

Whenever the criminalisation of male demand is raised we are told by pro-prostitution campaigners that society ought to consult with prostituted women before it introduces any such legislation. There is a problem with that. As we can see from the quote below, taken from the 2010 independent Swedish inquiry,[23] women's perspectives of the criminalisation of demand are markedly different depending upon whether they are still involved in or have freed themselves from prostitution:

'It is clear, and it seems logical, that those who have extricated themselves from prostitution take a positive view of the criminal-

---

23 The inquiry stated its 'remit has been to evaluate the application of the ban on the purchase of sexual services and the effects that prohibition has had'.

isation, while those who are still exploited in prostitution are critical of the ban. This pattern is reflected in many different reports and is also confirmed by the contacts that the inquiry has had with women with experience of prostitution.'

Had the criminalisation of demand been enacted in Ireland during my time in prostitution I would have been very satisfied that the men who bought my body were criminalised, but I also would have worried and have wondered about how it was going to affect my life. So I am in no way surprised that many prostituted women oppose the criminalisation of their punters, mainly because of the way criminalisation lays bare the actuality of the prostitution experience. The criminalisation of a prostitute's client strips away the smoke and mirrors game of pretence that often exists between them; it forces him to accept the reality of his role as an abuser—a reality many men who use prostitutes reject, dismiss, and concentratedly ignore. The criminalisation of their actions forces them to see that their behaviour is not considered acceptable. Men will resent this and any prostitute with more than a few weeks' experience will know that and be justifiably fearful of it, because the resentments of men who prostitute women are always vented on the women they prostitute. So yes, I would have worried about that.

I would have worried also about my livelihood. I would have asked myself a lot of questions, like how would I be able to earn a living in an environment where the punters were criminalised? But my understanding of the basic decency inherent to legislation like this would have prevailed over my worries and fears. When I was 'on the game' I would have known it was the right thing for the government to do. I believe that, deep down, the vast majority of prostitutes know it too.

The report of the Swedish inquiry into the effects of the ban has made very interesting reading, and has absolutely rubbished claims by pro-prostitution lobbyists that the ban was unwise and unworkable. Of course there are those who, predictably, have tried to strip the Swedish inquiry of its credibility. Its findings do not suit their agenda.

The Swedish inquiry reveals that prostitution in Sweden has plummeted in the years since the implementation of the 1999 ban, and states that: 'Since the introduction of the ban on the purchase of sexual services, street prostitution in Sweden has been halved. This reduction may be considered to be a direct result of the criminalisation of sex purchases'. It also reveals that the rises in online advertising for prostitution services since 1999 are in line with other countries and are attributable to the same technological advances seen everywhere else. If this legislation had simply moved prostitution indoors I would be suggesting alterations to it, but that has not been the case.

Ireland's 1993 Sexual Offences Act, on the other hand, made it an offence to 'loiter' with the intent of engaging in prostitution. That legislation had the, I believe, *intended* effect of driving prostitution indoors. It was never about eradicating prostitution; it was about obscuring it. It was about removing this ugliness from the sight of those who were not involved and did not wish to see it, and, in large part, it worked. Many women, including myself, were forced indoors with, as I've said, disastrous personal consequences. There is hypocrisy and culpability in any legislation that makes prostitution available to men but invisible to the rest of society.

Sweden's legislation, conversely, targets prostitution in whatever form it is found. As a result, pimps and traffickers now regard Sweden as an unwise location to set up shop and are taking their trade elsewhere. The same situation has replicated itself in Norway. The immediate consequence of their legislation was a reported similar reduction in Norwegian prostitution.

The situation didn't run so smoothly in Iceland. After the legislation was introduced Icelandic police announced that they hadn't the means or the manpower to enforce it, and prostitution was reported to have increased rather than decreased. The women of Iceland have refused to accept that and have instead chosen to take matters into their own hands. A new underground movement called 'Stóra systir' ('Big Sister') has sprung up and has been active in collating the contact details of would-be prostitutors and then handing them over to the police; in essence, doing the work of the police for them. I am both pleased and amused by this, and I also find it very revealing because it illustrates with great clarity that as soon as women have been promised the removal of these shackles they are not disposed to the feeling of having them snapped back on.

Another tactic of prostitution promoters, in their effort to secure legalisation of prostitution, is to frame the prostitution experience itself as a human or civil right, and because the denial of human and civil rights is duly universally abhorred it is a tactic that the proponents of prostitution will continue to claim and to cling on to, despite it being embarrassingly inappropriate.

Being abused is not a right, human, civil, or otherwise; and any group that claims to frame abuse as a right for certain persons clearly has no concern for those persons whose 'rights' to be abused they would uphold; nor do they have any concern for the dignity of civil and human rights as a concept, clearly, since they are active in so polluting and distorting the terms that describe it.

To stand accused of stripping any group of their civil rights is considered an indictment, and a serious one. In today's world, with its shared collective history of refusing and denying civil and human rights to ethnic and religious groups, even the utterance 'civil rights' can create the illusion of elevating the speaker to a position of moral high ground. Where this has been employed as a trick it has actually worked to the extent that it seems to make sense to some people, despite the fact that prostitution itself is a violation.

Invoking that illusion is just another aspect of the shamefully misogynistic position of the pro-prostitution alliance, which attempts to hijack human rights and use it as a normalising tactic. This is just further evidence of a position which is toxic by its nature.

Remember, there is nothing immutable about prostitution. It is not a human characteristic. It simply cannot be compared with the tone of a person's skin or other such unalterable attributes, and in fact it is an insult to humanity to attempt to compare it so.

The policy which seeks to promote prostitution based on a 'human/civil right' to be prostituted is nothing more than an attempt to remove all legal barriers to conducting the business of prostitution. It is not in any way based on the human rights of prostituted women. It presumes only one right: the right of prostitution to exist.

I have learned through the experiences of my prostitution and post-prostitution life that those who invent a case for prostitution are very often prostitution enthusiasts with a definite agenda and a correspondingly fixed perspective. They will row in and merge their arguments with those well-intentioned but misguided people who propose legalisation and regulation as a form of social control, and they will hide behind the reasoning of those non-invested parties who assume these controls to be beneficial to prostituted women. It is frustrating and saddening for me to know that there are many people who, out of genuine care for prostituted women, argue for legalisation in the mistaken assumption that it would take what is wrong about prostitution and somehow make it right.

Those who advocate legalisation for the benefit of men are sometimes pimps but more commonly prostitutors—men who buy women's bodies themselves. People who argue for the benefit of men usually benefit either sexually or financially from the bodies of prostituted women. They also often have no real understanding of the consequences of prostitution in the lives of prostituted women, nor do they care to, as they realise this knowledge would directly confront their agenda. They bang the legalisation drum and talk about the supposed benefits to prostituted women despite having no basis to do so. The only benefits they are interested in are their own, and those benefits involve either filling their wallets or emptying their scrotums.

There will, of course, be people who espouse legalisation who do not fit either category. In the absence of a referendum on the matter, the percentage of Irish people who would support legalisation is something I do not know. What I do know is that if they pursue and advocate for legalisation in a genuine attempt to make prostitution a safer and more tolerable place for prostituted women, they are not only wasting their time but striving for a legal structure which will deliver the opposite of their well-meaning intentions.

The sphere of life such laws attempt to regulate is so far outside the nature of what it is to relate as humans that it is actually incongruent with the laws of most Western nations. For example, sexual harassment laws, which are enacted to protect women in all other areas of work, simply cannot be made to apply to prostituted women. I have already discussed at length the way in which a majority of a prostitute's clients gleefully transgress any physical boundaries she may attempt to set. Outright sexual abuse is a matter of routine. Legislation here is futile. You cannot legislate away the nature of the prostitution exchange, but you can legislate to get rid of the market.

There are Irish voices who argue against Swedish-style legislation on the grounds that we ought not import a foreign solution to what is, as they see it, an Irish problem. What this argument fails to recognise is that this is not a specifically Irish problem. This is a global problem, and it is a global problem because it is a problem of gender inequality. What we need is a global response to a global problem.

I witnessed a radical shift in the thinking of one of my own sisters after the conversation I related earlier in this book (when she'd asked me had I ever been sexually assaulted or raped in prostitution). She had gone away and thought about the legalisation issue from the perspective of paid abuse. She later said to me: 'I would always have thought that legalising prostitution was the only real answer, until you explained how it was basically paid sexual abuse. I couldn't support that. I couldn't support sexual abuse in any form. If a woman doesn't want hands on her, in her own heart, then that is sexual abuse regardless of whether there's payment or not.'

She was right. I was so relieved to hear her say that and I told her so. There was the sense of being heard, of being seen, of being suddenly listened to in that moment. There was the sense of being acknowledged, contrasting with the feeling I've had every time I've had to listen to pro-legalisation arguments, which is the feeling of being disappeared.

In country after country where prostitution has been legalised something has occurred which is an embarrassment to the pro-prostitution lobby: it is the refusal of prostituted women to engage in legalised prostitution and it is expressed as a sharp rise in *illegal* prostitution. Women in these countries routinely refuse to register and work in secret to avoid being on record as prostitutes. The pro-prostitution lobby attempts to explain this by attributing women's reluctance to be officially documented as prostitutes to 'whore stigma', in an attempt to project the source of women's behaviour as coming from outside of themselves. Their rejection does not stem from some outer-imposed 'whore stigma'. The reason for women's refusal to collude in legalised prostitution is simple: the fact is that we women simply do not want to be labelled prostitutes. Most women want to get in and out of prostitution without any trace of their ever having been there. Many insist on working outside of the legal frameworks in these countries in order to preserve that precious anonymity. This is a classic of practical dissociation tactics, and people are actually mobilising politically to avoid having to be documented as prostitutes, as these words from a Dutch press release show:

> Petition—Stop Forced Registration of Sex Workers in the Netherlands
> Monday, 2 July 2012
> ICRSE Coordinator
> 'Several organisations and individuals, sex workers and allies, who work together to support the interests of sex workers in the Netherlands, have started a petition in protest of the proposed registration requirement for sex workers. A large number of women, transgender persons and men working in the Netherlands sex industry have already indicated that they DO NOT want to register, because they experience this as degrading and stigmatizing. Mandatory registration seriously violates their right to privacy. Moreover, there is no evidence that mandatory registration of sex workers helps to combat abuses such as trafficking.'

I can certainly relate to the position of anyone who refuses to be documented as a prostitute. Far from removing stigma, legalisation forces them to be compliant in accepting the tag 'prostitute' on an official level. I understand exactly why many reject that and work illegally to avoid it, because if I had been forced to choose between working in secret or being officially tagged a prostitute I would have done exactly the same thing. The pro-prostitution lobby would say I was suffering from the ill-effects of 'whore stigma'. No. The only ill-effects I was suffering from were the ill-effects of prostitution, and I wouldn't have wanted that to become any more fixed, set or established in my life than it already was. Those who would support legalisation on compassionate grounds need to consider this: 'prostitute' is not a label most prostituted women want to have follow them around forever, and it should not be forced on them. There is no compassion in that.

There is also this to consider: under State-sponsored prostitution, men are absolved from responsibility because it is legally, and we are to assume morally, perfectly acceptable to pay to use the body of another for sexual gratification.

To be prostituted is humiliating enough; to legalise prostitution is to condone that humiliation, and to absolve those who inflict it. It is an agonising insult.

Chapter 21 ∽

THE NORMALISATION
OF PROSTITUTION

It's hardest to see what's wrong about what seems normal.

JANE FONDA, *MY LIFE SO FAR*

For prostitution to be normalised, it must be sanitised. Its inherently harmful nature must, at all costs, be concealed. It could not be considered normal otherwise.

Several tactics are used to achieve this. The first I will discuss is the not-so-subtle terminology which has been deliberately introduced in recent decades with the aim of attempting to frame prostitution as ordinary work. The terms 'sex worker' and 'sex work' sound unnatural, and they sound unnatural because they suggest a correlation which is unnatural. Human nature is not attuned to an association between sex and work. However, though they inevitably strike the listener as odd, they do not shock with the potency of the terms 'prostitution' and 'prostitute', which conjure up all the mental imagery fitting to a sexually exploitative exchange. The imagery 'sex worker' calls to mind is of a woman in a sanitised situation; a masseuse's table perhaps, with clean cotton sheets and soft fluffy towels. A uniform, necessarily, something akin to a nurse's but with a much shorter skirt. White, of course, and matching spotlessly white tissues to wipe the semen off the floor.

Everything is clean in the imagery this terminology suggests; everything is above-board, and proper, and sanitised: but when we look at the actuality of what a 'sex worker' *does*, that is when we see the snag. The semen is the fly in the ointment, the singular clue that there is something not quite professional going on here; and its significance is not perceived as diluted by the disinfected imagery that surrounds it. Rather the starkness of this contrast belies the notion of ordinary work here.

It might be helpful to imagine what is suggested as rational here in another context. Imagine a woman in the throes of passionate intercourse with her lover, who suddenly gets out of bed, casually flips open her laptop, and sends an email to the office. Work is incongruent with sex, as sex is incongruent with work.

There are many aspects of prostitution that make it incongruent with the term 'work', but one of the most important and telling of these is that it is the only form of so-called 'work' in which a person is both the service provider and the product at the same time. As one prostitution survivor responded to the claim that prostitution is no better or worse than flipping burgers at McDonald's:

'In McDonald's, you're not the meat. In prostitution you are the meat.'[24]

The term 'sex worker' is a rhetorical weapon in the normalisation of prostitution. No doubt there are those whose agenda would be served if society wholly embraced it, but I have yet to hear a person, conversationally, with no agenda behind it, say 'sex worker' when they mean prostitute. The term 'sex worker' was received with a knowing snigger among the prostitutes I've known, including myself. We were all very well aware of its objective and equally aware of the pointlessness of trying to achieve it. Prostitutes and former prostitutes are instinctively attuned to these blatant attempts at whitewash. We know that they are not designed to dignify the women in prostitution; we know that they are designed to dignify prostitution itself. Further to that, we know that they are about as useful as tits on a bull, and we know it from the most reliable source of all—personal experience.

24 Janice G Raymond, 'Prostitution on Demand: Legalizing the Buyers as Sexual Consumers', 2004.

Trying to frame prostitution as legitimate and normal work opposes logic on innumerable levels, one of the most obvious (and almost laughable) being that European Union health and safety legislation prohibits sexual harassment, violence, and work that causes work-related stress! Needless to say, these negatives and many more besides are so intrinsically entrenched here as to be understood by those in prostitution as occupational hazards.

> '. . . If prostitution is ordinary work, we should be able to speak about what the skills of prostitution are. According to WHISPER (Organisation of women who have survived prostitution) such skills would include: performing sex acts, feigning sexual enjoyment, enduring all manner of bodily violation, and allowing your body to be used in any imaginable way by another person. Such acts are labelled harassment and abuse when money does not change hands. Prostitution is not recommended as a career option to young girls. It is not promoted as a career option by guidance counsellors and parents. Work experience at brothels is not recommended, unemployed people are not asked to work in prostitution.[25] The actual reality, which the sex industry tries to obscure, is that those with the power and personal agency to do so would not choose prostitution as a way of life.'[26]

The quote above points out that if we are to accept prostitution as ordinary work, then we should be able to speak about what the skills of prostitution are. This addresses a pertinent point in the issue of the normalisation of prostitution. There are particular skills necessary to the implementation of every job on this earth. That is a fact. If prostitution is to be framed as ordinary work, then we do indeed need to discuss the skill-sets necessary to perform it. I will describe the three which are most frequently used (as in every single day) from my own experience.

When a man has agreed upon a sexual act and the fee he is prepared to pay for it, very commonly, in fact more often than not, he will not be

---

25 Although this can become obscure where prostitution is legalised, as we have seen in the case of Germany.

26 Ruhama research report on prostitution as so-called free choice, Ireland, 2006.

satisfied to stay within the boundaries of the agreed sexual exchange. This will result in him shoving his fingers, roughly, suddenly, and without lubricant, into your anus or vagina. It will result in his snatching off the condom just before he orgasms so that he can ejaculate into your mouth and/or over your face/breasts. It will result in his grabbing the back of your head and shoving it downwards as he thrusts his penis down the back of your throat to its fullest possible extent. In these situations there is intense nausea, and the resulting skill necessary to prostitution is the ability to control your reflex to vomit.

Sometimes these attacks are prolonged in order that the paying client can revel in the deeply pleasurable satisfaction he derives from your degradation. In these situations there is an intense urge to cry, and the resulting skill necessary to prostitution is the ability to restrain it.

In any given week there will be many times where there is the urge to panic, to flee the situation. This is the natural flight response experienced by all humans in threatening or sexually repulsive situations. In prostitution, it cannot be indulged. The resulting skill necessary here is the ability to psychologically dissociate from your surrounds; to cut yourself off from your immediate reality; to pretend that it is not happening.

To summarise:

The ability to control your reflex to vomit.
The ability to restrain your urge to cry.
The ability to imagine your current reality is not happening.

These are the skill sets of prostitution. These are the skill sets necessary to perform what some people would like to see normalised as 'sex work'.

Obviously because I have suffered and survived the realities of prostitution but also I believe it is because I love words and writing that I find it so hard to stomach the message of those who try to misshape the prostitution experience through the deliberate distortion of language. Luckily these messages are prone to contradiction.

Many groups deny the intrinsic harm of prostitution while at the same time advocating a 'harm-reduction approach'. If prostitution is not violence towards women, and if it is not harmful, then what harm is it they are proposing to reduce? How can any group commit to combating harm if they strive to deny the harm exists in the first place? That discrepancy was birthed at the starting point, in the moment the harmful nature of prostitution was denied.

Another of the tactics in the normalisation of prostitution is the attempt to divide prostituted women into two separate camps: those who are supposedly 'free' and those who are 'forced'. 'Forced' referring to those women who have been enslaved bodily; who have been duped, often trafficked, forcibly detained, raped by their pimps and then sold as sexual meat to a succession of strangers. And 'free' of course indicating those women who have supposedly exercised free will and are happy as larks with their lot. It would be useful to question why, if prostitution is a choice for women which can be taken with such ease, so many women have to be deceived and enslaved in order to do it.

The prostitution experience of the trafficked woman most commonly involves force followed by the trauma of commercial sexual abuse. The prostitution experience of the non-trafficked woman most commonly involves coercion followed by the trauma of commercial sexual abuse.

Both of these situations are reactionary. Both result in sexual abuse as a result of something that preceded them, and both share the consequence of a woman having sex with strangers that she has no desire to have.

Precisely because these women's situations have been so divided in the popular consciousness by way of focusing on the differences that set them apart, attitudes towards them have been correspondingly divided. The woman who has been physically forced may be the focus of pity and compassion. By distinct comparison, the woman who has been coerced by life circumstances is the subject of criticism and derision. It is not the end-place, then, that frames the nature of the attitudes towards them—it is the route by which they got there.

A woman is derided as a whore if, like myself, she came to prostitution from a place of homelessness paired with male manipulation; but had I been duped to go to a foreign country under the promise of a non-existent au pair job and physically confined once I got there, I would have found myself the recipient of a very different attitude. This is difficult for me to know. Its very unfairness makes it difficult, because it is the woman who was *not* physically forced who has a far greater weight of inwardly directed shame to deal with. It is a shame that rests on the charge of her perceived culpability.

Had I been forced I could comfort myself with that knowledge at least. I could partake in the blameless mentality of the victim, free of guilt or accountability, with no questioning shadows flickering at the back of my mind and no internal voices whispering, 'Could you not have found another way?' I could offer a short retort to anyone who dared say (and there are very many who dare say), 'Well, nobody forced you to do it!' The woman who was trafficked can say: 'Well, actually, somebody *did* force me to do it'—she can outwardly direct her recriminations and she can look outside herself, rather than inside herself, for answers.

Women like myself who were forced by no*body* need to find our voices and assert that this does not mean we were forced by no*thing*. It is a very human foolishness to insist on the presence of a knife or a gun or a fist in order to recognise the existence of force, when often the most compelling forces on this earth present intangibly, in coercive situations. My prostitution experience *was* coerced. For those of us who fall into the 'free' category, it is *life* that does the coercing.

People concentrate so much on the differences between prostituted women and trafficking victims that they forget there are far more similarities than differences. Probably the most fundamental of these is that while the trafficked woman had her sexual autonomy stolen from her, the prostituted woman had hers bought; and so both sets of women have lost their sexual self-governance.

While individuals and organisations argue about whether the issues of trafficking and prostitution should be dealt with separately or together, the punters have already made their minds up. They use both sets of women, and they make no distinction.

There are some men who, bizarrely, think that because they buy sex from women, they have a right to speak on behalf of those women. 'She's happy', 'She enjoys it', etc. The men who use women in prostitution do not have the authority to speak for them. They are seeing the situation from the alternate perspective, and this will never lend to understanding. If you are looking down one end of a funnel and I am looking down the other, I am never going to see that funnel from your perspective; not as long as I keep looking from the opposite end.

Some men frame their view of prostitution based on their own behaviour within it. If a man is prepared to restrain his sexual impulses to fit within the boundaries of the woman whose body he's using, he may well form the opinion that her experience of prostitution is shaped by similar expressions of restraint; that his behaviour typifies what she commonly encounters. If he assumes so he couldn't be more wrong. Men who curtail their impulses to fit within the bounds of what a prostituted woman deems permissible are the exception, not the rule.

No man should measure the prostitution experience by his behaviour alone. Prostituted women do not process their experience by the behaviour of one man: they process it by the behaviour of thousands.

Nevertheless, there are male users of prostitutes who say they know prostitution is not damaging and who use their proximity as supposed evidence to support this. They ignore a vital fact: proximity means nothing here. It is a matter of perspective, not proximity. The same is true of all the experiences of life that separate the people involved into two polarised camps. Prostitutes' clients have no business speaking on behalf of the women they use. They simply do not know what they are talking about.

Another of the lies geared towards the normalisation of prostitution (and this one is not modern, it is very old) is the notion that the presence of prostitution directs male sexual aggression away from the non-prostituted female population. Susan McKay, former Chief Executive of the National Women's Council of Ireland, rubbished this myth when she said:

> 'There is an argument that the existence of prostitutes acts as a safety valve for male sexual aggression, thus protecting other women. This disregards the rights of all women to live without sexual violence,

but it is also untrue. Studies show that men who use prostitutes regularly are more likely to become violent to women with whom they are in a relationship. Men who use prostitutes are not men who respect women.'

The rape-prevention theory has persisted because it is very useful to the proponents of prostitution, and it is very useful because it is a multifaceted tool; it has a number of viable functions. Firstly, of course, it advises that prostitution is a necessary evil. It does this by portraying prostitution as the only remedy to a frightening and horrible alternative. By way of this fiction, prostitution is framed not only as a social necessity, but as a calming influence and, therefore, a desirable one.

In Simone de Beauvoir's book, *The Second Sex,* a quote from which prefaces this book, the author makes reference to an attitude I had never known existed in America's Deep South. I had often wondered as a child how American whites had justified slavery to themselves. It seemed incomprehensible to me that there could have been rational justification expressed, and I was right, because the justification they espoused was not rational. American proponents of slavery attempted to vindicate it by maintaining that it afforded them the opportunity to '. . . maintain the most democratic and refined relations among themselves'. *Among themselves*? Where is the justification in that? In the same way, the notion that prostitution protects the general female population serves to support prostitution by focusing on those outside of it, while giving no conscience-driven thought to those within it.

In any case, both sets of women are lied to, because the notion that prostitution protects other women is false. It doesn't. It does the opposite. It operates in a manner that is subtle and sinister and the only reason the non-prostituted women of the world don't know this is because what's happening is happening elsewhere, behind closed doors. It is true that there are men who indulge the fantasy of raping women, and there is no shortage of them. It is also true that many of the men who entertain these desires act out their fantasies on the bodies of prostitutes. What is *not* true is that prostitution is capable of containing these sadistic propensities within the walls of its own institution; it is no more capable of doing that than a prostitute is capable of containing it within the walls of her own vagina. The notion that prostitutes prevent rape is a fallacy; they do not prevent it. They are like magnets to whom are drawn the first physical enactments of these fantasies, but nothing stays as it was in its initial inception. Everything evolves and grows. Rape fantasies are no different.

Those men who do not rape prostituted women outright, but rather pay to use their bodies as instruments for their rape-fantasy enactments, will be somewhat gratified by what they do, but they are all-the-while very well aware that they've had to hand over money in order to do it. This counteracts their sense of control, which in turn dilutes the potency of their rape-fantasy experience. Since the thrill of sexual violation is defined by a sense of control, the most extreme sexual violators strive for the most potent sense of control available to them, and they do not interpret that as being found in the prostitution exchange. I know this because of the amount of violent perverts I met over the years and the one thing that was common to them all was their belligerent and bitter resentment of having to pay to enact their fantasies.

When the malignancy of their fantasies reaches a more potent level these men will not pay to enact them; they will simply rape prostituted women. Then there are men who wouldn't bother indulging these fantasies on the body of a prostitute because they wouldn't view a prostitute as being rapeable in the first place. (Here, again, more evidence of the prostitute's perceived insignificance.) And so enacting rape fantasies on the bodies of prostitutes is enough for some rapists, but not all.

For some, because raping the body of a prostitute is not quite real enough, they can and do move on to what they regard to be 'the real thing'. These men bypass prostitutes and rape non-prostituted women, and the supposedly saving powers of prostitution can do nothing to stop this.

These are frightening prospects for non-prostituted women, but many prostitutes and former prostitutes, including myself, have seen the faces of rapists and sexual abusers publicised in the media who were once particularly vile clients of ours. I was not at all surprised when I first saw the face of one of my paying abusers in the newspaper. How could I be, when I know prostitution is a training academy for misogynists?

The truth is prostitution cannot, by its nature, quell or contain perversion. In an atmosphere where malignant sexual domination thrives and cannot be discouraged, it should be clear that perversion cannot be quelled or contained. It can only be fed, and what is fed grows, and what grows unchecked increases in amount and intensity until it is too large to be contained in the confines of what once housed it. Prostitution does not, because it *cannot*, contain the perversity of sexual violence; it can only feed and unleash it out into the rest of the world.

In de Beauvoir's quote, one line interested me most. It was '. . . man vents his turpitude upon her'. It interested me because I didn't know what turpitude meant, so I went to the dictionary. When I sourced its meaning I realised I knew everything I wanted to know about turpitude except its name. The term describes 'depravity' and 'wickedness' and has its origins in the Latin term '*turpis*', meaning 'disgraceful' or 'base'. What is happening in countries that legalise prostitution is a shift away from the expectation of decency and towards the acceptance of turpitude, and this is done by denying the principal elements of prostitution, which are disgraceful, depraved, wicked and base.

Since prostitution is stylised as tolerable through the denial of its principal elements it is clear that it is made permissible only by way of the denial of its own nature. This aggressive rebuttal of the nature of prostitution is the mantra of prostitution enthusiasts, but what the proponents of prostitution do not realise is that their position strongly ratifies the position of the anti-prostitution movement. Refusal to recognise the presence of depravity etc. as integral to prostitution only confirms the wrongfulness of prostitution. If there is nothing wrong with prostitution, then why deny the presence of the fundamentals that make up its lived experience?

In fact, the notion of prostitution as free of a depraved nature is so glaringly fictional that most women who've never spent a day in prostitution can see straight through it. The offer of money for sex to most women would be met with offence and perhaps a swift smack in the mouth. This is true because women do not need to think about it; they instinctively sense the deeply derogatory nature of the proposal—and those who must strip prostitution of its true nature in order to frame it as acceptable are fooling nobody who would not prefer to be fooled.

The depraved nature of prostitution can be found in every single element of it, from those that are so obvious a non-prostituted person can see them, to those that are apparent only from the perspective of personal experience. For example, elsewhere in society there is a universally accepted rule, which is that it is not acceptable to encroach upon a stranger's personal space. This is not so in prostitution. Not only do prostituted women not own their own bodies but they have no rights to the space that surrounds them. This is another area of social normality from which they are excluded.

Often when I was working on the streets prospective clients would walk up to us and stand so close that we could smell the sweat off their skin. They would stand within inches of us, centimetres even, and peer and leer at us as if inspecting something particularly enticing that they might be choosing from a supermarket shelf; a rib-eye steak, for example. All aspects of our physicality would be inspected, but particularly the breasts. This behaviour on behalf of men was simply a consequence of our commodification and their interpretation of it. Their attitude expressed that we were not regarded as people; we were things to be bought, and like anything else that's for sale, we were liable to be held up to the scrutiny of intense consumer inspection. Also, as with a slab of meat, there was no consideration as to how sensitively that commodity ought to be scrutinised or inspected.

In brothel prostitution women are sometimes expected to line up while a punter inspects them to decide who he's going to fuck, and the dehumanising attitude is no different indoors and is in fact often worse, because there are no 'normal' members of society around to be appalled by it.

If prostitution is to be normalised then we must normalise all of the abnormal attitudes and interactions contained within it, but the base reality is that it is not normal to treat people like this. The attempt to normalise prostitution is therefore an attempt to normalise the abnormal, and because these abnormal ways of interaction cause human suffering, it is also an attempt to endorse the immoral.

For the normalisation of prostitution to be rejected its tactics must first be recognised and understood. These tactics are deeply ingrained in the communal psyche. Prostitution is often referred to as 'the oldest profession', as though, like a wise and aged individual, legitimacy were conferred on it by its years.

It is a tactic in the same vein as trying to whitewash the prostitution experience as 'sex work', and it is in the same vein because they both share the same objective. Make no mistake, behind these depictions is deliberate intent: it is the intent to marry prostitution with respectability, and here is the reason for that: what's respectable is acceptable.

There has also been an attempt by some to include prostituted women with gay men and women in order to frame the prostituted as a sexual minority. This is erroneous, because prostitution has nothing to do with sexual orientation. Any attempt to frame it so is akin to suggesting that an impoverished person in the developing world is engaged in a sexually expressive activity as they sew clothing for those in more affluent parts of the world.

This tactic constitutes an attempt to influence thinking in relation to prostitution while relying on the false premise of a moral high ground, and to alter the political landscape in relation to prostitution by assuming the rights of legitimate sexual minorities, to which it has no rightful claim. At an extreme level, pro-prostitution groups have caught on to the idea and have even taken this fiction so far as to march in Gay Pride Festivals! It is a wonder they are welcome to do so. It is a wonder the gay community cannot see how it is being used.

This attempt to reframe the prostitution experience is found in every endeavour that is complicit in the normalising of prostitution, so it is useful to have so stark an example of what to look for. As for the prostitution advocates who march in Gay Pride Festivals around the world, they know as well as I do that what they're doing constitutes a deliberate

PAID FOR

and calculated alignment with sexual minority groups, with the hope
and the intention that the legal and civil rights currently being conferred
on those groups will rub off.

Quite simply, the pro-prostitution lobby is trying to pull a fast one
here, and it is lucky, both for those who know the truth about prostitution and for those who want to know it, that their efforts so clearly
constitute a square-peg/round-hole scenario. I can absolutely assure the
reader that, not only did we not see ourselves as a sexual minority, but
the suggestion never even raised its ridiculous head.

|PART THREE

Chapter 22 ∾

INTEGRATING MYSELF INTO SOCIETY

*The natural flights of the human mind are not from plea-
sure to pleasure, but from hope to hope.*

SAMUEL JOHNSON, *THE RAMBLER*

If anyone supposes that leaving prostitution ought to be met with
some sort of jubilant mental fanfare, I cannot say they are mistaken
in all cases, but they are certainly mistaken in mine. On leaving
prostitution, I swapped the daily living of it for the daily reeling from
it. I swapped enduring it for examining it. Both were uniquely painful,
and the latter had its own flavours of fragmentation, new ones to contend with. For example, I could make no link that seemed worth making between my present-day self and the fourteen-year-old girl who'd
walked out of her mother's house eight years before. Who was she any
more? And who was I? And how in God's name could we be in any way
related when the one thing that spanned the distance between us was a
rotten foetid experience that had morphed her out of all existence? That
wasn't growing up. That was growing out, out of myself. It took a very
long time to accept that what was good about me had survived prostitution; that the more basic elements of my fourteen-year-old self still
existed and that they still existed inside me.

When you grow through the stages of adolescence into adulthood in
prostitution, you've literally grown up in prostitution. It informs everything you know. It was hard for me to face that I'd grown up in that, and
harder still to identify what was left of my original self. I felt like a girl
who'd gone to a party in a beautiful new dress, lost hours she could not

number, and come to consciousness covered in dirt and clothed in rags. I could not connect to myself. I'd lost the view of who I was. Dissociation had become concrete.

I had thought to title this chapter 'reintegrating myself into society', until I was struck by the realisation that progressing into prostitution from a childhood where I was never socially assimilated in the first place means that I did not re-integrate myself into society. I began the task of integrating myself into society at twenty-two, for the first time. Needless to say, this was not easy. Much of what made it difficult was the daily assault of memory. This did not lessen easily. It took years before a lessening even began.

It is said that time is a great healer, but I am inclined to think that maybe time heals nothing. Maybe all it does is create distance between you and that which you wish could be healed. There is comfort in this distance, and I think it is possible that people have mistaken the comfort of distance for the comfort of healing. In any case, for a long time I thought that was the only comfort I could take, and I was happy to take it.

I spent my first year out of prostitution cultivating this distance without knowing that was what I was doing. I had begun my last cocaine binge on 16 June 1998. It was a short one. It only lasted two days. That was no credit to me; it stopped for the same reason it had always done: the cocaine had run out. Once I began a binge I never stopped for any other reason, but I had spent months before that trying to stop taking cocaine in the first place.

Most of my attempts were pitiful. I would get two days clean, maybe three. I even got five days once or twice. These were big deals, those clean days; bigger than I can express. If you've lived in a madhouse of the mind for four years there's a lot to be said for a three-day reprieve. I kept going, and then I'd got one week, one month clean, and then I packed up my child and whatever else was worth taking and got on a bus that would take us out of Dublin to the house in the countryside I'd rented for a year. That was some year.

An immediate after-effect of cocaine abuse is a well-documented crippling depression. It passes within a couple of days. What is less spoken of is the milder but longer-term sadness that lingers after you've spent years abusing your body and mind with a narcotic substance. I'd wake in the morning in our weirdly quiet home, get my child ready for school and walk the considerable distance to its gates: I didn't drive at the time and no bus passed that way. This year away from Dublin was supposed to be an exercise in getting my life together, but when I returned from the school and sat alone with my thoughts I felt that my life was anything but together. I saw, really saw, what my life amounted to. The summer that had just passed was a time when I'd felt I had no other choice but to get drug free. It was because my only child was about to start his first year at school. That was the reason why. It's a reason every parent will understand.

In those days I was a mother with nothing else to hold onto but instinct, and I am so glad to say that instinct prevailed and served us both. But as for that first year of clean living, that was spent in the sort of contemplation inevitable for someone kicking a drug problem on her own. I wonder now how different it might have been had I had some professional support, but I know as quickly as I raise the question that the answer doesn't matter. I got through it without rehab, or counselling, or any other service luxurious and non-essential to a rabbit bolting out of a trap. I spent that year looking at the sitting-room wall, and in all that looking, I found some way back to the idea of living a drug-free life.

Before that first year was out I knew I had to get back to Dublin. I missed home, and I was tired of being reminded I was an outsider by some of the locals, who were so clannish-minded they couldn't cope with the understanding that I came from an hour's drive away. I found myself, again, packing up my child and our belongings, but this time, thankfully, heading for home.

I rented an apartment on the north side of Dublin. I felt very positive about this new start, and about the future, but as soon as my child started the new school term I found myself living on social welfare again and staring at the wall all day wondering what to do with myself.

The time between wondering was spent watching daytime television shows and reading British women's magazines, until one day it occurred to me to write something for one of them, so I did. I amused myself that day by writing a scandalous piece of imagination about a woman whose husband passes out drunk on their wedding night and who decides, while drunk and feeling sorry for herself, to consummate something other than her marriage with someone other than her husband. I waited a couple of months and then forgot all about the piece. Long after I assumed it had been dismissed without even the courtesy of a rejection slip, a cheque for two hundred and fifty pounds sterling dropped through my door. It had been nine or ten months since I'd posted my story and that cheque wasn't only a welcome financial surprise, it was an affirmation that I was capable of making money by doing something I enjoyed rather than something I detested. I can scarcely express the surprise I felt at opening that envelope. I'm sure it didn't cost a thought to the person who posted it, but opening it gave me such joy, confidence and hope.

My mind then began to operate on a different level. I began to imagine things that hadn't felt previously imaginable to me. I began to want things I hadn't dared want before, at least not overtly; not in the sense that I could imagine them manifesting in a real and tangible way. The first thing I knew I wanted to do was to learn how to type.

When I'd been arrested at sixteen I'd spent a short time in a technical school in south Dublin under the order of the children's court, during which time I'd discovered word processors. Within weeks I'd moved on from the technical school and before long was back on the streets, but I never forgot about the word processors. I had watched in amazement as the words were manipulated on the screen and I realised I had just come across a fascinating invention. I saw this as a way I could process not just my words, but my thoughts; I saw it as a perfect way to put order on the writing experience.

I had always written. As a teenager I would scribble on bits of paper and cardboard and the back of beer mats. My bag would be full of loose scraps of paper, hurriedly torn from notebooks and flyleaves and anywhere else I could think of. Every receipt was unravelled, pressed flat, and the back covered in my semi-legible scrawl. I was once arrested by a policewoman and had to endure the embarrassment of her reading my poems and verses, before turning to me wide-eyed and asking: 'Did you write this?' The humiliation evaporated. I had thought she was going to

sneer at me. Instead I was moved because she was moved. It was nice to
know someone thought I wasn't suited to the life I was living.

During those post-prostitution afternoons when I sat alone in my
flat, I didn't know what I might possibly do in the future, but I knew
I had a feeling those word processors ought to have something to do
with it. The problem was, at twenty-three and knowing nothing about
the education system, I thought myself too old to return to learning. I
thought that because I hadn't got the Leaving Cert, I hadn't got a chance
of being accepted anywhere. I'd never even heard the term 'mature student'. It simply wasn't used in the circles I'd grown up in.

At exactly that point there occurred one of the oddest things that's
ever happened in my family. I had always known that my mother was
adopted; she had been adopted by a Dublin couple in the late 1940s
and raised as an only child. In 1999, her half-sister tracked her down
through her marriage records, so she came to find my mother through
my father's sister, whom my mother hadn't spoken to in the best part
of twenty years. My brother called in and told me about all this and
I could scarcely believe what I was hearing. In fact, it sounded to me
very much like another of my mother's schizophrenic fantasies. Sadly,
many of them focused on her family of origin, and anyway, you might
expect the family of an adopted woman to come looking for her in her
late teens or in her twenties; you do not expect it in her fifties. But my
brother assured me it was true.

I passed my number on for my mother's sister to call me, which she
did, and the situation turned out to be very much authentic. The upshot
of all this was I went from having no aunts to having two, one from my
mother's side and one from my father's, and the important point in that
was that I suddenly had something else I'd never had: two older female
relatives to advise me. They wasted no time in influencing me to return
to education and I was stunned to learn that anybody over the age of
twenty-three could apply for further education without having a Leaving Certificate.

I enrolled for a course at a Post-Leaving Certificate college for the
following term. I remember shaking, probably visibly, as I was sitting in
the college hall waiting for the interview. I got a place on a course spe-

cifically for adults returning to education that taught typing, communications and computer applications, including word processing.

Although I was terrified, I advanced quickly. We were all given electronic typewriters to bring home to practise on and we were advised to practise for forty minutes a night. I never practised for less than an hour; it was a joyous experience to be learning how to type. I was the fastest typist in the class when we graduated at the end of the year, and I got four distinctions out of the five modules we studied, gaining a merit for the fifth (which was Microsoft Excel—figures have never been my strong point).

By the spring of the following year I had decided what I wanted to do in the future and so I applied for a place on a journalism degree course at Dublin City University. This was no small thing. There isn't a word or any combination of words that could adequately describe my fear at walking into that university for the first time. When I went in for an interview, I was walking into the unknown. I was attempting to shove myself into a mould that didn't fit, that didn't recognise me; or if it did, I felt, recognised me as something that didn't belong; but to hell with it, I thought, I would stick my square self into the round hole, because some part of me knew I had to be there. I was trying, attempting, *determining*, to attain for myself a new life, a new existence; a new way of relating to the world and, for the first time, framing the terms I expected the world to relate back to me. I felt just as I'd done approaching the PLC college, only much more amplified, and the huge imposing buildings of DCU seemed to reflect back that difference.

I was successful at the interview, and then hurled straight into a different sort of nerve-wracking time. I had been offered a place but it was conditional on my grades from the PLC course being high enough to secure it. I needed a majority of distinctions, so I was told, but I wouldn't know my results until late that summer. I had to spend most of the summer waiting to see if the grades from my PLC course would be high enough to get me into DCU. They were, thankfully, and I went to university in September of that year.

There were problems for me in university that I hadn't foreseen coming. I had been worried about my academic capabilities, but those for the most part weren't a worry. I did fall down badly in a couple of subjects but I just took grinds in those. The real problem was in making myself believe I had a right to be there. I always had this sense that I was about to be found out; that I would soon be discovered as ineligible and unworthy. It had been just over three years between the end of my prostitution life and the beginning of my university one, and I still was so mired in a negative view of myself that I would sit sometimes alongside my classmates and almost wonder how they could not recognise me as an imposter. How they could not spot the prostitute in the room.

To assimilate into this highly regarded social setting was very difficult, because being a drug-addicted prostitute positions you at the very bottom of the social scale; you just don't get much lower than that. So any woman in my former situation has a lot to come back from and there were great tremors of insecurity involved in the climb. I remember one of my classmates saying during a first year seminar: 'It is much easier to fall than it is to climb'. Another classmate traced his finger down his face, as if indicating an invisible tear, and laughed. It was a joke and it was not directed at me, but still, it stung the hell out of me. I wanted to break his face for him. Those kinds of feelings were enormous, but I got by with them and I graduated with them too.

One of the difficulties I had no way of foreseeing was figuring out how to behave when setting boundaries in normal mainstream situations, like going to college and then going to work. I had a very strong sense of how to handle myself in prostitution, of how to deal with people and how to protect myself; but I had a very damaged sense of how to frame the boundaries of what was acceptable to me in these standard social situations.

In college, I see now looking back, I was inappropriately aggressive. The only time I ever hurt anyone physically was when one classmate shoved his tongue in my mouth while drunk in the student bar. I stewed on the sense of violation for days, and head-butted him the next time I saw him. Apart from that, I never hurt anyone physically in college, but I occasionally felt like it, and I was relentlessly verbally forceful. I realise that I came off as mouthy and, most likely, a bitch. The truth is that I was frightened, intimidated, and trying to find my feet in a place I only half-believed I deserved to be.

I remember making a remark one day in class in response to something the lecturer had said. I forget what she'd said, but my response was: 'But what if you got into college by the back door?' This was supposed to be funny. Nobody laughed, and I was embarrassed. When she next saw me alone she remarked that I seemed under-confident, and that there was no reason for me to be. I was mortified that she'd picked up on that, but I also thought it was sweet of her to have said what she said. I thought as well, for obvious reasons, that she didn't know the half of it.

So that was one of the ways my prostitution history affected me and those around me while I was trying to live the life of a 'normal' young woman in third level education. Sometimes I would just sit on the campus benches between classes, smoking and wondering how I got there, while staring at the big university buildings all around and trying to measure the distance between them and the houses on Waterloo Road, in a way that had nothing to do with miles.

By the time I began working I had the opposite problem; I no longer reacted with verbal aggression when I felt insulted or demeaned. I had figured out that that wasn't acceptable in the real world and that it didn't make me feel good either, but what I hadn't figured out was how else to handle those situations. So instead I retreated silently into myself when treated badly or spoken to abruptly and just took it, because I didn't know what else to do. If I was out and about in public I would react as I'd always done, that is to say aggressively, to such slights, but in work, where I was expected to conform to social norms, I hadn't the first idea how to enforce healthy boundaries in a reasonable and appropriate way.

Thankfully, I have since learned how to do that. I have learned how to calmly state that I am offended by something that's been said to me, and more often than not I can resolve things without the need for any further discord.

It was only in recent years I learned that people who have been sexually violated, especially in childhood, almost without exception present a skewed and unhealthy understanding of boundaries, with their ideas of boundaries being either far too rigid or far too lax, and I see now how I swung between those extremes, as I tried to find my own balance in the world. As I find my way towards that equilibrium, I find that I am feeling more balanced and centred in the core of my own self.

Integrating herself into society is not the only challenge for the former prostitute. There is a larger, more important and more difficult one: she must also learn to integrate herself into herself. Sex is the first stumbling block and here is the problem with it: we women have learned, over the course of countless encounters, to remove ourselves mentally and emotionally from the sexual act. We have gotten so used to divorcing ourselves from our feelings and so attuned to the small acts which signify when it is time to do that, that we are left in the position of Pavlov's dogs, where the unbuckling of a belt causes us to shut off and shut down. This position must be regarded as reversible if we are to hold out any hope of living a normal life. There is one element which makes this possible: it is deep trust between the formerly prostituted woman and her partner.

For my own sake, I was not so damaged that I could not think of trusting a man, though I've known some women for whom this would have been very unlikely, if not impossible. But I had not lost the capacity to love men, and I am very glad of it. As far as my relationships are concerned, I have a very firm necessity to feel respected by a man I am involved with. If I do not feel respected in a relationship I cannot stay in it. If I did, I would begin to hate myself. I think it is true of all of us to a greater or lesser extent, that if we stay with somebody who treats us with contempt we will internalise that contempt, and it becomes a part of us; it becomes a part of our view of the self.

This is something I think of like the circular stain on a table left behind by a hot mug. It has been accentuated and stamped on me by my prostitution experience. No matter; rejecting contempt is one thing I'm good at. Appreciating the difference between sexual contempt and loving intimacy is another. A powerful truth is that when men express their love through sex, they can bring incredible healing, and I want men to know that and to understand that, and to know and understand too how much heterosexual women love and appreciate them for it, especially if we have ever been prostituted.

Another of the problems I've faced in moving on has been in how those close to me process my prostitution past. I think what we do sometimes as humans is to interpret what we encounter in line with what we already know or believe; or, more frequently, to superimpose upon these things the shape of our own present needs. I do it myself. I think that's what I did the first time I read the Desiderata.

Recently one of my sisters gave me a copy of that beautiful verse on bronze-coloured canvas with a brown paper label attached informing me it had been screen-printed by hand in Bali. I hadn't read the Desiderata in many years and didn't read it for many months after she gave it to me, instead rolling it up and putting it away, knowing I'd be moving to a new home soon and would find a place for it when I got there.

When I eventually unpacked it and hung it by my computer I sat there reading it, in anticipation of the closing line, which has always been my favourite. I was surprised and disappointed to read that it was not the line I remembered. I'd had that verse hanging on my wall many years before, when I was sixteen and living in a little flat in Rathmines, a year after I'd entered prostitution. I had often repeated that line to myself during tough times, for the sense of comfort I drew from it. The line I'd repeated was: 'With all its shame and drudgery and broken dreams, it is still a beautiful world; be careful, strive to be happy'.

The actual line, as I've recently discovered, reads: 'With all its *sham*, drudgery, and broken dreams, it is still a beautiful world; be *cheerful*, strive to be happy'.

I was disappointed to read this because the line I'd been comforting myself with for many years did not exist as part of the Desiderata, as I'd always taken for granted that it had. I think what happened was that line hadn't rung true for me. It was not what I had needed. Shame, after all, was far more relevant to me than sham and to be careful was far more appropriate and realistic advice for me than to be cheerful!

I think this is what we do as humans. I think that, in many areas of our lives, we look at what's in front of us and take from it what we need at that present time. That's the only way I can explain my having misread the closing lines of the Desiderata every one of the many times I read it hanging on my wall, and it's the only way I can explain my having morphed prostituting myself from something that horrified me into a matter of courage: because that's what I needed prostitution to be at that time.

There is nothing unusual in this. I was once disturbed and devastated by the drunken comment of a former lover when he said that he 'found something erotic' about my having worked as a prostitute. I felt so angry and let down and hurt that I immediately began to cry. I confronted him with the reality of my prostitution experience, between sobs, and it was only as I watched the guilt build in his eyes that I could calm down, as I could see him begin to understand the nature of my experience and the monstrous inappropriateness of his finding eroticism in it. I don't hold that against him. I can see what he was doing. He was morphing prostitution into something he needed it to be. He had processed my prostitution past in the way that best suited him and given it the shape and texture of something much more palatable. This is what we do as humans; we process it the way we need to process it and this is true of very many people who give thought to prostitution. As for my then-partner; it was easier, much easier, for him to find something sexy in my past than to confront the fact that the woman he loved had been ritually sexually abused.

I am learning now to harness this capacity to interpret things in line with what I want and need; to acknowledge the positives and the signs of moving on that can be found in just about anything, and it really is astonishing that these interpretations can be found in the most everyday and commonplace routines. I was standing recently in the street reading a notice for planning permission and I turned for some reason and saw a man watching me as he walked on the other side of the road. It occurred to me immediately (probably because I am immersed in writing these pages) that had I been standing just like this in a place very unlike this, he would have assumed that I was a prostitute. There is a great privacy, the privacy of anonymity, afforded to people as they stand on a normal street. I think you have to have experienced its opposite to fully appreciate it.

So this is one of the positives of my post-prostitution life; this new reality; this new quiet understanding that I am regarded just as a woman. Not a whore of a woman or a slut of a woman or a promiscuous morally-stained or dirty woman; but just as a woman.

I had already been a woman several years before I knew what it felt like to be considered one, with no adjectives attached. But this, now that I am finally experiencing it, is a new reality in which I and my new non-prostituted identity have moved beyond the first steps of tentative acquaintance and are becoming intimately linked. It has a calming and peaceful texture, this feeling of just being a woman.

I want to hold onto this and to build on it so that I can move closer to thinking of myself in this way at all times, and I hope for a time when I can look at my prostitution experience, but not stare at it, and finally disentangle where I've been from who I am.

| DEPRESSION AND SUICIDE

Suicide is a significant consequence of prostitution.
C STARK AND R WHISNANT, *NOT FOR SALE*

Of course, with a history like mine, I suppose it is only natural that, down the years, I would have had my struggles with depression. Those years started very early actually, from that first suicide attempt aged eleven, and I now perceive that I was in a state of depression for all of my adolescence and much of my childhood.

Depression affects the sufferer negatively in numerous ways. You can become so paranoid and withdrawn that it is a huge psychological effort to mix in society, even if it is as simple a thing as buying something inconsequential, like a cup of coffee or a packet of cigarettes. Eye contact can be excruciating. But those moments are, thankfully, in the minority for me and it has been years since I've suffered from them badly. I usually carry myself with a confidence that doesn't require effort.

But my post-prostitution life has operated in cycles; at times I did not like to be alone. I would think too much and often my thoughts were not kind to me. There have been long stretches of time when I did not like or enjoy my own company. Sometimes, there was the near panic-filled desire to get out and away when I was in company, only to come home and dislike my own company even more. There was sometimes the sense of running and running, ceaseless running, and no matter where I arrived at, not being contented anywhere at all.

For quite a stretch after I got out of prostitution, I was ashamed of the lack of people in my life, but most of my old friends were either dead or dying of drug addiction and, in both cases, couldn't keep me company

any more. In more recent years, I have made new friends, but for a long time after I left prostitution, I told myself that I didn't make friends easily, and a part of me didn't even want to. At the same time, though, I often felt isolated and lonely. I am glad I am over that now. It's no way to live. I spent over three years in counselling and I first made the decision to go there because I could no longer deal with the fact that, at a very base level, I was still desperately unhappy. These were feelings that kept on resurfacing and had done over and over ever since I'd gotten off narcotics and could no longer numb them that way any more. Not all days are good days but I don't feel miserable the majority of the time any more and very often, I thank God for it.

One of the saving graces about psychotherapeutic counselling is that it makes you much more self-aware. I am much more connected to my feelings these days and I'm much better able to come to terms with some of the things that happened in the past.

It's a pity it took me so many years to go to therapy; it's something I think I should have done earlier, but then, as my therapist said to me one day: 'Don't "shouda" all over yourself!' What I did in the ten years between the time I left prostitution and cocaine and the time I entered therapy was to keep on moving forward in practical terms, securing an education and employment and a home, but what I failed to do for all that time was to try to remove the awful sadness that had dogged me all my life. Perhaps I came to that when I was ready.

I believe that words are powerful however we choose to use them. Great pain can be caused by the telling of an innocuous lie, but I believe another thing: words are at their most powerful when used to deliver truth. The problem and the conundrum for prostitutes is that the power behind the truisms we tell ourselves is as often negative as it is positive. We sometimes tell ourselves, while still embroiled in the business, that our experience is hateful and as true as this is (unless we use it as the impetus for change) it can do nothing to brighten our daily existence. The very truth of our situation is damaging and so if we tell ourselves the truth, we are victims of our own honesty.

This puts a woman in a situation whereby she can either begin to practise lying to herself (done usually by omitting to acknowledge the exactness of her experience) or sink further and further into depression. Most women choose the former for as long as they can get away with it, as I did. The truth, however, becomes more and more difficult to evade on a conscious level, and it has been impossible to evade on a subconscious level right from the start, because our inner selves always intuitively sense what is right for us and what is wrong. Depression dogs the prostitute from the start, because the core of her knows and feels this damage to the most private part of herself. The truth has been there right from the start and depression arrived right alongside it, as it did for me, on the first night I prostituted myself and went to sleep weeping.

The Diagnostic and Statistical Manual of Mental Disorders is the guide most commonly used by psychiatrists and other mental health professionals in the diagnosis of depressive disorders. I was shocked to read the list of symptoms. I was shocked because, during my last episode of depression (which was post-prostitution) I experienced and exhibited every last one. Had I been asked, I would have said that I was depressed, but had I been asked to quantify that on the scale used to measure this illness (mild, moderate to severe), I would never have thought to say that it was severe. I would have thought that it was moderate, middle-of-the-road depression. That is frightening to me. It is frightening to realise that I vastly underrated the depths of my own despair and it is saddening to understand why: I had felt so bad for so long that I had come to normalise those feelings.

For example, I was chronically indecisive. I would sometimes consider going to the shop and then allow the whole day to pass without my going. When night time came and the shop had closed, I'd feel lousy about my inability to make it there. That is another of the crueller aspects of depression, that way it has of causing the sufferers to berate themselves for exhibiting its symptoms. In this way depression multiplies, but it doesn't feed on itself; it feeds on the person it inhabits.

When a person is in the grip of severe depression, they are not mentally capable of making the distinction between shame-based feelings which have their roots in reality and those which arise as a symptom of their illness. Nor are they capable of identifying negative feelings which arise from outside the remit of the illness as distinct from those which are actually induced by it. During my last bout of depression, I didn't feel guilty about being depressed; I felt guilty because I couldn't make it as far as the local shop and my house was in chaos. That my perceived 'laziness' was symptomatic of my illness didn't occur to me. All I knew was that I felt lousy about myself and here was more evidence that I was quite right to do so. The very nature of depression dictates that the depressive will give credence to any negative feeling, no matter where it comes from.

I believe that depression is widespread among prostitutes and, while I am certainly not medically qualified to diagnose it, I don't believe a person always needs to have been medically trained in order to recognise its symptoms, particularly when they've had a ritual recurrence of it in their own lives. What I saw around me in prostitution was a consistent very low mood and what I saw almost as regularly was the abuse of alcohol and other mind-altering drugs. Depressives are notorious for self-medicating with alcohol and other substances.

A 2005 Ruhama research report on barriers affecting women in prostitution states: 'Studies in Ireland have found that 38% of women involved in prostitution have attempted suicide and 25% suffered from diagnosed depression and were in receipt of medical treatment.' It is my personal conviction that the twenty-five per cent of prostitutes recorded as having depression in Ireland is a significant *underestimate* of the true figure and that many prostitutes have not been diagnosed simply because they have not presented their symptoms to a doctor. I have good reason to think that. Any talk of doctors during my time in prostitution usually centred around STI health checks, and in the cases where it didn't, it would involve some other physical ailment, such as trips to A&E to have bones set, since some clients were apt to break them. That was where our health concerns began and ended. It was about keeping ourselves functioning physically; nothing to do with keeping ourselves functioning mentally or emotionally. In my experience prostituted women did not even consider their mental health and this never surprised me. It is a situation that exists, I believe, because women know going to a doctor for antidepressants while they're in prostitution is about as useful as being treated for lung cancer while you're smoking your brains out. As long as you are in proximity to it, this is not a malignancy you can ward off with a packet of antidepressant pills.

There is an inconsistency in the figures relating to depression among Irish prostitutes and they are worth taking a closer look at, because there is evidence here that depression is much more widespread than has been diagnosed and documented. Irish statistics prove that *thirty-eight* per cent of prostitutes have attempted suicide while only *twenty-five* per cent have been diagnosed with depression and received medical treatment for it. It's clear that there is a disparity between the number of prostitutes who have been diagnosed with depression and those who have attempted suicide. People who are not depressed are not usually given to attempting suicide, are they? And given that only a portion of those with depression actually attempt suicide, this obviously indicates that the percentage of prostitutes suffering from depression is significantly *higher* than the number of those who have tried to kill themselves. Horrifyingly so, I am sure.

Chapter 24 ❧

THE DAMAGE TO RELATIONSHIPS AND SEXUALITY

Consider the fact that I learned what sexuality meant from johns and pimps before I could find out what it might mean with the girl I loved. This lesson is not erasable. My body remembers all of it.

TOBY SUMMER IN *LESBIAN CULTURE: AN ANTHOLOGY*
BY JULIA PENELOPE & SUSAN WOLFE

I have found the act of sexual intercourse to be profoundly more pleasurable when experienced between two people who are in love. I didn't experience the depth of that disparity until I was twenty-two, and I had been having sex for seven years at that point. I can only imagine how much more intensified that ecstasy would have been had I not worked as a prostitute prior to that.

He and I went on to have a loving relationship and became engaged to be married. The marriage did not happen, but we are still friends to this day.

I will say, though, that I remember going asleep that first night I slept with him in what I can only describe as a state of exquisite shock from this powerful new discovery and waking up the following morning in exactly the same mental condition. It was as though every voluntary sexual encounter I'd ever had within relationships had been experienced in drab shades of grey and now I'd been made aware that in fact they were supposed to have been experienced in this vivid and glorious technicolour. It wasn't that I hadn't loved men before; I had, but I'd grown to love them, slowly and over time, whereas with this man I had fallen in love in the most rapid, passionate and classically romantic sense of the term.

I understood the place of the word 'fallen' in that term, then, for the first time, because falling is exactly what it's like: you are in a state of freefall where you cannot exercise any control whatever over the intensity of your own feelings, nor would you want to. Of course the thing about falling is that you eventually hit the ground, as he and I did, but it was worth the fall.

The sex though, that happened in those first three or four months, were spiritual experiences; of that much I am absolutely sure. I cannot say how exactly, or why, I can only say that they were; there was so much more going on there than the satisfying of a physical urge. It satiated an urge that was outside of and above my physical self and yet pulsated through me at the same time. It was a more pleasurable pulsating than I could ever have imagined prior to having experienced it and the satisfying of it gave me to understand the true meaning of terms like ecstasy, rapture and bliss. For me, there was a powerful romantic love entwined with a very great depth of caring in that relationship. This, for me, is the ultimate intimacy, and it is as far removed from prostitution as it is possible to imagine.

It is no coincidence that I left prostitution a few short months after making this discovery. There were several factors involved in my leaving, but a crucial one was that continuing to experience the opposite of joy through my sexuality was too much to bear.

A history like mine can be detrimental to romantic relationships. It fractures even the possibility of every relationship before it begins. It fractures your worth, as partner material, in the eyes of the men that you meet. I can accept that, up to a point. Few men would wilfully go looking for a former prostitute as a mate, just as few women (including myself) would deliberately go looking for a former gigolo; but I tell myself that if a man, after having gotten to know me, still held fast to his prejudices, well then he'd be the sort of man I wouldn't want to share my life with anyway.

Prostitution doesn't just hinder the likelihood of a woman settling down; it actually hinders her ability to do that. But it does not always impede her desire to conduct a normal healthy loving relationship; for me at least, it increased it. This is because when a woman regularly experiences the sleazy, disrespectful and debased side of male-to-female sexual relations it can create in her a longing for the respectful, principled sexual love that can and does exist between men and women. In short, a woman begins to yearn for prostitution's opposite; and she does this because she misses the romantic sexual gentleness a man who's in love with her can provide. This is especially so if she has had profound experiences of that in her past. The reason for that is simple: we all miss what's missing.

Most older prostitutes will tell you that nothing a man did or requested her to do would surprise her any more, and some have lost all their faith in men and in relationships as a result. Psychological scarring is inevitable in prostitution and one of the most common forms of it is in a fractured capacity for relationships, but psychological damage so severe that a woman is wholly incapable of conducting a relationship on any level is, thankfully, not the norm from what I've seen.

It seems to be assumed that embittered, aged prostitutes are incapable of forming or maintaining relationships and are generally found among street-walking women. But I met many women during my street-walking days, decades older than me, most of whom were returning to husbands and male partners at the end of each night. A general distrust of men is a natural consequence of prostitution and this distrust usually runs very deep, but that is not the same thing as hatred.

I think most women experience the recognisable human desire to 'settle down'; to strive towards a place with her mate where they are both enveloped in the security of commitment, which acts both as a comforter in its own right and as a buffer against loneliness. I am, like many women, someone who craves devotion and particularly the respectful sexual loyalty that monogamy brings. I think that mutual commitment is coveted by both genders, but I suspect that it is more strongly desired by women. Many females seem to desire commitment to a degree that transcends want and is so suffused with requirement as to be actually experienced as need. The influences that encourage women to think and feel this way are far outside the scope of this book, but let me just say that prostituted women are no less inclined (and are probably more inclined) than any other group of women to need companionship to counterbalance the loneliness of their working lives.

The problem for prostitutes is that they are not pegged on the lowest point on the scale of desirable partners; they are not placed on the scale at all, so they do not play out the fear of rejection, as some women do, only in their minds; they live out the authentic reality of romantic rejection in their daily lives. It is not hard to see why.

Germaine Greer, in her 1969 classic, *The Female Eunuch*, made the case for women's sexuality having been unnaturally downgraded to being merely reactive and responsive. It is true that it has been and it is true that social conditioning has been responsible for it. It is also true that in no other group of women has sexuality been so hobbled as in prostitution. Where sexuality has been hobbled, intimate relationships inevitably share in the handicap.

One of the principal handicaps of the formerly prostituted woman is the conditioning that causes her to keep on slipping into the role of the pornified objectified female—the subject of the sexual encounter, rather than an equal participant. This is a disabling tendency that has been learned by relentless repetition. It is detrimental to true intimacy and it must firstly, painfully, be identified, before we can ever even begin to work towards its eradication.

Reclaiming my own sexuality in the aftermath of prostitution has been an ongoing process. For me, it was initially a matter of reclaiming my sexual autonomy. On leaving prostitution, I had simply been programmed to be sexually pliable. This is necessary in prostitution. The woman who is not sexually pliable leaves herself open to vicious violent assault; but the upshot of this unnatural programming meant that it would never have occurred to me to refuse my partner sex, regardless of what sort of mood I was in or how I felt about it. I didn't even ask myself how I felt about it.

I was so young and so sexually inexperienced when I became involved in prostitution that those formative years of sexual growth and learning were spent absorbing a very skewed and unnatural depiction of adult sexual relations. It wasn't simply a matter of my experiencing sex within the client/prostitute dynamic and superimposing that image above the one that ought to have existed in my mind; my sexual schooling was much more subtle than that. I was not stupid; I understood that this was not normal natural sex, but the way that it led me to feel about myself and also about sex was so suffused with negativity that somewhere in my mind the link was forged between sexuality and duty (the 'just do it' mentality) and though my conscious self was not utterly submerged beneath it, I was wholly unexposed, for a long time, to the link between sexuality and loving. I was aware enough of it to miss it, but enough unused to it not to go looking for it either.

And so my feelings didn't enter into the equation. In this, I had taken the most fundamental reality of prostitution with me into my personal life. It took me several years to set about breaking that habit; and in fact it needed to be pointed out to me before I even became aware of it. I also had the unfortunate tendency of taking my arousal from my partner's arousal; that is, I would very rarely become aroused in my own right but rather would become aroused by feeling his arousal. I would quite literally feed off his feelings in the sexual sense and I did that because very often something inside me was absent and I would have, for long stretches of time, no independent sexual functioning of my own.

Thankfully, one of my post-prostitution partners worked up the nerve to say to me, 'I never know if you're enjoying sex. Because you say yes all the time, I never know if you want it or not'. I went over our sexual encounters in my mind (we'd been together about nine months at the time) and I saw that in each of them I had reacted to him in the same way. There was no variation. I had always responded positively to his advances, and always with the same degree of intensity, regardless of my mood, the extent of my passion, or complete lack of it. So how could he have known if I was enjoying sex, or even if I wanted it?

He sensed something of the wooden doll I had been made into and felt compelled to remark on it. What that comment caused me to do was to start spending time observing my own sexual behaviour and responses. As soon as I had shone a spotlight on them, I found that I was behaving like an automaton, or a car with only one gear. The first thing I began to do to rectify the situation was to say no to sex when I was not in the mood. Rather than allow myself to be coerced I'd simply say: 'No, I'm not in the mood'. How strange it was to find that I (usually a fairly determined woman who does not allow herself to be talked round) had spent all the years of my post-prostitution life relating to my partners in a way that negated all my sexual autonomy! It was a tremendous relief to begin to give voice to my true sexual feelings, and giving them voice first made them become real to me and then made them become my own again. It brought me back in touch with my own sexuality, and of course, it made the encounters when I said 'Yes', all the more meaningful also. As well as that, it allowed me to initiate sex in a new way, with the heightened level of confidence that comes from being utterly sure about something. But I am still moving towards my sexual self by increments. It is, and probably always will be, an on-going process.

The damage to female sexual autonomy that Greer speaks of is amplified many times in the sexuality of the prostituted woman. Not only has she been socially conditioned to overlook her own sexual autonomy, as women generally have been; she has been trained, in the name of self-preservation, to actively refute and deny even the possibility of its existence. This is because the notion of female sexual autonomy in prostitution is a dangerous thing. It counteracts the majority of male fantasy and is known to provoke reactions ranging right the way through from mild annoyance to extreme aggression and all the way to murderous rage. It is safest to refute that it exists, and where it does manifest it is only in a bawdy caricature, in the cases where a dominatrix is required, at the request and for the pleasure of a man, of course. I could not always contain my sexual autonomy, as I have already explained. Pulling away from clients who mistreated me was something I felt compelled to do at times, and when I did, I always paid for it. This also damages the sexual psyche. It trains the mind to continue with sexual activities regardless, even if they have become painful or in any other way unpleasant. This, too, manifested in, and further damaged, my personal sexual relationships.

I do not want to talk in this work too much about partners and lovers, because this book is not about them, but it is important to say that I have felt profoundly comforted in the emotional sense by experiencing monogamy in my post-prostitution life. I've only had sexual encounters with four men in the last fourteen years and all were in relationships, two of them long-term.

I agree with the findings of international prostitution research which conclude that: 'It is impossible to preserve yourself and your emotional life when you are involved in prostitution.'[27] Women do conduct relationships while in prostitution (as I did and as I witnessed others do), but they are inevitably affected by the polluting dynamics at play. These dynamics do not stop operating on the day a woman leaves prostitution and the influence they exert does not entirely end any time afterwards.

This continuing pollution can also be seen in women's non-intimate female-to-male interactions and relationships. For example, with women, I am a very tactile person. If I see that a woman is at all upset, I am moved by compassion to comfort her physically. I will, almost without thinking, rest my hand on her arm or her shoulder or her back. I find these gestures from women comforting also. They are welcome to me because they are soothing and consoling and never cause me to feel anything but a sense of being reassured; but the same gesture from a man who I am not very close to will cause me to jolt with discomfort and reel from the sense that my body and physical space have been invaded. It is a sad truth that a man's benign and gentle intentions usually have no mitigating power for a woman here. They are more often no match for the brutal force of the lessons prostitution has taught her.

And as for intimate acts, oftentimes during personal sexual experiences in a woman's post-prostitution life she will be assailed by intrusive memories of physically similar acts within prostitution. This damages her ability to be intimate with her partner. I have had this happen in all of my intimacies with men since leaving prostitution. Sometimes he'll put his hand on your breasts, or his lips to your nipple, or his hand on your thigh, and you'll be nearly overcome with a flood of unwelcome and uninvited memories, each of them mirroring what you are now

27 Relayed in 'The Next Step Initiative', Ruhama research report on barriers affecting women in prostitution, Ireland, 2005.

experiencing. They don't knock on the door of your mind, these memories; they let themselves in. You cannot prevent them, and this is one example of the lasting damage of prostitution in the lives of the women it touches.

An example of this would be the way I experienced a near inability to give one of my post-prostitution partners fellatio. For a good chunk of that relationship, I just could not go down on that man. It began as a faint sense of unwillingness that would have faded away on its own if it had been allowed to. Instead it rapidly escalated in response to his constant persistence. I felt trapped. It was, in fact, very little to do with his penis and everything to do with the feeling of *having to*; the feeling of not getting a say in the matter; the feeling of *having no choice*. I'd imagine having the emotions of my prostitution life recalled will always be traumatic enough to provoke these sorts of sexual shut-downs, but, as I have since discovered, they are sometimes avoidable.

After that experience (and mainly because of it) I told my next lover that I had been abused in that way, and that consequently I found it very difficult to give fellatio if I felt compelled to do it. He told me that was all he needed to know and that he'd never pressure me on that point. He never did. The issue of blow-jobs never even came up until I approached him, and when I did it was out of the pure desire to pleasure him. It was such a relief to experience again the deep arousal I had occasionally felt during that sexual act, and I know it could only have happened because the man I was with was patient, caring and understanding. It could only have happened, in other words, with a man whose behaviour did not imbue in me the feeling of *having to*. It takes a measure of maturity for a man to know how to bring out the best sexually in a woman whose body has been abused. I was lucky to become involved with a man like that.

Thankfully, I continue to find men erotic and arousing. For me, there is nothing more sexually seductive than watching a beautiful man sleep. I have had it asked of me: might this be true because the fear of danger is negated for me while a man is sleeping? I don't think so; or rather if that forms any part of it I think it is a very small part. I've always felt that there was some hidden vulnerability in masculinity that becomes exposed when a man is sleeping, and this is both deeply alluring and endearing to me. It is alluring on a sexual level and endearing on an emotional one, and because these two things combine here, sexual arousal and emotional connection, I know that my sexuality and capacity for relationships has not been damaged beyond repair.

There are big hurdles though, before a relationship can even begin. Firstly, forming the wrong relationships out of a simple lack of self-love is one of the major stumbling blocks for formerly prostituted women; I have experienced this in my own life and seen it in the lives of others. My first post-prostitution relationship was with a man I was deeply in love with, but who could not have a functional relationship due to his chronic alcoholism. I persisted in trying to make things work, in trying to make something healthy flourish with someone who was simply too sick to be in a relationship, and I cut lumps out of myself emotionally in the effort, before I eventually walked away.

The second of my post-prostitution relationships exemplifies how formerly prostituted women are drawn to damaging emotional situations probably more clearly than the first. He was simply incapable of receiving love, never mind returning it. The result was a relationship that was relentlessly emotionally traumatic.

We spent several years together but any expression of loyalty or devotion to me would have been to capitulate to me, in his strange and unfathomable mentality. I was consistently placed last in his life, in ways that were publicly degrading and demeaning and seemed almost designed to be so.

There was a consistency of contempt that is sickening to me now, more in the memory of my accepting it than anything to do with its being levelled against me. There were enough of these incidents to compose a small book in itself, and of course they are not worthy of that attention. I was affronted beyond belief and ripped my own mind to shreds trying to make sense out of these situations, all the while I could not or would not grasp that he was simply emotionally violent.

Moving out—that was his favourite thing. We only lived together for eighteen months but I could not count the times he moved out. Folding clothes, throwing books into bags, stacking letters and papers, packing ornaments; he loved the ritual. Every action that communicated 'I'm leaving you' had both a deeper message and a real objective. The message: you're not worth staying with. The objective: cause maximum possible hurt.

It was a wonder we ever got to the point of moving in at all, as pretending I did not exist was another favourite of his, practised with dedicated regularity. After every single row he would not call for one week, two weeks, three. He dragged it out for five weeks on one occasion, after I'd dared to question a smutty message from an Australian woman that had popped up on his computer screen. When he eventually decided to make his reappearance in my life, he questioned, with genuine perplexity, why I had lost twenty pounds in weight. Weeks later he mentioned, quite casually, as though there was nothing in the world wrong with it, that he had contacted the sister of his Australian laureate, who he was also exchanging emails with. I said nothing, and was ashamed of myself for saying nothing.

Tolerating contempt *is* shame-inducing, but I see today why I kept silent. I couldn't go through another five weeks of his manipulation by withholding. He practised it with ruthlessness and regularity and I responded to it, for about the first half of our time together, by obscuring my very self; by superimposing a meek and agreeable character over my own, like a child trying to be pleasing in order to avoid a beating.

Eventually instinct began to draw me back towards my sense of self and then followed the most serious tremors in the fault line our relationship was built on. I simply would not accept being left to sit alone, wondering what sort of relationship this was supposed to be, while he was out five nights a week. He could not bear his interpretation of my emerging self, or the requirement for basic respect that came with it, which he translated as 'being dictated to'.

I ask myself now how could I have gone back, again and again, knowing as I did, better than anyone, the deliberate emotional cruelty I would be subjected to? How do we rationalise an internal acceptance of emotional abuse? The bog-standard 'I loved him' is embarrassingly inadequate here. It is more truthful, and so of course more essentially painful, to admit it had little to do with my feelings for him. The aching truth is sometimes freeing and the truth here is that that relationship was only sparked by my love for him. It was sustained by my lack of love for myself.

So that is one of the damages of prostitution—you've been trained to regard yourself as dirt, so you don't expect love from those who are supposed to love you. As skewed as your mind may be, you hold onto something of logic, and something inside yourself asks, who would find something worth loving in a piece of dirt?

So that is what we formerly prostituted women sometimes do; we find ourselves in toxic relationships with others who slowly poison them in an active or passive aggressive manner and we often do a good deal of the poisoning ourselves. We doom our own relationships by entering the wrong ones to begin with and we torture ourselves by being drawn to situations where we recreate the familiar feelings of being alone, insignificant and disrespected. When those feelings intensified in me to the point where I could no longer stand them I responded in the one way that was sure to accelerate our demise: I drank like the day before Prohibition.

Of course you move on and you learn and it is unlikely that I will find myself dealing with those dynamics again. Certain red flags are identifiable to me now, but the point is they would have been identifiable to a woman with a healthier view of herself to begin with. A woman with a healthy view of herself does not spend years of her life with somebody she thinks is her best friend, only to discover that he hasn't behaved like any kind of friend.

Looking back now I see why that relationship was always going to end. When you long for commitment and devotion, the evidential manifestations of love, and are wretchedly disappointed by their absence, there is no way forward from there that I can see or imagine. And yet there was no accepting that then, because I didn't just love him: I adored him.

So there are all these hindrances and hurdles before a formerly prostituted woman can even begin a relationship, and if she has found someone with whom she can form a worthwhile bond, that is not the end of the obstacles either. Telling him about your past is nearly the hardest part. Your throat constricts with fear. The words feel like tangible things; big lumps of words you must heave up to where your Adam's apple would be if you had one. And you have one today. You can feel it in your throat like a tightly compressed collection of rocks, digging into you until you've managed to choke it out, that collection of words, and then you do, and then comes the hardest part: the look in his eyes.

Disillusionment. Simply that, and from that everything else grows. Disappointment, now, in his eyes. The love draining out of them. The hurt trickling in. The rapidly growing conviction that no, this is not the woman I thought she was, and in you there is just the building of panic and desperation and the awful urge to cry out: 'I'm still here, I'm still me, and I AM the woman you thought I was!' But you don't say that, because you know there's no point saying it, and you look at the floor because you can't stand to look in his eyes any more. This is the truth about sharing your past with the man you want to share your future.

Chapter 25 ⌒

| AFTERSHOCKS

The effects of prostitution abuse have been found to
resemble post-traumatic stress disorder.
'THE NEXT STEP INITIATIVE', *RUHAMA RESEARCH*
REPORT ON BARRIERS AFFECTING WOMEN IN
PROSTITUTION, IRELAND, 2005

During the writing of this book, while enquiring into ances-
tral names as possible pseudonyms for it, my aunt (who I was
talking to) told me that she didn't want her mother's maiden
name on this book, but that I could use her paternal grandmother's
name. She didn't say this outright at first; I could see that she had a problem with my suggestion of using her mother's maiden name. I thought
perhaps she didn't think the name suited as well as the other one we
were discussing. This was either down to an uncharacteristic naïveté or
the effects of the two glasses of wine I'd just drank, either way, I hadn't
seen it coming when I pressed her on it and she responded, softly but
firmly: 'I don't want my mother's name on that book'.

Immediately I understood. 'Oh,' I said, 'that's OK. That's understandable.'

'Is it?' she shot straight back.

'Yes,' I said, 'it is'. And it was.

Obviously she hadn't wanted to hurt me. I had to drag it out of her
and I could see from her need for reassurance that she felt guilty about
that reluctance on her part, but I understood it. I understood it better
than she could have known and she had no reason to feel badly about it.
A person will not comfortably watch any connection, however tenuous,

be made between prostitution and a woman they love. She did not want her mother's memory tainted by an association between the name of her birth and the world of prostitution, and that reaction is so natural and so ordinary that in fact I don't know what I was thinking of when I made the suggestion. So yes, her position was understandable to me. It was as understandable as it gets.

I also thought it was interesting to note the ease with which she gave her blessing to an association between prostitution and a name that came from her *father's* line. His memory, it seemed to me, was not corruptible by such an association. Being male, it seemed, protected him from such an outcome. It put him beyond that sort of reproach. This too is understandable given that the shame of prostitution is overwhelmingly and unquestioningly apportioned to females. It is understandable given that people make a very clear link between prostitution and the pollution of a woman's sexual self, however unaware they may be about the instinctual association they are making.

I thought about all these things that night while talking to my aunt. And it has just hit me now that I have to worry that, though I have not used her name, my aunt may be upset that I have mentioned her mother here at all. I have only done so in order to make what I believe to be a very relevant point and all I can do now is hope it doesn't anger or upset her. So here is yet another tremor—the anticipation of discord prostitution may yet cause in my life. These are your aftershocks, these realisations that come plop plop plopping into your mind and your life like pebbles into a pond. You know why they are there, but that does nothing to prevent the ripples forming on the surface of the water. Sometimes all you can do is observe them.

The dictionary definition of the word 'aftershock' is: 'a smaller earthquake following the main shock of a large earthquake'. Therefore the term is not entirely appropriate here. Post-prostitution aftershocks are sometimes more consciously painful, sometimes more acute, and always more prolonged than the main event. There is a reason for this: we become so adept at camouflaging our reality from ourselves that it is sometimes only in the aftermath that a woman can fully engage with the proportion and the nature of the original trauma. For me, it has been in the retrospective processing of prostitution that I have been able to face the fullness of its numerous individual traumas and have come to a true and thorough consciousness of the depth and gravity of it as an experience.

Experiencing the aftershocks of prostitution is to experience the act of dissociation in reverse. It is uniquely painful, mentally and emotionally. There is an element of the overwhelming contained in the experience. Recently I described this psychological assault to a friend, this sense of being overwhelmed. I said that I couldn't quite put it into words for her on the spot, without taking a long pause for thinking, but that I would try to illustrate it by way of an analogy. I told her that I imagine myself as a woman who is out hunting on the African plains. It is pitch dark, night, and all can be seen only in its outlines against the night sky. I am holding a hunting rifle and looking for my quarry; a medium-sized beast, shorter than me, but dangerous and strong, like a hyena or a wild boar. I feel a presence, turn, and look. Here is the beast at my shoulder. It is an elephant.

This describes the time when the enormity of prostitution hits you, and you realise there is more lost to you than is possible to process at that point. Dissociation once concealed the fullness of prostitution's nature from you, because that was necessary, but it has also built a barrier between you and truth which must now be dismantled. The process is painful, but utterly necessary.

Just like any other form of sex abuse, the true essence of the prostitution experience must be understood before it can be overcome. Prostitution is a particularly cruel form of sexual abuse because, though sexual abuse that manifests in other forms (particularly incest) also hammers home the message, 'there is no sex abuse going on here', only in prostitution is this message still respected after the facts have been uncovered. The silencing voice of prostitution abuse speaks with great conviction, and much of the world believes it.

If there is no abuse then surely there could be no requisite for healing? There certainly is a requisite for healing here, but the prostituted must navigate through much more confusion and complication in the seeking of it. Society's misplaced certainties around the essence of prostitution seriously impede the former prostitute from moving on and moving beyond it. Cash is not only a legitimiser and a silencer; it is an *obscurer*, and a ruthlessly effective one. With her victimisation itself blurred and shrouded in obscurity, how much more difficult is it for a woman to arrive at healing, when her first hurdle is in reaching the understanding that she even deserves it?

Conversely, I came to a fuller understanding of prostitution's role in my life by coming to an understanding of my role in prostitution. I realised that I too had been culpable; I too had hurt people by my involvement in prostitution. It then came to me that because I was guilty of my particular role at any one time others were guilty of their momentary roles also. The lines between the innocent and the guilty can be indistinct and blurred, because society directs them to be, but also because they occasionally switch roles, the innocent and the culpable.

I'll explain: any time I deliberately paid special attention, with conversation and an added edge of caring, to a young man who had troubles relating to women, I did so in order that he would continue to return to see me. I did this any time I came across a young man with this feature of character and I did so because they were always shy and non-intimidating and easy to manage; in other words, because they exhibited perfect qualities for a regular client. This was not done out of compassion; it was a falsified mockery of caring. I seldom thought long about what was best and healthy for him, although I instinctively knew what that was. I seldom (although I did occasionally) advise that he find himself a young woman and form a healthy relationship. I seldom pointed out that his fear of rejection was disproportionate to reality. I usually thought only of myself and of the fact that, if I had to see a number of men for money each week, my week would be somewhat less stressful if he featured in it. Was I not culpable, at least of not discouraging emotional frailty, for the sake of satisfying my own requirements? Of course I was, and not in those cases only; as I have already said, every time I engaged in prostitution with a committed man I colluded in hurting some woman somewhere who had done nothing to deserve it.

For someone who is well aware that she was involved in a system in which she was victimised, to discover that at times the opposite has also been true comes as a shock. This was one of the aftershocks of prostitution as I experienced it. It was a valuable shock, in that it moved me closer to an understanding of the fullness of prostitution's negative nature. I see now that prostitution was an experience by which my own moral codes were being eroded and in seeing that, I now perceive the true depth of its corruptive and corrosive character. This is not to be mistaken as directing disproportionate blame towards the exploited. It is to be taken as it is meant—that I see if my experience were a prism, then negativity shone through every single facet of it.

For me, this realisation has been a necessary part of moving on. Some women try to move on from prostitution by erasing its presence from the forefront of their minds, by batting away the memory of it every time it occurs to them. Separation and compartmentalisation are thoroughly necessary in prostitution, as is the suppression of memory; these are old and well-learned habits. It is understandable that women would carry them with them into their post-prostitution lives. After some time, however, these habits either will or will not begin to be discarded, depending on whether or not the formerly prostituted individual continues to use the defence strategy of dissociation in her own life.

There was a deconstruction necessary for me here that would not have been possible had I continued to practise my old habit of dissociation, and deconstructing the experience was, for me, a necessary component of healing. I found really *examining* what had happened to me an essential factor in healing from it. I had to understand it, and to do so I had to fully remember. I had to open the door on a lot of things I really didn't want to.

I believe that you can never facilitate the moving beyond any experience by the suppression of its memory, but many women try to do this. Many women conceal the fullness of their experience from themselves. It is a predictable reaction to a painful history. I believe this is a natural tactic in women and I understand their motives thoroughly because I practised exactly this type of avoidance technique for the first couple of years after I left prostitution, but I believe today that it is a damaging and useless tactic. It is useless because you cannot expunge the past; you can only understand it—and it is damaging because it is only in confronting the past that a woman can loosen prostitution's grip on her present day self. Those memories will not stop coming and if you do not turn around and face them they will come after you forever. This is a process best conducted with the aid of a therapist, in my experience. There is a lot to work through.

The psychological impact of prostitution is incalculable for the women involved. Disturbances manifest in many ways; for me personally, and among those I witnessed, there was the heightened propensity to inflict violence paired with the heightened capacity for enduring it. I have my own theories about this. Violence, in my opinion, stems from unexpressed grief, and I strongly suspect that violence reflects the parameters of the cage that contains it. The structure which detains and deforms grief is simply the human inability to express it, and our inability to grieve is itself a negative influence in our lives. No group I can think of is less able to express their grief than prostituted women; apart from being paid to keep that to themselves, it would be very dangerous not to do so.

That the inability or unwillingness to express grief is a negative thing is borne out by the fact that it gives rise to negative consequences. Grief is released when it is expressed. Its purpose is to be released. When it isn't, and instead is forcibly contained, it deepens and worsens and eventually manifests as violence, which is either inwardly or outwardly directed.

But this inability to express grief is just another necessary component of the prostitute's armour: had I been able to grieve each incidence of prostitution directly after it happened, I would never have been able to continue in prostitution. Coming to terms with the level of my own unexpressed grief and the damage it has caused was itself a monumental aftershock, and one I am still grappling with.

I was, in my pre-prostitution life, always the girl who pushed the boy's hand away. Refused to go up the laneway, or when I was cajoled into it, kissed tentatively and shook with shock when he moved his hand to my breast; to let him go lower than that was unthinkable. So it was with a very great deal of belated shock that I began to trace the outlines of my experience, to try to connect the dots between who I had been to start out with and who prostitution had forced me to become. God knew what he was doing when he made it impossible for us to see the future. I am being in no way melodramatic when I say that if we could, I believe my fourteen-year-old self may well have committed suicide.

To experience an aftershock is to have some part of you triggered, whether it is your memory, your perception or your insight, to cause you to recognise and reflect with the jolt of a sudden, usually discomfiting, understanding. This book is going out at a very pertinent point in Irish history. We are deep in recession and have an exceptionally high unemployment rate. Homes are being repossessed every day. For many families, it is not a matter of cancelling the summer holiday—it is a matter of cancelling the future as they'd planned it. In circumstances like these, destitution is the proverbial wolf at the door, and there comes a point when you have nothing to sell but yourself. This is an aftershock for me, to know that I am now living in a country where women, probably in great numbers, have had prostitution recently cross their minds. And if they have, I know exactly what they'll have thought immediately after it. They'll have thought, could I? Could I really stand it? And they will have felt shudders at the very thought of it, but many of them will have kept on thinking about it anyway, because it's either think about that or think about the stack of unpaid bills in the kitchen next to the letters from the bank about the mortgage arrears.

So what would I say to those women? Firstly, what I'd say I would say gently. There are no lectures to desperate women that I feel entitled to give. I know what destitution feels like, and I know from the lessons of my own life that the fear of its imminence is outweighed only by the agony of its arrival. What I'd say is what I wish someone had been there to say to me: please do not do this. You are considering selling the last thing you have of value, but just remember, the last thing worth selling is also the last thing worth holding on to. You can buy other things for the price you'll get for your sexual self, yes, but then how will you ever know you wouldn't have found other ways to buy them? But this sale you are contemplating is beyond the laws of capitalism. No matter what happens in your future, no matter what way things turn out, you will never accrue the means to buy back what you have sold here. There is no buying your way back from this. There is no currency that can ever re-forge the broken link between a woman and her private essential self.

I have read a lot about prostitution in the closing months of writing this book. It has been interesting to educate myself as to the social politics of what happened to me. But also I know that there has been something else going on here; there is a two-pronged reaction to all this research. At times I have felt overwhelmed by the horror of it all, just paralysed by the magnitude of the tsunami before me. At other times, when reading text relating to aspects of prostitution that are less traumatising to me (or perhaps I have been inured to) there has been an inevitable removal from the personal. I have to question whether this is dissociation sneaking in the back door.

Sometimes I find myself spliced somewhere in the middle, in a land even I struggle to understand. For example, it is put forward statistically that 'only' one in fifteen Irish men are purchasers of female sexuality. I do not know if I am supposed to feel cheered by this. Obviously this situation is preferable to its opposite, but if one in fifteen women commodified the bodies of men, I do not suppose that this would be a statistic expected to put men in good spirits.

In this country, where 'only' one in fifteen men buys women, it is worth remembering that these are the pool of men from which a prostituted woman must draw on to frame her view of males, given that these make up the vast majority of the men she interacts with. It should be clear, then, that prostituted women have seen the worst of what men have to offer, and they have seen it far more often than not.

When this is your reality you will naturally withdraw from men generally. You will recoil from little pleasantries. Your eyes will narrow in suspicion at the man who offers to carry your shopping bags. You will shy away from the elderly man who says 'good evening' in the park. You will withdraw from small kindnesses, and men will feel you withdraw. We, men and women, have lost each other in all this. Is it not pitifully obvious that we have lost each other?

The perspectives I have put forward in this book are put forward by me as a woman, and most specifically as a formerly prostituted woman, but it has been amazing for me to read the evidence of other people (mainly women) whose writings communicate that they feel the same way. It is amazing because for quite a long time I had seen no evidence that any non-prostituted persons could understand the wrong of what was happening to us.

These, too, are the aftershocks of prostitution—to find with surprise that though certainly we were alone, there were non-prostituted others out there thinking of us and writing of us. I had no voice. I knew I had no voice; what I didn't know was that there was a whole movement out there trying to speak *for* me.

It was comforting and relieving to find that the writings of these women were so often in line with my own. For example, since early on in the writing of this book I realised that I preferred to use the term 'prostituted woman' as opposed to 'prostitute'. I didn't know why exactly that term felt more appropriate for me; I just knew that it did. Now I know why: a woman can only be a prostitute when she has been prostituted by somebody else, and it hardly makes logical sense to refer to the former while ignoring the latter. I think about how that would work in other areas of commerce. Is a butcher still a butcher if nobody buys *his* meat? No. He is an aspiring butcher— nothing more. A woman must be prostituted in order to earn that title; a woman must be bought before she is made into what she is.

This comment by Australian academic Sheila Jeffreys, which I came across long after I'd started using the term 'prostituted woman', clearly reflects my own thinking: 'The term *prostituted woman* brings the perpetrator into the picture: somebody must be doing something to the woman for her to be "prostituted".'

It was with the pleasant shock of relief that I found evidence, in reading writings like these, of the existence of those who really are able to understand my experience of prostitution. And so I find, in the closing chapters of this book, that in fact I owe a debt—and now that I have a voice, I hope this book goes some way towards repaying it.

Does it qualify as an aftershock, I wonder, to find in my readings that there are those outside the prostitution experience who recognise the link I always felt between prostitution and slavery? I think that it does. I was not accustomed to aftershocks presenting in positive formats, but it was, again, with the shock of relief that I found I was not alone in this thinking.

Prostitution, to me, is like slavery with a mask on, just as it is like rape with a mask on, and we were no more recompensed for the abuse of our bodies by our punters' cash than slaves were recompensed by the food and lodgings provided by their slave masters. The function of food and lodgings was to keep enslaved people alive (physically present) in order to be used for the benefit of their abusers. The function of cash paid to us was to keep us cooperative (physically present) in order to be used for the benefit of our abusers.

No doubt there are those who will find any likening of the prostitution experience to the enslavement experience a very contentious one. No doubt there are those who would fear insulting the descendants of enslaved people by doing so. I hope that this is not the case, because I have no desire to add insult to injury, but I *must* speak my own truth. The truth is there was something in prostitution that always called to my mind the essence of slavery as I understood it. The dehumanisation of people was a prerequisite of slavery, and slavery then went on to be both a cause and a consequence of the dehumanisation of the enslaved. I experienced this double-barrelled dynamic in prostitution.

I see that, again, my thinking has been in line with that of some feminist theorists all along, as quotes like the ones below have shown me:

'Consent to violation is a fact of oppression. Any oppression. All oppression . . . If, for example, consent was the criterion for determining whether or not slavery is a violation of human dignity and rights, slavery would not have been recognised as a violation, because an important element of slavery is the acceptance of their condition by many slaves.'

KATHLEEN BARRY
THE PROSTITUTION OF SEXUALITY

'Barry explains that 'consent' is not a good divining-rod as to the existence of oppression, and consent to violation is a fact of oppression. (1995, p. 65). Oppression cannot be effectively gauged according to the degree of 'consent', since even in slavery there was some consent if consent is defined as inability to see, or feel entitled to, any alternative.'

SHEILA JEFFREYS
THE IDEA OF PROSTITUTION

Barry and Jeffreys lay out one element of the link between the system of prostitution and the system of slavery here. Others contend that prostitution actually developed in and from the slavery of ancient times and that makes sense to me, because these are the only two areas of life I am aware of where one person exercises total dominion over the physical body of another. Feminist historian Gerda Lerner, in *The Creation of Patriarchy* argued that prostitution was the result of slaveholding and Jeffreys comments that: 'If prostitution did in fact originate in slavery, then it is not at all surprising that there are so many past and present parallels between them.'[28] Regardless of whether it actually originated in slavery or not, it is widely historically recorded that prostitution abuse was an element of the lived experience of slavery.

Black American feminist Vednita Carter expresses a view on the subject that is particularly interesting to me, and it is not one that is liable to be mistaken:

'[S]trip joints and massage parlours are typically zoned in Black neighbourhoods, which gives the message to white men that it is alright to solicit Black women and girls for sex—that we are all prostitutes. On almost any night, you can see them slowly cruising around our neighbourhoods, rolling down their windows, calling out to women and girls. And we got the message growing up, just like our daughters are

---

28 For a more thorough dissection of the parallels between prostitution and slavery, see chapter six of Sheila Jeffreys' *The Idea of Prostitution* and Kathleen Barry's *Female Sexual Slavery*.

getting it today, that this is how it is, this is who we are, this is what we are for.

'Many people have said that prostitution is tolerated by the black community. They are wrong. We do not tolerate prostitution; it has been imposed upon us. It has been imposed upon us since the days of slavery, when the master came out to the field and chose whichever Black woman he wanted to have sex with. Light-skinned slaves, known as 'fancy girls', were sold at high prices in the marketplace and later 'rented out' or sold to brothels.

'Today, middle-class white men from the suburbs drive through the ghettos of America to pick out whichever Black women or girls they want to have sex with, as if our cities were their own private plantations. No, prostitution is not tolerated in the Black community any more than African-American slaves tolerated it on the plantation; it is imposed upon us.'

VEDNITA CARTER

MICHIGAN JOURNAL OF GENDER AND LAW, 1993, VOLUME 1: 81–89

The words above are taken from a speech presented by Vednita Carter (formerly Nelson) at the University of Michigan Law School in October 1992. In that speech, she also queried:

'How can mainstream feminists claim to care about Black women and racism when they fail to speak out against the white men who pay for the right to sexually abuse our daughters and sisters, or against the police who target these same women for arrest and imprisonment, while their abusers, the johns that prey on our community, go free?'

My answer to her would be that they can't. Any white feminist who fails to speak out against the white men who so abuse black women cannot, with any credibility, claim to care about black women or the particular racially-related form of sexual abuse for which black women are singled out.

One of my post-prostitution aftershocks was experienced in considering the way other women are hurt in prostitution. When you are prostituted in a mono-racial society (as Ireland was at that time), it is unlikely that you will deeply consider the hurdles facing other women in multi-racial societies. Those issues, quite simply, are not your issues. You have enough to contend with in what you're dealing with yourself. But in my post-prostitution life, and especially during the writing of this book, I have had cause to consider the experiences of other women and have been horrified by much of what I've found. Carter's words chill me, because they lay out so clearly the systematic nature of prostitution as it specifically relates to African-American females, and it is a cold and brutal system that embodies the essence of the double-bind. A black American woman may turn one way to escape from prostitution only to have society, through many of its structures, conspire to turn her around and send her right back where she came from, and to do so *because* she is black. The system which ensnares black women is doubly cruel, doubly coercive and naturally doubly difficult to escape from, and this is so because black American women's prostitution experience is lived, as Carter says, in: 'That very difficult, tight space where Black women attempt to survive—that space where racism and sexism intersect'.

It should never be ignored that prostituted black women report the majority of their clients to be white. To do so is to ignore the context in which their bodies are abused; it is to ignore the racist/sexist nature of their double-bind.

In prostitution, you lose ownership of yourself through the mechanism of having been bought and sold, but you cannot turn to the slave-master with a bitter accusatory stare because society has constructed the belief that if you were to look in those eyes, at least one of them would be your own. It does not matter, says the world, that prostitution was chosen for you through poverty and all the spin-off social disadvantages that come with that; *you* chose it, says the world, so if you want to blame someone, go blame yourself. And you buy into this to a great extent, because it is such a prevailing concept; and you do not rail openly against your having been *bought* because there is such strongly implied personal culpability in your having been *sold*, and, though you feel it in every fibre of your being, you consciously are very far removed from identifying with prostitution's enslavement element, because the world says you have sold yourself, and who would ever sympathise with a slave like that?

There are other systems of oppression that work in tandem with sexism to copper-fasten prostitution as inevitable in many women's lives. The position of prostituted Thai women sickens and appals me. The impoverished circumstances of these women have turned parts of Bangkok into an open whorehouse. Much of the world turns a blind eye to the ritualistic sexual abuse of Thai women and girls, which is indulged by local men and by western men for the price they'd pay back home for a daily paper.

While all the female participation in prostitution I ever came across, by its nature, owed its existence to economic constraints, in Thailand a massive percentage of their country's economic viability is dependent on sex tourism. It is a horrifying situation. To know this is an aftershock to me. To really *consider* what this means, as a former prostitute, is to be reminded of the presence of a monster and to be near struck-dumb by the immensity of its size.

The 'monster' I refer to is normalised prostitution and industrialised prostitution is just one facet of it; examples of this are to be found with abundance across the globe. Industrialised prostitution services the sexual appetites of men at military bases in developing countries worldwide. Taking the Philippines, for example, it is customary to subdivide prostituted women into regular prostitutes and 'three-holers'—those women who are described so, as Kathleen Barry reports after having spent time with them—'because no orifice of the human body is protected from sale and customer intrusion.' Often the young women and girls who find themselves put to work as 'three-holers' will not have heard the term before living the soul-destroying reality that it applies to them.[29]

There will probably always be aftershocks I will have to process and deal with. One of the more recent ones was my reaching a point where I began to interpret my prostitution abuse on an intellectual, as well as a deep, personal level. This was a new way of understanding; sometimes

---

29 See chapter one of Kathleen Barry's *The Prostitution of Sexuality*.

it meant being removed from the emotional and sometimes it meant being violently pulled back into a sense of immediate trauma. It was always beneficial, but often disturbingly revealing. I had always felt prostitution's malignance, but being able to decode and comprehend its structure and the way it operates is to reach an understanding of its dynamics on a level that both terrifies and saddens in an altogether new way. The deep fear of what lurks beneath the mask morphs into the starker and more immediate fear of what *is* beneath it, because you can see that clearly now, and if anything it is worse than your senses had forewarned you. I am thinking now of the point of payment and what that is seen to mean, as opposed to what it *really* means, for the prostituted woman. The cash transaction is the legitimiser, as I have said, and this is true as far as the rest of the world is concerned; but the world's legitimiser is the prostitutes' silencer: it is the veil behind which women are abused every day.

This explains to me why I never saved anything I earned in prostitution and why I, in common with so many other former prostitutes, was as poor coming out of it as I was going in to it. The concept of 'dirty money' from the perspective of the prostituted comes up time and again in prostitution literature, and I can certainly relate to that.

Another of the great aftershocks of prostitution for me was to come to find that the reality of my prostitution experience would be aggressively denied and that prostitution itself would be equally defended. To come to find that the money we'd been paid was seen to have, as Catharine MacKinnon wrote, 'a magical quality' which 'dissolved' our sexual abuse; that it was supposed to evaporate the psychic anguish of having to imagine ourselves elsewhere while reams of contempt-driven strangers masturbated on and inside us.

These opinions, naturally, disgust me, and when I hear them my mind presents me with a flurry of images to contradict them. They are very great in number and each as horrible as the next, but as I sit here now and type, one stands out from the rest. It is an image that has returned to me many times since I first saw it. It is the look in the eyes of a fellow-prostitute hunched down on all fours while a man kneeling behind her is ramming himself into her. I had walked in on them in the brothel, not knowing anyone to be there, and she was positioned on the floor facing the door I'd just walked through. Her eyes met mine just for a moment before I closed the door, but what passed between them in that split-second was a depth of understanding that couldn't have been better conveyed in a full-length conversation. It was the moment when I saw my abuse in her eyes and she acknowledged hers in mine. That look was a sharing of the purest disturbance, and it was a moment of connection that has never left me. It was the acknowledgement of the prostitution experience.

Chapter 26 ❧

| THE LAST QUESTION

. . .'tis misfortune that awakens ingenuity, or fortitude, or endurance, in hearts where these qualities had never come to life but for the circumstance which gave them a being.

WILLIAM MAKEPEACE THACKERAY, *THE HISTORY OF HENRY ESMOND*

That every prostitute I've ever known wanted to get out of prostitution is something I deduce from many things, mostly direct comments but also more subtle reactions and attitudes I witnessed while still in prostitution. The responses of prostitutes I've run into since exiting the business have been equally revealing. I've yet to have a post-prostitution conversation with any of them who didn't say something along the lines of: 'Good for you', 'Fair play to you', 'I'm proud of you', 'I'm glad to hear it'. Could the women who say these things be thought to consider prostitution a positive place to be? And if they don't consider it a positive place for me, could they be presumed to consider it a positive place for themselves?

Since the first question always seeks to know how a woman gets into prostitution it is logical to record here, near this book's end, how I got out of it. I have already explained the mechanics of that, the practical steps I took to remove myself from it, but none of these would have been taken had I not felt a deep inner urging to extract myself from that hideous way of life. This urging is truly the first step, though it is not consciously taken, and yet it is one I have never known another prostitute not to take.

I always felt myself being reminded by this urging that my current lifestyle was one which I needed to turn away from, which was not right for me, and which was a path I'd never been intended to stay on. It was, in one of its aspects, a deeply spiritual yearning. I needed that peace back, the peace I'd had in childhood when walking in woodland, surrounded by the beauty of the world. It was the peace of knowing exactly who I was, and being content in that knowing.

There is no peace in prostitution. There is no peace in your body or your mind. There is no peace anywhere within you. I think, by nature, I am a peaceful person. I am someone who craves to be at peace within her own self. Since that was not possible in prostitution, I feel that my own necessity to be at peace with myself strongly contributed to my leaving.

Recently, while having a bath, I became very aware of my own nakedness and was filled with a sense of loathing. 'Think of all the horrible places this body has been', I thought to myself, and immediately my mind swam with images of punters: fat, heaving, sweating, or skinny, vicious, belligerent. Rooms, beds, cars, streets, brothels, hotels: the imagery was abundant, and loathsome. For some reason I fought it. For some reason I insisted to myself: 'Think of all the lovely places this body has been'. I remembered the touch of lovers, soft, gentle, erotic; remembered affection, hugs, cuddles. I saw myself cradling my newborn son; saw myself walking not long after dawn while the dew still glittered on the grass. I felt the tension begin to seep out of my body and immediately clasped my hands gently on either upper arm. It was a hug of the self I suppose. I was okay again, safe again to be in my own body. I realised that this place, where we are safe or unsafe, clean or unclean, is not in the body. It is encoded in a much deeper part of ourselves, and when that is triggered by memory its last port of call is in the body. This results in the felt bodily experience of either joy or revulsion reverberating through us physically, and washing over and through us, either healingly or damagingly, like waves.

When I think back on my time in prostitution and the women I knew then, one thing marks for me most potently what we were among the memories of our prostituted selves. I see now what we were with the clarity of a painful understanding. It would have been too painful, while it was true in my life, to acknowledge with such a blatant comparison; but it was true nonetheless. I am thinking now of the wind-up toys I remember me and my brother playing with as very young children in my grandad's flat. I had a tin penguin and he had a motorbike with a rider attached. We would wind them up at the back and my big penguin would walk unsteadily around the room while his smaller motorbike would whiz around it. When they'd used up all their energy they'd stop, frozen, inanimate objects again until someone (not they) decided it was time again for them to start moving.

I see now that's what *we* were, us young women and girls. Money was our wind-up mechanism. That is how we were controlled and made to behave according to the whims of whoever dictated our movements. That is what we were, both to them and deeply, damagingly, to us; and the interplay of our actions made clear exactly what we were: we were toy humans. And we toy humans played out limitless scenes that were the direct opposite of equality. Those scenes are still played out every moment of every day, for the benefit of the toy masters who do not hold puppet strings, because they do not need them. They hold purse strings instead.

I don't imagine the degrading depressing lifestyle of prostitution as being innately suited to any woman and I have never seen the remotest spark of evidence in prostitution to suggest that it may be. In terms of the degree of negativity a woman is able to contend with and process, I imagine that there are differing degrees here as in all of life, so I think another of the reasons I left was because, to put it simply, I hated it too much to stay.

I think the thing that most strongly induced me to leave was the perpetual sense of 'wrongness' to the whole thing; that was a hugely discouraging factor for me. I hated, above all else, the bodily invasion that is integral to the prostitution experience.

I knew that as long as prostitution was in my life drugs would be there also and I desperately wanted to be rid of drugs. I would never have gotten off drugs while I was in prostitution. I know that now and I knew it then.

I've had it remarked that it must have taken great personal strength to extract myself from prostitution. I don't know about the place of inner strength in that process, where it sits and how much of it can take credit for the end result, but I know with certainty that it was in no way the only factor at work. I think I was motivated as much by the fear of spending a lifetime in prostitution, so in that sense you could say that my leave-taking was motivated every bit as much by fear as by strength. It was a very clear-sighted fear though, I see now, and it indicated an ability to envision a different future.

There was also defiance associated with the fact that I was a prostitute and a drug addict and I didn't want to die like that; I didn't want those to be the points that defined or invoked memories of me, but prostitution and drug abuse were so entwined in my life at that point that one could not be without the other.

The realisation of the urgent need for change is really only transition's (or recovery's) first step, but it is obligatory; it is not a step you can bypass. There are no 'start at stage two' concessions for latecomers or awkward-truth-dodgers and in that sense its importance is not to be overlooked, but that comprehension alone does not assure success; many a drug addict has died with that realisation alive and kicking in their consciousness. I managed it with some resilience and much good fortune and I count myself very lucky; I've loved some who were not.

By the summer after my twenty-second birthday I had to deal with the fact that I'd spent almost a third of my life in prostitution. It was a disturbing realisation. I knew that it was true but I so badly wanted to reject that reality. It felt deeply depressing and utterly pathetic and my feelings urged and spurred me to leave in that they fuelled the impetus for change. It is not enough to desire change. I had spent seven years desiring change. There must also be the will for momentum, the drive for moving forward. Putting these two things together, the desire for change and the will to provoke it—that is the magic formula of action, I've since realised; that is the gunpowder and the naked flame.

When I was a little girl my mother had for years a particular poster hung on the kitchen wall. It was of a climber on the snow and ice-covered face of a perilously steep mountain. The caption beneath it read: 'Where there's a will, there's a way'. I remember her commenting on it and repeating that caption when she was faced with great difficulties, some of which were as pitiable as how to make ten pounds stretch to feed five kids for the whole week. This instinct for overcoming was obviously innate to my mother's nature. It would have to have been, given that she managed to navigate raising five children in the desperate circumstances she was in for as long as she did. I don't know whether I inherited that same impulse or whether she instilled it in me. It may have been a bit of both. In any case, I know it was in large part responsible for guiding me out of prostitution, so I have a lot to thank my mother for.

My parents' illnesses and addictions furnished me with an unenviable childhood and a young adulthood fraught with difficulties, but their wellness, the decent sides of themselves, the positivity inherent to their own deeper natures, was in large part what gifted me with the tools to overcome the inheritance of their misfortunes.

This book was, for me, among other things, an exercise in overcoming. I have always felt in response to traumatic or difficult events a desire to overcome or to surmount. I have written this book, in part, in order to satisfy that need. This inclination is a behavioural pattern that I became aware of early in life. It is generally positive but has not always been for the good. It has certainly been of assistance in helping me navigate my way through difficult times, but it has also kept me captive in harsh circumstances when I misinterpreted 'overcoming' for 'enduring'. I see that I was, for quite a long time, confused on that point; but I know now that the latter is not always a position of strength and these days I pay careful attention to the distinction between the two.

I never felt that I had overcome prostitution simply by way of having left it. That was not nearly enough. I had to dissect it as an experience, for myself. I had to understand its effects on me and on other women and on society as I had seen it and then lay what I had found of understanding before others to dissect and make sense of what they may. I had to hope, and still do, that the sense others make of prostitution after having read this account will be somewhat enlightened by my experiences. There is, decade upon decade, more and more tolerance of prostitution and other sexually exploitative practices in much of the world. It is my hope that after having read this book at least some people will come to a fuller understanding of the simple immorality of prostitution, the damage of it, the pain of it, and the necessity of eradicating it from our world. If I achieve that, that will be another level, another layer, of overcoming.

This has not been an easy book to write. The voice in my mind that has been encouraging me to record these things all this time has been telling me: sit down and be calm, be rational, be focused, and be driven. But to be focused and driven to write this book has also been to be troubled and disconcerted; that is the inevitable corollary. It has been rather like attempting to concentrate your vision on a target in the middle of an irrepressible blizzard and feeling confused and anxious as you are caught between the necessity to focus and the fear of being overcome by the storm. I had many moments like this and had to think many times: 'Be calm, be rational, be focused, and be driven'.

Some days I have been able to take this sort of advice from myself and some days I haven't. Some days my depression has come back in waves and left me fit for nothing; hardly any days have I been able to work on this book and feel few ill effects.

On bad days I've been confined to my home, just crippled with depression, fear and self-doubt, and on others I have felt inwardly calmed by the sort of feeling that assures me I don't need to look in a mirror to know who I am. These feelings are produced by way of a psychological distancing from prostitution. Usually the act of writing about this draws you back into it. In later days it has produced the feeling of letting go. I am looking forward to typing the last full stop. I look forward to the feeling it will evoke in me. I know it will be a positive one.

Men who buy the bodies of women are aware on an inner level of the wrong they do and some of them struggle with self-loathing because of it. Though they may not know it, this is good news for them: if there is self-loathing here on the part of a punter it comes from a positive source. Most of us feel low about ourselves when we know we've done something lousy. Men do not feel low about themselves when they know they've done something lousy here because they are intrinsically bad: they do so because they are intrinsically good and hate the part of themselves that has brought them to abuse the females who share their world. I know this in my heart. I think some part of me has always done, and I am glad to know it.

Prostitution might have made me cagey, wary and guarded, but it never robbed me of my love of men. I am glad to know that also. My hate is directed, not towards men generally, but towards prostitution and all the other misogynistic structures in our world which ask questions like: 'What is a woman?' and answer: 'A support system for a pussy.'[30] These attitudes are the building blocks of prostitution and similar structures erected and maintained by men and for men.

A deeper understanding of these things came about after I had gotten out of prostitution, but it was in the sensory understanding of them as they occurred, the inner knowledge that I was being abused *while* I was being abused, that helped build in me the impetus to get out of prostitution. So, in short, I knew I had to get out, because that's what my gut told me; and it never stopped telling me that.

There is enough left of the authentic me to say what happened to me, and how, and why, and for that I will always be thankful. But does it give me back to myself? There are still parts of me I do not recognise as my own, though I surely know how they got there. This invulnerability, for example, was never me. It was never part of my original make-up, but instead it has become encoded, rewritten into me, one track laid over another as if on a rewriteable CD.

I have begun to make peace with my past, though I do wonder how much of who I would have been is eroded beyond restoration. I cannot measure that, and I am partially glad that I can't. I'm also thankful I'm left with enough to mourn what's missing.

There is a feeling that I can never move on; that I'll always be in phase one; that I am a neophyte in life and that I am condemned to stay that

---

30 These words are taken from a sign nailed up in public outside a red-light bar in Angeles City in the Philippines, as reported by Kathleen Barry in her book *The Prostitution of Sexuality*.

way, however long I happen to live it. And then another voice rises up in me, a blessed voice, which doesn't talk softly, but instead rebukes in scolding tones and cautions strongly against self-pity. Get up, it says. Get on with things. It's a lovely day. Take your dog for a walk.

EPILOGUE

My sisters, my daughters, my friends—find your voice.
LIBERIAN PRESIDENT ELLEN JOHNSON SIRLEAF—
AFRICA'S FIRST DEMOCRATICALLY ELECTED FEMALE
PRESIDENT—ON COLLECTING HER NOBEL DIPLOMA AND
MEDAL AT A CEREMONY IN OSLO, DECEMBER 2011

So much of what I've written here describes the prostitution experience as an experience which is *lived*, which is made up of the different things that happen to you and the ways you respond bodily, soulfully and psychically to them. All of this is true, but there is something else I must not leave out because it is important: it is that the prostitution life is shaped very much also by what does *not* happen as well as what does. In my adulthood, these things began to hit me. They arrived as aftershocks, particularly poignant ones.

I remember several years back while in the home of newly made friends, watching a group of teenage girls, the daughters of the house, getting ready to go out bowling. A year or two after that, in the same house, I watched the eldest daughter get ready for her Debs while her younger sisters crowded round her. Those images—teenage girls laughing, messing, heading out to have fun—stirred feelings buried very deep in me. They were good images, and I smiled for the girls in them, but there was an inner eye watching another scene, and there was no smiling to be done for the girls in that one.

The eye cannot appreciate a picture without considering what is left out. The lace on a woman's dress, for example, would not be lace but for

the little gaps between the cloth. Those little empty spaces are as necessary as the material to the pattern of the lace. All the things we did *not*
get to do, those too made up a part of our picture; they were the gaps in
our lace.

And that is how it was: all the teenage things we never got to do also
defined our experience and shaped, by their absence, how we existed in
the world. And because they were the things that 'normal' young women
our age did, that caused to further separate us from a particular type of
meaningful connection with the world. It was psychically a very strong
sense of disconnection. It caused the feeling of being thoroughly removed.

This has left from its soul-level injury the mark of a lingering scar that
presents as the need to remind yourself of your own place in the world
and, crucially, of your having any right to it. There may always be days I'll
have to consciously haul myself back from that feeling of being removed.
I am glad I am learning how to do that, but I will not stop hoping, and
working, for the day this lesson no longer needs to be learned.

This book was written over the span of more than a decade, between
the years 2002 and 2012, and the ages of twenty-six to thirty-six. It was
a long, slow and painful process. It has been very different to writing
creatively. I enjoy that; I find it's like trying to unfold the feelings inside
of me. But writing creatively is so different from the process of writing a
memoir. With creative writing you have no template, no factual truisms
you must stick to. It is freer. It makes me think of dancing in the air.
There is no 'you must do this' driving you, though I believe the urge to
write fills some secret need that drives every book.

I have already explained most of the reasons I wrote this book. There
is one more. It is probably the most important one. I see in my mind the
metaphor of a burning building, and I know if you are lucky enough to
escape a burning building it is only right to alert others that there is a
fire in that house. That way, there is some hope for those still trapped
inside.

This is far from the only book that needs to be written about prostitution. I want to see many other women wrench the truth from their
guts about what prostitution has done to them, and what it will continue

to do to other women and girls until the world wakes up to the simple wrongness of it.

This is not the only *type* of book that needs to be written about prostitution either. The book has not yet been written, in my awareness, that deals with the type of sexual healing specific to survivors of prostitution abuse. I am certainly not qualified to write it, but I do hope that someday it will be written, by someone with the necessary balance of training and experience in psychoanalysis or a related discipline, and, preferably, personal experience of the text material. In the absence of that, the author would need in-depth experience of working with prostituted women. We women frankly *need* a book like that to be written, but we need the right person to write it.

There has been so much damage done, and I am proud to add my voice to the voices of those who have been a long time trying to fix it. The comforting truth is that women are not alone in this. One of the most heartening sights I've ever seen was a group of men sitting together in a row, fronting a campaign for the criminalisation of the demand for prostitution in Ireland. They were recognisable men: artists, writers and heads of trades unions. They were part of the Turn Off The Red Light coalition, which calls for the eradication of prostitution in Ireland,[31] and I would take it as a personal favour if anybody reading this who wants to be supportive contacted their TDs and pressed for their support of the Turn Off The Red Light campaign.

As a former prostitute, watching that small group of men, seven of them, I was drawn back by instinct and memory to the comforting presence of men I could trust. Men like my father, my brothers, my closest male friends. Those men standing up that day, in the full glare of the Irish media, brought a healing to me that I could never expect them to understand. What they did that day was more precious than they can know, and so of course I don't have the words to thank them for it.

As well as being healing, it was enlightening. It reminded me of something important. It reminded me that women, all women, including

31 www.turnofftheredlight.ie

those with histories like mine, should never consider men the enemy. We are all humans on this earth and we need to work together to make it a better place to live.

I don't know what else to say of where I am today, except that I am almost happy. Before I can be, there is something else I need to see begin to happen.

There are many factors which support prostitution in our world, but there is one above all others that has assured its continuance throughout the ages. It is the driving force of demand. As Simone de Beauvoir wrote in the last century, 'Prostitution will be suppressed only when the needs to which it responds are suppressed.' Janice G Raymond commented in these modern times: 'A prostitution market without male consumers would go broke.'

These facts have not changed. They are as true and as relevant today as they were a hundred years ago, and they were as relevant a hundred years ago as they were since time immemorial before that. If we do not want them to be relevant any more, we need do only one thing, but do it seriously: we need to address demand.

Prostitution first fell sharply in one place and one place only. That is in the nation which suppressed demand. A global implementation of Sweden's laws, which criminalise demand, is the one thing I'd most like to see before I die. It will be ridiculed, of course, by prostitution promoters as unrealistic. It is not unrealistic. If it was unrealistic it wouldn't have happened in Sweden and it wouldn't have gone on to happen in Norway and Iceland and if it can happen in those nations, it can happen elsewhere. The qualities of wisdom, equality and human integrity are expressed in the legislation enacted in these countries, and that is why I would like to see it spreading.

It may well be rejected, however, and if it is I believe that would be a disaster for humans as a race and for females in particular, because it is also the only hope this world has of making very serious inroads towards ridding itself of prostitution. This will almost certainly not happen in the short term and may not even have happened a hundred years from now, but I dream that someday it will happen, whether or not I am here to see it, because it ought to happen and because on the day that it does humanity will have moved closer to the purest expression of its essence.

It will not be helped to happen by anyone sitting back and hoping that it does, myself or anyone else. That is another of the reasons I wrote this book. I wanted to do my part by drawing attention to the true nature of prostitution, to give a face and a shape to the hideous nature of being molested for money.

This has not been an easy understanding to carry, nor an easy message to convey. I have felt for the longest time like a woman screaming in a glass box where nobody can hear me. This book has been about shattering that box; it has been about giving voice to that scream. Yes, it has been a painful process; but it is done now, and now that it is, I hope some people will have heard me. I hope they will have lent their ear to that scream.

I have some more things to hope for, as stepping stones on the way to fully implemented criminalisation of demand. One is that people, no matter in what nation they reside, will begin to lobby their politicians for the implementation of Swedish-style prostitution laws. Rejecting the commercialisation of sexual abuse needs to be a global effort. Another is that people will remember to support financially, in any small way they can, charities and agencies set up to support the prostituted and the homeless. These are crucial services. Many more women would enter prostitution if not for services which help the homeless and many prostituted women would never get to fight their way out but for the agencies set up to support them.

It is important to note, though, the nature of the help that is offered by an agency and to make sure it is of the necessary sort. Some offer this sort of support and some don't. I was given plenty of help in prostitution, if help consists of free condoms and STI testing. I was given plenty of assistance that recognised, and by doing so unintentionally *reinforced* my position in prostitution; but I was given zero assistance in getting out of it. An agency offering just healthcare as a form of support can only, by its nature, fail to challenge the status quo. That is another important thing I'd like to see changed. Agencies need to offer education and training and help with housing and childcare; they need to offer *a route out* if they seriously intend to support prostituted women.

And that brings me on to my last hope: I hope I live to see government-funded prostitution alternatives programmes every bit as accessible to women as prostitution is, because only in a world like that would women and girls like my teenage self experience some of the 'choice' the world keeps telling us about.

AFTERWORD

Rachel Moran was one of three Irish members of SPACE International who gave evidence to the Irish Government on 6 February 2013. That summer, on 27 June, the Joint Oireachtas Committee on Justice, Defence and Equality returned the recommendations that the Nordic Model be passed into Irish law.

On 27 November 2014, the Irish Government announced their decision to implement the tenets of the Nordic Model.

SPACE

(SURVIVORS OF PROSTITUTION-ABUSE CALLING FOR ENLIGHTENMENT)

INTERNATIONAL

SPACE is a new international organisation, formed to give voice to women who have survived the abusive reality of prostitution. SPACE now includes members from Ireland, Germany, Denmark, France, the UK, USA and Canada. It is an independent organisation and its founding member is the author of this book.

SPACE is committed both to raising the public's consciousness of the harm of prostitution and to lobbying governments to do something about it. We press for political recognition of prostitution as sexually abusive exploitation, and, as a response, for criminalisation of the demand for prostitution.

Membership of SPACE is restricted to formerly prostituted women, from any country, who believe in the right of all people to live free from the oppression of paid sexual abuse. We call for enlightenment because before we can expect social change, prostitution must be recognised for the abuse that it is.

You can contact SPACE in the utmost confidentiality at info@ spaceintl.org or visit our website at www.spaceintl.org

ABOUT THE AUTHOR

Rachel Moran grew up in north Dublin city. From a troubled family background, she was fourteen when she was taken into State care. She became homeless and got involved in prostitution at age fifteen, and was exploited in Dublin and other Irish cities for the following seven years.

In 1998, at the age of 22, she liberated herself from that life. At 24 she got on the path to further education, gaining a degree in journalism from Dublin City University, where she won the Hybrid Award for excellence in journalism.

She speaks internationally on prostitution and sex-trafficking and volunteers to talk to young girls in residential care about the harms and dangers of prostitution. She lives in north Dublin.

http://theprostitutionexperience.com